D1497908

HELL'S KITCHEN

HELL'S

KITCHEN

THE ROARING DAYS OF NEW YORK'S WILD WEST SIDE

BY RICHARD O'CONNOR

Old Town Books

New York

This edition published by Old Town Books,
a division of Barnes & Noble, Inc.,
by arrangement with McIntosh & Otis, Inc.

1993 Old Town Books

ISBN 1-56619-328-1

Printed and bound in the United States of America
M 9 8 7 6 5 4 3 2 1

AUTHOR'S NOTE

WHAT IS HELL'S KITCHEN? The designation has worked its way into the language as a sort of back alley of the underworld and summons up the image of a thug with turtleneck sweater lounging under gaslight with a blackjack sticking out of his rear pants pocket. It was more than that, as this book seeks to show. It has been the home of many generations for the past century. Geographically speaking, it is one of the many neighborhoods which make up the Borough of Manhattan, on the Middle West Side between Eighth Avenue and the Hudson River. Its northern and southern boundaries are a matter of vigorous dispute but the outermost limits allowed by anyone are from Twenty-third to Fifty-ninth Street. Brevity is a virtue in book titles, but *Hell's Kitchen* does not quite indicate the geographic and historic scope of this excursion, which includes Chelsea, lying adjacent to and south of Hell's Kitchen, and the now vanished but seldom mourned Tenderloin which adjoined it to the east from Twenty-fourth to Fortieth Streets.

But let the buyer (and the book borrower) beware. This is not a sociological textbook, nor a work of formal history winnowed out of mounds of scholarly research, but an informal account of some of the lively, the deadly, the saintly, the mischievous people who have lived there.

Contents

HELL'S KITCHEN

1

The Flash Age

HELL'S KITCHEN, the section of New York's West Side long notorious as a seedbed of violence and gangsterism, once was a quiet nook of Manhattan Island. A century ago wealthy New Yorkers still maintained summer estates along its cobbled streets. Before that it was an enclave of rural peace and solitude; its green meadows, sloping to the Hudson, were hospitable to lowing herds, barefoot boys and strolling lovers. By 1855, however, the city was expanding northward, and homes and business establishments were being built up to Forty-second Street.

With the coming of the Civil War, with vast migrations from Europe and rapid industrialization, the countrified charm of the section vanished forever, and its streets were invaded by jerry-built rows of tenements, grogshops, slaughterhouses, railroad yards, warehouses, gas reservoirs. Gangs of hoodlums battled police for supremacy in its streets. Riots and disorders were fomented along its noisome thoroughfares. The Middle West Side, as sociologists have termed the section, became to New York what "south of the slot" is to San Francisco, parts of the Vieux Carré are to New Orleans, and the near North Side is to

11

Chicago. It was the domain of Bully Morrison, who used lamp-posts as shillelaghs; of Battle Annie Welsh and her corps of female goons; of the spring-heeled lads who banded together and called themselves the Gophers, the Gorillas, the Parlor Mob; of Owney Madden, Duke of the West Side during Prohibition days, and Mad Dog Coll, who scared even the underworld; of the boys who marched off with the Fighting 69th in the First World War, and of writers and artists who lived there in their salad days before they became famous.

The geography of Hell's Kitchen, even the derivation of its name, is a matter of controversy. The most enduring of legends concerning its early history is that "Hell's Kitchen" first cropped up in a conversation between two policemen, one a veteran of the force and the other a rookie, while they were observing a small riot in West Thirty-ninth Street.

"This place is hell itself," the rookie is supposed to have remarked.

"Hell's a mild climate," the veteran supposedly replied. "This is Hell's Kitchen, no less."

The less picturesque probability is that the designation was imported from England. A section of London noted for its crime and disorder once was called Hell's Kitchen, and the generic phrase may well have been brought over by English immigrants, who were among the first to settle in the neighborhood.

The title of Hell's Kitchen, strictly speaking, was first bestowed upon a rookery full of violent characters which stood on an outcropping of rock in West Thirty-ninth Street near Tenth Avenue, then to the whole block of that street between Ninth and Tenth avenues. Soon the name, or epithet, was applied to the district between Eighth Avenue and the North River (as New Yorkers call the Hudson). Its north and south boundaries are a matter of dispute. Theodore Dreiser (*The Color of a Great City*) defined Hell's Kitchen as the section between Thirty-sixth and Forty-first streets; Lloyd Morris (*Incredible New York*) voted in favor of Twenty-third Street as the south boundary, Fortieth Street as the north; a number of other authorities believe Hell's

Kitchen takes in the whole section between Twenty-third and Fifty-ninth streets. No two authorities can be found in agreement on the point. Just to the south of Hell's Kitchen is Chelsea, which lies between Fourteenth and Twenty-third streets, Eighth Avenue and the North River. Chelsea's boundaries, too, are a matter of vigorous dispute, with some historians placing them as far north as Thirtieth Street. The old Tenderloin, also known as Satan's Circus, established itself near by, between Fifth and Seventh avenues, from Twenty-fourth to Fortieth streets.

Long before these neighborhoods came into being, the section was part of what Dutch settlers called Bloemendael, "Vale of Flowers," testifying to its pastoral charm. The Great Kill, a stream running along what is now West Forty-second Street, drained the brooks coursing through its meadows. The roads traversing its fields and meadows were favored by coaching parties. By the beginning of the nineteenth century Bloomingdale, as the Anglo-Saxon successors translated Bloemendael, was broken up into a number of tracts, including the Eden Farm, where Hell's Kitchen later cropped up. In 1803 the Eden Farm was acquired through foreclosure by John Jacob Astor for $25,000, according to the New York historian Hopper Striker Mott (*The New York of Yesterday*). He knew a real-estate bargain when he saw one: fifty-odd years later the Astor farmland was raising a lucrative cash crop of tenements.

In 1851, the Hudson River Railroad opened a station at Thirtieth Street and Tenth Avenue, the line then being in operation between East Albany and New York City. Commodore Cornelius Vanderbilt, who acquired control of the railroad in 1863, did not join those who ridiculed the idea of building a rail line through such "unpromising" country. "Put the road there," he observed, "and people will go there to live." In a few years the Hudson River Railroad's trackage was surrounded by lumberyards, stables, distilleries, brickyards, warehouses and slaughterhouses, as well as the tenements of their laboring forces.

And by 1859, West Thirty-ninth Street was known as Abattoir Place, and the bawling of cattle being herded to the bludgeons and knives of the butchers, not to mention the special aroma of the stockyards, filled the once sweet and quiet air of Bloomingdale. No longer was the school in West Thirty-seventh Street— built in 1854 and still standing today as Public School 127 between Tenth and Eleventh avenues—a place where its pupils could run barefoot, hear the melody of a lark through open windows on a drowsy spring afternoon, or watch white sails maneuvering down the Hudson. To replace such simple pleasures, the railroads and the encroaching water front, the mushrooming of industry and the influx of immigrant labor brought the rumble of trains, the clatter of horse-drawn trucks, soot and smoke, and the malty fumes of the breweries. A few years later *Leslie's Magazine* was crusading against the alleged practices of dairymen in the district, who were accused of feeding brewery mash to their cows and selling milk which made children groggy.

In the wartime 'sixties, with 203,000 natives of Ireland and 169,000 of Germany in a total population of 813,000 in the city, living conditions deteriorated still further in Hell's Kitchen. The wooden houses and shanties of the district were torn down and replaced by tenement rows, and it became one of the most wretched slums in North America. The landlords prospered on rents collected from rookeries with overcrowded rooms and medieval sewage disposal systems. Protests against housing conditions in Hell's Kitchen first arose in 1864, but corrective measures were feeble and inadequate. A Select Committee of the state legislature subsequently reported that cattle were better housed than human beings in Hell's Kitchen.

Under such conditions the Draft Riots of 1863 erupted out of the metropolitan stews, including Hell's Kitchen, at a cost of two thousand lives and property damage running into millions of dollars.

The Draft Riots broke out ten days after the battle of Gettysburg, and from July 13 to 17 mob anarchy ruled most of the streets of New York. Historians generally have provided a rather one-sided picture of the uprising of New York's immigrant population as an unpatriotic outburst fomented by Copperheads and other

Confederate sympathizers. The other side of the story is less creditable to the Union itself. At that stage of the war, with weariness and despair infecting both sides to an extent greater than is now acknowledged, the Union armies could be kept up to combat strength only by enlisting or conscripting the recent arrivals.

Both the Irish and Germans had contributed liberally to the process of fleshing out the Union armies decimated by the campaigns in northern Virginia and the fighting along the Tennessee, Cumberland and Mississippi rivers. The Irish Brigade, recruited mostly in New York City, had performed one of the most gallant and futile exploits of the war in charging to the crest of Marye's Heights at Fredericksburg, and German-speaking regiments from Wisconsin were among the staunchest fighters in the Army of the Potomac.

The Conscription Act of 1863 was aimed at family men, the only large source of manpower left untapped—except for the politically untouchable thousands who had purchased exemption from military service. Under the provisions of the new draft no man could claim exemption on the grounds that he was the sole support of his wife and children. "Just as specifically," a historian has pointed out, "anyone who could pay three hundred dollars or could hire a substitute for less was automatically exempted. Never before since the birth of the nation had the people been served notice so arrogantly that the privilege of dying in battle was reserved exclusively for them—that moneyed men owed no duty to the nation that could not be discharged with a trifling payment in cash, not even the primary obligation of defending it."

There was a strong current of resentment against the new draft throughout the North, but nowhere was the indignation greater than among the immigrant Irish of New York. (The Germans, for the most part, were passive during the Draft Riots, sympathizing with the Irish but by nature less inclined toward civic disorder.) Irish mothers with large families told their men to fight it out in the streets rather than leave them to beg, steal or live on charity.

The first draft-lottery took place Saturday, July 11, 1863, and on Sunday the lists of those tapped for military service were published in the newspapers. Over that troubled weekend the nabobs of the city completed their plans for suppressing the disorders they anticipated when the draft lists were published. Three separate forces were ready to put down the disturbances. The metropolitan police could muster 2,297 men of all ranks. A dozen regiments of infantry and cavalry were in or near the city. The third force was a corps of Volunteer Specials, private citizens enrolled as an auxiliary police force. Not all the volunteering for this special force was enthusiastic; white-collar workers in the banks and commercial houses had to be threatened with loss of their jobs, in many instances, before they would sign up. Finally a thousand men were enrolled as Volunteer Specials and armed with pistols and nightsticks.

The rioting broke out Monday morning, July 13, and continued for four days, with an estimated fifty to seventy thousand men, women and children participating. Most of them were armed only with bricks, paving stones and clubs. Some of the mobs numbered ten thousand apiece, and the sight of them swarming down a wide street and filling it from wall to wall and as far as the eye could range was blood-chilling and unforgettable. The people surged out of the Five Points, Mulberry Bend, Hell's Kitchen and the Upper West Side and set forth to burn, kill and loot; they attacked the draft offices, the New York *Tribune* building, the mansions along Lexington Avenue, the Negro Orphan Asylum. All of Manhattan above Mulberry Street was in the hands of the rioting mobs, the police concentrating below that line to protect the business and financial district. Uptown the police detachments took cover in their station houses.

With the army pouring regiments into the city from all directions, the authorities strove to regain control of the streets. Batteries of field artillery were lined up hub to hub and loaded with grapeshot and canister. They proved to be most efficient in clearing a bloody path through the mobs.

The newspapers were unanimous in demanding the employment of all possible force to crush the insurrection. Henry J. Raymond wrote in the *Times:* "The mob is not the people, nor does it belong to the people. It is for the most part made up of the vilest elements of the city. It has not even the poor merit of being what mobs usually are—the product of mere ignorance and passion. They talk, or rather they did talk at first, of the oppressiveness of the Conscription Law; but three-fourths of those who have been actively engaged in violence have been boys and young men under twenty years of age, and not at all subject to the Conscription. Were the Conscription Law to be abrogated tomorrow, the controlling inspiration of the mob would remain the same..It comes from sources quite independent of that law, or any other other law—from a malignant hate toward those in better circumstances, from a craving for plunder, from a barbarous spite against a different race, from a disposition to bolster up the failing fortunes of the Southern rebels. . . . The mob must be crushed at once. Give them grape and plenty of it." This was a comparatively mild expression of the savage reaction of New York's ruling classes to the savagery of the mobs.

Against the volleys of trained infantry, cavalry charges and artillery barrages, the rioters were helpless, but they soon devised new tactics for street fighting which were tried out first in Hell's Kitchen. The people of Hell's Kitchen already had marched down Eleventh Avenue en masse and wrecked the Hudson River Railroad's depot and yards at Thirtieth Street; they attacked and disarmed a company of soldiers in front of Allerton's Hotel on Eleventh Avenue between Fortieth and Forty-first streets, and they burned the Weehawken Ferry building at the foot of West Forty-second Street. Instead of massing in the streets and challenging the army and police firepower, they lashed together wagons, telegraph poles and heavy beams to form barricades closing off Eighth Avenue between Thirty-seventh and Forty-third streets.

A strong force of Volunteer Specials supported by infantry attacked the barricade at Thirty-seventh Street. They were unpleasantly surprised when the few armed men behind the barricade riddled the Volunteer Specials' ranks. The latter took cover behind the infantry and declined any further part in trying to root the rioters out of Eighth Avenue. That left it up to the soldiers, who, having no choice in the matter, advanced and fired by volleys. Under heavy and controlled fire the barricades could not long be held, because few of the rioters were armed with any-thing more lethal than bricks and stones. They held each barri-cade as long as possible, then retired to the next, taking a heavy toll of the military each step of the way and using Eighth Avenue as Wellington used the lines of Tôrres Vedras. Between twenty and thirty rioters were killed behind the barricades of Eighth Avenue. When the infantry had finally cleared that avenue, the Volunteer Specials took up a task more suitable to their talents than the direct assault—clubbing to death the wounded rioters left behind the barricades.

Barricades sprang up all over the city, but police and troops were hesitant to assault them.

In four days of fighting, the authorities were able to maintain control only of the southern tip of the island. The rioters still ruled the city and would not be lured back into civil obedience by false announcements that the draft had been suspended.

Two factors were responsible for the appeasement of the mobs on Friday, the fifth day of New York's insurrection. The Common Council voted to appropriate millions of dollars to pay the draft-exemption fees of poor men with dependents. (Less than two weeks later the appropriation was vetoed by Mayor Opdyke.) That morning also the Roman Catholic Archbishop Hughes ad-dressed an orderly enough crowd from the balcony of his resi-dence at Thirty-sixth Street and Madison Avenue. He urged that the rioting be halted, saying, "Every man has a right to defend his home or his shanty at the risk of life. The cause, however, must be just. It must not be aggressive or offensive. Do you want my advice? . . . Is there not some way by which you can stop these proceedings and support the laws, none of which have been enacted against you as Irishmen and Catholics? You have suf-fered already. No government can save itself unless it protects its citizens. Military force will be let loose on you. The innocent will be shot down, and the guilty will be likely to escape. Would it not be better to retire quietly?"

The rioting ended that day after taking a toll of two thousand lives, eight to ten thousand wounded, five millions in property damage. The Volunteer Specials, who had lost only three men out of a thousand in the fighting, boasted openly that—thanks mostly to their efforts—"the Irish cattle have had impressed on them a respect for order." One of their spokesmen belatedly took note of the fact in a statement to the *Tribune* that many Irish had fought with the police and the military to suppress the disorders: "The Irish in the police department have won the respect of good citizens. They nobly shot down their fellow countrymen and women."

The draft proceeded without further protest from the tenement districts, and New York was peaceable enough for the duration, as thousands of men who had fought in the streets in July of 1863 went on to answer their summons to military service.

Those draftees who survived the war found on their return home that Hell's Kitchen and the other tenement districts were still rotting away in utter squalor and that nothing had been done to curb the rapacity of the slum landlord, except to establish a metropolitan Board of Health, followed by mildly regulatory legislation on the construction of tenement houses. In 1867, multiple dwellings were required to have fire escapes, banisters must be attached to all stairways, either a water closet or an outside privvy must be furnished for every twenty tenants. The Board of Health subsequently ordered that transoms be provided for forty-six thousand unventilated rooms, but this work was delayed until 1874 by recurring epidemics of cholera and smallpox in the tenement districts.

During the postwar years these rookeries on the Lower East Side and the Middle West Side, with smaller patches of blight elsewhere in the city, were crowded by continuing waves of immigration, including growing groups from eastern and southern Europe and the Levant. Gangs of homeless children lived in tenement basements. Street-fighting gangs ruled whole neighbor-

hoods, encouraged by Tammany politicians and undeterred by
the police. "For more than twenty-five years the criminal classes
revelled in an orgy of vice and crime," Herbert Asbury has written of the post-Civil War period.

With unparalleled vulgarity, those who had profited by the
war held sway in the city until the severe depression of 1873.
Before the war there had been only a few actual millionaires in
the United States—now there were hundreds. Most of them descended on New York as the center of frivolity this side of Paris.
Some of the New Yorkers had done well for themselves, too. J.
Pierpont Morgan provided backing for one Simon Stevens who
bought the obsolete rifles of a New York militia regiment and
sold them at $22 apiece to the Union arsenal in St. Louis. A sub-
sequent investigation by a congressional committee uncovered
the fact that soldiers who fired the obsolete rifles had had their
thumbs blown off. Commodore Vanderbilt also was somewhat
less than choosy about his business associates. One of them,
T. J. Southard, sought to defraud the government by leasing un-
seaworthy vessels to the army as troop transports, which had to
be condemned without ever leaving their harbor graves. Other
New Yorkers did well for themselves at selling condemned arms
imported from Europe, shoddy uniform cloth, paper-soled shoes,
rotten beef . . . the whole sorry list of trade goods favored by
profiteers in all wars.

In spending their ill-gotten wealth, the parvenus displayed
such monumental vulgarity that New York suffered by compari-
son even with the crassness of Washington in the Johnson
and Grant administrations. Contemporary historians aptly termed
it "The Flash Age." In the *Valentine's Manual* for that period it
was observed, "In its endeavor to keep pace with the Second Empire the Flash Age took note only of the superficial and, like all
imitators, failed in the matter of good taste, a quality inherent in
the French. The march of Prussian troops through the Arc de
Triomphe brought New York's era of false prosperity and extravagance to its close, but it staggered on for two years without a
guide, then collapsed with equal suddenness."

At the routs given by the newly rich, which were shunned by members of real New York society, a low premium was placed on sexual morality, according to Frederick Longchamp *(Asmodeus in New York).* Just as the parvenus were trying to crash the old-line society, lesser creatures were eager to secure a footing among the well-heeled upstarts. "Among the fair sex here," Longchamp wrote of a typical party attended by members of the raffish, newly rich group, "many ladies really deserve that name for their decency . . . but the dresses of many others, the most elegantly attired, have not been paid for by their husbands' money. How could it be otherwise, when most of them spend, in tinsel and jewels alone, the salary of these poor men, or the profits of their business. I firmly believe that of the three hundred male guests, one half of them earn hardly $2,000 per annum—about the rent of the houses they live in; and how they are enabled to face their other expenses is a problem that Euclid himself could not solve. . . ."

The Tweed Ring, with Tammany Hall as its citadel, was permitted to plunder the city for years without effective opposition from the "better people." Edward Crapsey, a journalist who produced a somewhat ill-tempered study of Flash Age amorality *(The Nether Side of New York),* described in acrimonious detail how the Tweed Ring and its satellites and beneficiaries were "rioting in suddenly acquired wealth, and constantly exhibited themselves to the public gaze loaded with diamonds and guzzling costly wines, like the vulgar knaves they are. . . . Men who were fit to be ushers at minstrel shows were made State Senators, and the keepers of gin-shops were manufactured into legislators for the great State of New York. Among the police magistrates were the meanest of political tricksters, and a man who had been brought back from a distant State to answer for a felony was made Auditor of the public accounts.

"There was not only general acquiescence in this government, but general desire to share in its booty. It came to be accepted as a matter of course that all governments were corrupt, and that of New York was no worse than others. The people seemed contented with being swindled, and at any rate they could not be roused to defend themselves until, in 1871, they were confronted with evidence that could not be doubted. They then rose in their might and crushed the Ring as a giant would break a straw."

Of the giants of journalism thundering from their headquarters on Park Row, Horace Greeley in his *Tribune* was foremost in crying out against Boss Tweed and his associates. The Tweed Ring depended for its power on the resentments of the oppressed thousands in the tenement districts, and constantly put forward the argument—true enough—that the rich were Tammany's worst enemies. The corollary, of course, was that the rich hated Tammany because it fought for the poor. Greeley denounced this reasoning in one of his more celebrated and telling editorials:

"It is generally believed that the rich pay all the taxes upon houses, lots, grounds, etc., in a great city like ours. Hence many poor men give little thought to the constant and rapid growth of municipal extravagance and corruption. *They* are not dunned by the tax-collector—no part of the vast amount paid into the city's treasury is wrung directly from their hands. In their view, taxation is the concern of landlords and capitalists, not of journeymen and laborers who own no homes and, of course, pay no taxes.

"But they *do* pay; they *must* pay. If a tenement house is valued by the assessors at $50,000, the tax on it at two percent is $1000 per annum. Who pays it? The landlord immediately, the tenants ultimately. All of us are subsisted upon the fruits of labor; all taxes are paid therefrom. He who has made millions by office and politics may well give back to poverty a part of it in alms; but he cannot give so much as he has taken and have anything left. If he scatters gold coins among the poor as though they were pebbles, he must have made it by some means inconsistent with old-fashioned honesty and fidelity to public trust. Every dollar taken from the public treasury, in payment for services not required, is so much money unjustly wrested from private citizens for the aggrandizement of the wielders of power."

The people, however, were in no mood to listen to the avuncular sermons of Horace Greeley, who had been one of the prime targets of the Draft Riot mobs. The rich were too busy enjoying themselves to work up much indignation over the Grand Sachem of Tammany and his raids on the city treasury. The poor only knew that when they needed a relative sprung from the Tombs, or a few buckets of coal, or a basket of groceries, it was the Tammany district leader or his ward bosses who came to their rescue. The rather inconsiderable middle class was inclined to abdicate whatever responsibility it bore for political and social conditions.

Even then—it all has a curiously familiar ring—the substantial citizens were flocking out of Manhattan and heading for the suburban towns across the Hudson and elsewhere to escape their less fortunate neighbors. As Crapsey wrote in 1872, "Every man of moderate income saw that while he could house his family more decently and at less cost in any one of the suburban towns of New Jersey, he could reach them sooner and with less hardship, even if twenty miles away, than he could if they were only a tenth of that distance uptown. Therefore, an exodus began to these towns which has continued for several years, to the detriment of the city to a degree that is hardly yet realized. . . . With its middle classes in large part self-exiled, its laboring population being brutalized in the tenements, and its citizens of the highest class indifferent to the common weal, New York drifted from bad to worse, and became the prey of professional thieves, ruffians, and political jugglers. The municipal government shared in the vices of the people, and New York became a city paralyzed in the hands of its rulers."

In this general abdication of responsibility, Tweed flourished amazingly. Reputedly broke at the outbreak of the Civil War, the Grand Sachem of Tammany was worth $12,000,000 by 1870 and was the city's third largest owner of real estate. He was president of the Board of Supervisors, and had Mayor A. Oakey Hall, dubbed The Elegant Oakey, in his hip pocket. His philosophy of government had the sole virtue of frankness: "This population is too hopelessly split up into races and factions to govern it under universal suffrage, except by the bribery of patronage, or corruption."

Except for Greeley and the *Tribune*, the city's newspapers seldom roused themselves to a show of indignation over the undisguised thievery of Tweed and his associates. The pre-Pulitzer *World* was a Tammany organ. The *Post* was on the Tweed payroll for $5,000 a month. The *Times* was tolerant of "The Boss" editorially, one of its three directors being a partner of Tweed's in a printing concern. Only after this director died early in 1870 were the editors of the *Times* allowed to follow their natural distaste for Tweed and begin publishing the facts of his corrupt dictatorship of the city. The celebrated flaying performed by Thomas Nast's cartoons in *Harper's Weekly* was a major factor in the eventual destruction of Boss Tweed's power.

The Tweed Ring's judges—Albert Cardozo, John H. McCunn and George G. Bernard—were quite as venal as their co-conspirators in the municipal offices. They sold writs of habeas corpus, receiverships and court orders as openly as any pushcart merchant crying his wares, and used the Tombs as their private Bastille for political and personal enemies. Cardozo, by far the most rapacious of the three, was revealed to have taken bribes to release more than two hundred clients of one law firm alone, that of the notorious William F. Howe and Abe Hummel, before he resigned from the bench in 1872 to escape impeachment. For private reasons, Cardozo once kept two women in jail incommunicado for seventeen days. A lawyer who attempted to intervene on behalf of the women was warned by Justice Cardozo, "Do not touch this case. If you do, you will displease me. If you take this case, you need never expect any favor from me while I am on the bench."

Crime and vice flourished throughout the city with the amiable permission of the police and the politicians, who shared in the proceeds, and the indifference of the supposedly responsible electorate.

In 1870, seventeen thousand sailors were robbed in Manhattan. It was a fairly average year for this sport. The favorite method of separating a seaman from his pay was to administer chloral hydrate (knockout drops) and fling his unconscious body into the gutter. In the sailors' boardinghouses of Water Street and the vicinity the proprietors not only robbed their guests but shanghaied them for long cruises to the fever ports of the world.

Hardly an eyebrow was raised when the Reverend Henry W. Bellows told a public meeting in 1871 that New York sheltered thirty thousand professional thieves, twenty thousand "lewd women and harlots," two thousand gambling establishments, and three thousand grogshops. Or when Methodist Bishop Simpson announced in a speech at the Cooper Union that the prostitutes outnumbered the Methodists in the city. Or when the Reverend Henry Ward Beecher, later revealed as something less than a paragon of virtue, descended on Manhattan from his Brooklyn parsonage and described most vividly his tours of the West Side centers of depravity.

The observant Crapsey disputed only the reverend gentlemen's statistics on grogshops. He placed their number at 7,500 licensed, and many more unlicensed, and wrote that "the majority are dens where only the vilest stuff can be found." Another historian of the time agreed that the various types of saloons were largely responsible for the brutalization of all classes. "The money kings and the palaces of Broadway are worth visiting, but to get an idea of the people who rule this metropolis, one must go down among the tenements and the drinking saloons of the whiskey wards. . . . The drinking saloons were brilliantly lighted, and the girls were dressed in holiday attire, hoping thereby to entice many curious countrymen into their music dens. The barrooms did a wonderful business, and a constant stream of ghastly forms shuffled through the doorways. Now and then, in the midst of the tumult, one could not help pausing to watch the thinly clad girls as they emerged from the gin shops with a long black bottle of gin and disappear in the crowd."

Getting drunk and falling into the hands of the law was a bitter experience for the otherwise respectable citizen. Court officials and hangers-on did their best to make the occasion memorable in their parasitic fashion, according to Crapsey. "When he has not the money at hand [to pay his fine], he must communicate with his friends, and the court messenger never stirs without his fee. He is so unmanned by his new and dreadful position as a prisoner that he is an easy prey to the harpies in the shape of shyster lawyers who infest these courts and who persuade him that their influence or advocacy is a pearl of great price, and he pays for it accordingly. If in the end, when all expenses are counted up, he gets out for less than $50, he is fortunate, and the money is the least of the expenses entailed by his debauch. He has ever afterward the consciousness that he has been a criminal, however casually, and he has seen how great a mockery is the administration of justice which he enjoys, and he is never thereafter worth much to himself or the community."

Of the thieving class which swarmed all over the city, the pickpockets were "without equal in cunning and daring" in Crapsey's estimation. Most of them traveled in groups of three, one to jostle the victim, another to "hook" his pocketbook and the third to rifle it and dispose of it as quickly as possible. Crapsey told of an elderly gentlemen who became exasperated after losing several watches to pickpockets; he had an unbreakable chain made and anchored it and his watch to his vest so securely it couldn't be removed without ripping off his vest in the process. Boarding a crowded omnibus, he felt several tugs at his watch chain. Next to him was a man dressed as a minister. The latter left the bus in evident frustration, and the old gentleman crowed to his fellow passengers, "That fellow who just got out is a pickpocket. He took three pulls at my watch, but you see he didn't get it." He put his hand in a trouser pocket and a moment later was wailing, "But the rascal's got my pocketbook with $500 in it!"

About the only criminal in short supply was the professional killer, and that lack occurred, according to another commentator, because "murder was still an art, not an industry." Soon enough there was no lack of assassins for hire.

Eager understudies for all these criminals were to be found among the thousands of homeless children roaming, living in, and making their schoolrooms on the streets of New York. "Street sparrows," the more sentimental people called them. Most re-

spectable citizens were less kindly. Even Crapsey, usually a hu-
mane observer, wasted little sympathy on them, and wrote, "They
are casual criminals only during the brief years of boyhood, and
soon ripen into habitual vagrants, thieves or ruffians, and in each
case become public burdens. Sodden with vile liquor, ready to
give insult without provocation, indescribably filthy in language,
person and habits, they are entitled to a great deal less of grace
at the hands of the authorities than they get."

The earliest of the juvenile gangs, according to Charles L.
Brace *(The Dangerous Class of New York)*, was the Nineteenth
Street Gang, which roamed the district between Seventeenth and
Nineteenth streets, Seventh and Tenth avenues. A block on Tenth
Avenue called Misery Row was the "main seedbed of crime in the
quarter," according to Brace. The children in this gang, boys and
girls alike, were orphans or had been driven out on the streets by
their parents. They slept on hay barges in the North River, in
old sheds on Eighteenth and Nineteenth streets and around the
breweries. "They had never been in school or church, and knew
of God and Christ only in street oaths," Brace wrote.

The homeless children fought for existence only a few blocks
from the finest homes in old Chelsea, yet "society hurried on
selfishly for its wealth and left this vast class in misery and temptation." The city was shocked when a boy named Rogers murdered "a respectable gentleman named Swanton" while the latter
was walking with his wife in a street of the district. Another boy
gangster slew "an unoffending old man, in open day, before his
own door." Brace was contemptuous of the city's surprise at these
events: "Now these children arise and wrest back, with bloody
and criminal hands, what the world was too careless or too selfish
to give. The worldliness of the rich, the indifference of all classes
to the poor, will always be avenged." Influential citizens were
moved to establish the Eighteenth Street Lodging House for Boys,
which provided bed and board for eight hundred boys annually.

Ten thousand of the homeless children roaming the streets were
under fourteen years old, Crapsey estimated. Most of them, he
believed, had been abandoned by parents who fell victim to the

thousands of grogshops. "At least $15,000,000 are swallowed up every year by these grog shops, and $3 in every ten come out of the pockets of the tenement classes. The $5,000,000 thus wasted, if legitimately used, would more than provide a home for every vagabond child in New York." Many of the homeless children joined gangs dominated by Fagins who taught them to pick pockets, snatch purses and fur muffs, and burglarize homes. Others, not bold or nimble enough for criminal pursuits, begged for pennies outside theaters and saloons. "It is these forlorn creatures whose naked feet smear the gutter ice with blood, whose hands eagerly search the garbage barrel for morsels of refuse food which the homeless dogs will not touch, but which they devour; it is they who are found at night under stoops, in wagons, in lumber yards, or timidly asking for lodging at the police station."

The respectable world, for all the piety which spilled from pulpits, the press and popular literature in the 'seventies, either ignored the plight of these children or treated them with a chill inhumanity. The New York Prison Association found a fifteen-year-old boy who had been convicted of petty theft still in jail after three years had passed. The sentencing magistrate proclaimed that the boy was "an incorrigible young rascal—sure to be hanged." The Prison Association, which was one of the few organizations performing disinterested good deeds in any number, secured the boy's release.

Even the Children's Aid Society—now one of the finest and most efficient groups of its kind in the world—was not then notable for its generous attitude. It took pride in announcing that it had supervised the adoption of thousands of New York street children into "good homes in the west." Actually most of the children had been indentured to farmers who worked them, sunup to sundown, for many years without pay. Charles L. Brace, who long served as president of the society, wrote (in *The Dangerous Classes of New York*) of two starvelings who applied for help and were shown to the door by a staff member with the words, "Now, boys, just be kind enough to walk up that avenue for a hundred miles into the country, and you will find plenty of work and food." Brace explained that there was much fear among the charitable organizations that such children would "fall into habits of dependence." Brace wrote these words without conscious irony. It should be added, in all fairness, that the Children's Aid Society has come a long way in tolerance and true philanthropy since those days.

According to the works of Horatio Alger, the best way for a boy cast into the streets to avoid thievery and beggary was to join the hundreds of newsboys who swarmed over the city. Less inspirational writers of the period bear him out. Crapsey, from his investigations of the "nether side" of the metropolis, reported that the newsboys were in a class by themselves, characterized by "energy, independence, effrontery, cunning, and contentedness with the lot fortune sends them." Even so, their lot was not an easy one. They had to report at four o'clock in the morning to the circulation bosses on Park Row and work fourteen hours a day to earn a maximum of three dollars a week. Many of them lived in the Newsboys' Lodging House, where they were provided a cot and two meals a day for six cents.

Homeless girls specialized in selling flowers and matches on the streets. The "little match girl" standing on a street corner in the snow became a symbol of childhood wretchedness in New York. Some of the girls, however, improved their lot by peddling their wares in residential districts, gaining access to homes, and stealing whatever they could lay hands on before they were ejected.

No two persons better epitomized the Flash Age in New York than the city's leading abortionist, Madame Restelle, and Jim Fisk, its nimblest financier. Publicly at least, their paths did not cross, but they had in common the greed, boldness and amorality required for success in this free-wheeling society in which banquets were given in honor of lap dogs, the new plutocrats had their teeth set with diamonds, and stag dinners were regarded as dreary unless naked blondes popped out of papier-mâché pies for dessert.

Madame Restelle, in spite of or because of her vocation, was one of New York's leading citizens. In 1870 she was a woman of fifty-odd years, a score of which had been spent in her clandestine trade. She occupied a four-story brownstone residence on the northeast corner of Fifth Avenue and Fifty-second Street, which was staffed by seven servants. She advertised herself in the newspapers and the city directory as a "professor of midwifery," with offices at Chambers and Greenwich streets where she dispensed "infallible French female pills." She guaranteed a "cure at one interview." Occasionally she received clients at her home, in which she maintained a basement office for consultations. Sometimes a coach would draw up at her side door late at night to discharge a heavily veiled client. And sometimes, according to her neighbors, a hearse would roll up in the pre-dawn hours to remove a patient for whom the "French pills" had been less than "infallible."

"Madame Killer," as she became known in the newspapers, was a squat, dark-complexioned woman who had come to the United States some years before the Civil War as an English immigrant. Newspapermen who later traced her career reported that she had learned the abortionist's trade as the mistress of a New York physician during her early years in this country. Once knowledgeable, she shucked off the physician and set up her own practice. She was arrested and charged with murder in the death of one girl, but reportedly escaped conviction by handing out $100,000 in bribes. There were reports that the bribe money was raised, at her command, among people who had come to her with their problems. The Madame often boasted that she "knew the skeletons in the closets of many prominent people."

What with the generally feeble state of public morality, Madame Restelle was raking in the money both in her uptown and downtown offices. She charged from $500 to $1,000 per "consultation." A contemporary writer (Gustav Lening in *The Dark Side of New York Life*) wrote that "the families of the brownstone and marble fronts of Fifth Avenue were not blest very liberally with children. This, in connection with the '$500 to $1,000 per case,' clearly indicates the chief source of wealth of this woman."

As the newly rich invaded Fifth Avenue, many earnest efforts were made to buy out Madame Restelle but she clung to her elegant residence at Fifty-second Street and was indignant that some of these flashy newcomers should consider her beneath them in any way. Lening found it ironic that harassed New Yorkers who "do not hesitate to make use of the services of Madame Restelle exclude her most inexorably from their circles in social intercourse. This is all the more curious as Fifth Avenue very seldom inquires as to the means employed in obtaining wealth."

One day, however, the chatelaines of Fifth Avenue were relieved of Madame Restelle's presence in the neighborhood, thanks to Anthony Comstock, the anti-vice crusader.

Comstock, posing as the husband of a woman who "desperately" needed an abortion, obtained her agreement to perform the necessary services. He promptly arrested her and took her to the Tombs in a hack. On the way, he reported, she offered him a $40,000 bribe to forget the whole affair.

A few days after she was released on bail, one of her seven servants found Madame Restelle dead in her bathtub. She had slashed her throat with a razor.

Then came much private agony among the citizens of New York who had been able to afford her fees. The police seized the lists of her customers. Scandal-loving and sensation-mongering old James Gordon Bennett considered it a sacred duty that the names on these lists be published in his *Herald*, but never laid hands on them. Oddly and inexplicably enough, they "disappeared" from the police files.

The comic paper *Puck* published a double-truck cartoon titled "Fifth Avenue Two Years After Mme. Restelle's Death," showing

the thoroughfare thronged with baby carriages and nurse girls.
It served quite well as the diligent Madame's epitaph.

If there was one man who found his natural element in the
Flash Age, it was "Jubilee Jim" Fisk.

His piratical forays on Wall Street, the Erie Railroad and the
gold market may not have been forgiven by the people he victimized, but the general public viewed him with indulgence. For
one reason: he enjoyed himself. Dour little hypocrites like Daniel
Drew, crafty connivers like Jay Gould, consummate grabbers
like the first Astor and the first Vanderbilt never won much popular favor. But Fisk took such a voluptuous pleasure in his ill-
gotten gains, and carried them off with such a triumphant waddle,
that the public was able to derive a vicarious enjoyment from
watching him throw away millions on mistresses, French opera
singers, matched carriage horses, gold-encrusted uniforms. Even
Greeley's *Tribune*, which was appalled by the financial swash-
buckling of the times, conceded that he had one sterling virtue:
"He was no hypocrite. . . . When he devoured the widow's substance he differed from so many of his associates in refraining
from the pretense of long prayers."

In 1871, next to the last year of his suddenly terminated life,
he was thirty-seven years old, a stout, jovial, back-slapping fellow
"leading a life of half-barbaric prodigality." Napoleon III mus-
tachios sprouted dashingly from his porcine face. He wore, as
often as possible, the two flashiest uniforms in his wardrobe—
that of an admiral of the Fall River Line, which he controlled,
and of the 9th National Guard Regiment, the colonelcy of which
he bought with money and favors—not the wisest purchase he
ever made, as it developed.

The son of a Vermont peddler, Fisk was a circus roustabout
in his youth, finally settled down to a desk job with the Jordan &
Marsh mercantile firm in Boston. He married a Boston girl named
Lucy Moore, whom he eventually installed in a mansion in her
native city and to whom he wrote every day of his life, even while

hectically pursuing every sightly female in New York—the only known instance of fidelity in his feverishly disordered life. He was an almost immediate success, a fresh breeze blowing through the stuffy Boston commercial world, and obtained a number of large war contracts for Jordan & Marsh. During the war, suppressing his latent yearning for martial glory, he bought cotton in the South for a Boston syndicate, a venture of dubious legality. Just after the war, in league with Jay Gould and Daniel Drew, he obtained control of the Erie Railroad and milked its stockholders unmercifully. He and his fellow brigands, in the summer of 1868, increased Erie's stock issues from thirty-four to fifty-eight million dollars. Then, to cover up their short sales, a year later Fisk and Gould precipitated the Black Friday financial disaster by buying up seven to eight million dollars' worth of gold and cornering the market, banking on President Grant not to throw the United States Treasury's gold on the market. Fisk put too much faith in Gould's loyalty, too little in Grant's sense of responsibility. Behind Fisk's back, Gould dumped five million dollars' worth of gold on the market, and the Treasury released another four million dollars. Fisk was on the verge of ruin. Then Gould showed Fisk how to repudiate his contracts, slip out from under his commitments, and let hundreds of other people be ruined instead. A mob of unlucky speculators chased Fisk and Gould through the streets until they reached the sanctuary of Fisk's offices and barricaded themselves in with a gang of armed hirelings.

A congressional investigating committee demanded to know what had happened to the money involved in the attempt to corner the gold market.

"Gone where the woodbine twineth," was Fisk's impish reply.

Fisk established a sort of satrapy on West Twenty-third Street, near Eighth Avenue, on the uncertain boundary between Chelsea and Hell's Kitchen. He bought Pike's Opera House on the northwest corner of Twenty-third and Eighth; installed his No. 1 concubine, the velvet-eyed young actress Josie Mansfield, in a

mansion at 359 West Twenty-third Street, and himself in an
equally luxurious house adjacent to the opera house. The fickle
Josie's house cost the Erie Railroad stockholders $40,000, and she
was on the Erie payroll for $1,000 a month for services rendered
its chief executive. The opera house was paid for with $820,000 of
Erie funds, but the railroad's headquarters were installed on the
three floors above the theater as a sort of sop to the corporate
decencies. The corner of Twenty-third and Eighth, according to
Robert Hall, a native of Chelsea, soon became a turbulent scene.
Hardly a day passed without a flying wedge of summons servers
trying to crash into Erie's general offices with legal papers obtained by stockholders struggling to recapture the railroad. A
neighborhood stalwart named Tommy Lynch was commander
of the toughs enlisted by Fisk to repel such assaults on his sovereignty. Hall wrote of "stirring scenes, days of injunctions, man-
damuses, seizures with court orders and without them, and battles
in the hallways [of the Grand Opera House, as Fisk renamed
it] between sheriff's deputies and Fisk's and Gould's henchmen,
which gave special interest to the daily papers and were followed
by the readers as they do the war news of today. Every morning
the public looked first at the Fisk-Erie headlines to see what the
opposing armies had accomplished the day and night before. . . .
Many of Fisk's and Gould's smartest moves were made at night
through injunctions granted overnight by complaisant judges."
   The Grand Opera House, with Fisk as amateur impresario, was
the financier's most satisfying toy, aside from his fancy ladies.
He discarded the heavy German and Italian operas in favor of
French comic opera, engaged two separate ballet companies, one
blonde and one brunette, "just as he drove his horses in black
and white pairs." Less successfully he tried casting three prima
donnas in the same rôle, one for each act of the opera. Prima
donnas, in fact, generally resisted his porky charm. When Celine
de Montaland, the French opera star, arrived to fulfill an engagement at his opera house, he took her for a ride through Central
Park and pretended that vast acreage was part of his private estate. Instead of swooning with delight, Mme. Montaland snapped,

"If you're that rich, Monsieur Fisk, you can afford to pay me more money." Fisk had no alternative but to comply.

This was the Flash Age, the climate which nurtured Hell's Kitchen and its environs.

2

"What Makes You Irishers All the Time Fight?"

B Y 1871 a rather tepid form of social consciousness had
broken out among New York's middle and upper classes.
Distinguished-looking gentlemen in clean collars and
clawhammer frock coats and inquisitive bureaucrats
from City Hall began poking their way through tenement rows and Blood Alleys hitherto visited only by the police
in club-swinging platoons. The residents of Hell's Kitchen did
not always take kindly to the advice and admonitions which the
visitors dispensed in liberal doses. A man from the Sanitary Commission scolded a woman resident in Hell's Kitchen for not making her place more livable by applying "soap and water and elbow
grease." She immediately supplied him with some of the facts
of life in her ramshackle world. "What do you take us for?" she
demanded. "Do you think we are going to clean out the house
so the landlord can kick us out when it looks better and rent it
to people who can pay more than us?"

A health inspector's report indicated that the rapid industrialization of the section, as well as the poverty and ignorance of its

inhabitants, was creating conditions against which mere soap and water would have little effect. He spotted forty-six slaughter-houses, which drained blood and offal into the gutters instead of sewers. Children by the droves splashed in these same gutters. In his report he also cited the "offal dock" at the foot of West Thirty-eighth Street where dead animals from all over the city were unloaded and either burned or sent to the glue factory; "swill-milk" cow stables where the cows were fed on the waste from neighboring distilleries; and garbage and refuse piled into hillocks along the gutters of Tenth and Eleventh avenues.

So many goats were wandering around the Middle West Side that the matter came to the attention of the Board of Aldermen, difficult as they were to distract from consideration of paving contracts and other more profitable matters. A West Side grocer complained that "a goat could destroy $500 worth of shrubbery in an afternoon." The aldermen passed an ordinance decreeing, "No goat shall be at large in any part of the streets, avenues, lanes, alleys, piers, wharves or public places in the City of New York under penalty of three dollars for every such goat which shall be found at large, to be paid by the owner or person having charge, care, or keeping thereof." Cattle, however, could be driven along Forty-second Street from river to river, most of the city's slaughterhouses being located around the foot of West Forty-second.

The desolate atmosphere of the section was conveyed by the short-story writer and poet Fitz-James O'Brien (*Life, Stories and Poems*):

"This tract of land is perhaps the most melancholy and mysterious spot in the whole city. The different streets that cross the Island pull up, as it were, suddenly on reaching this dreary place, seemingly afraid to trust themselves any further. The buildings that approach nearest to its confines are long, low ranges of fetid slaughterhouses, where on Sunday bloated butcher boys lounge against the walls, and on weekdays one hears through the closed doors the muffled blow, the heavy fall of oxen within, the groan and the hard-drawn breath; and then a red sluggish stream trickles from under the doorway and flows into the gutter, where hungry dogs wait impatiently to lap it up. The murderous atmosphere, these streamlets of blood, seem appropriate, however, as one approaches the desolate locality."

All sorts of industries, attracted by Hell's Kitchen's real-estate bargains and cheap labor, were moving into the district. The Higgins carpet factory on West Forty-third Street become one of the nation's largest within a decade and was employing two thousand people by 1882. (When the Higgins company moved to Thompsonville, Connecticut, around the turn of the century, only ten per cent of its employes agreed to follow it out of Hell's Kitchen, despite the offer of cottages and gardens, free clubs, reading rooms, pool tables and bowling alleys. "Dark rooms, foul air, congested, dirty, squalid, all but unlivable home conditions, if only somewhere in New York, were preferable to the lonely monotony of a country town in Connecticut," it was noted by Otho G. Cartwright in his sociological treatise *The Middle West Side.*) The Metropolitan Gas Company settled down between West Forty-first and Forty-second and Eleventh Avenue and the North River, the Municipal Oxygen Gas Company between West Forty-fourth and Forty-sixth and Eleventh Avenue and the river, adding little to the beauty of the neighborhood. Rafts of logs were floated down the Hudson and collected in a boom at the foot of West Forty-fourth Street, around which many sawmills sprang up. Oyster fisheries were located along the North River between Forty-fourth and Forty-fifth streets.

Many of the German immigrants, expert cabinetmakers in their native land, found employment at Wessel, Nickel & Gross, the piano manufacturers on West Forty-fifth. Other piano factories, printing concerns, candymakers, iron foundries and ornamental ironworks, and carriage factories were established throughout the district. Shipyards were founded at the foot of West Forty-eighth Street. Dotted throughout the section were lime kilns and stone masons' yards. Much of the brownstone then in high fashion was cut into slabs in the yards of Hell's Kitchen. It was quarried across the river at Weehawken and Guttenberg on the Jersey shore, and every day at 6:30 A.M. a fleet of skiffs loaded with workmen pulled out from the Manhattan shore for the quarries.

The extension of the Ninth Avenue elevated railway above West Thirtieth Street in 1879 was filling up the Middle West Side with workingmen. It was also killing off the sedate neighborhood below Thirty-third Street, the clean and quiet streets of old Chelsea, and replacing its countrified old houses with rows of tenements. The Ninth Avenue El, the city's first rapid transit system, brought with it the unsightly trestle and the shriek and clatter of its steam locomotives. The streets were showered with cinders, soot and hot ashes. The El's trains could have been powered by electricity instead of soft coal, if only Jay Gould, the financier, hadn't been scared half to death by a mishap during a demonstration some years later of electric-powered trains. A fuse blew out close to where Gould was standing during the trial run. Gould leaped several feet off the ground, and came down screaming that he'd never trust electricity again. The result was that for twenty years "the faces of lady passengers were stenciled with smoky replicas of the patterns of their veils," and dignified old Chelsea, not to mention the newer neighborhood to the north, was subjected to the uproar of steam engines, whistles and brakes.

In the Chelsea of the gracious past, Lieutenant General Winfield Scott, first general-in-chief of the Union armies during the Civil War and conqueror of Mexico in 1847, made his last home at 136 West Twentieth Street. Edwin Forrest, the celebrated actor, established himself at 436 West Twenty-second Street with its ornate porch, wrought-iron gallery and formal garden in which he and his friend William Cullen Bryant sipped mint juleps during the summer evenings. Another leading actor, Edwin Booth, built his theater on the southeast corner of Twenty-third Street and Sixth Avenue in 1869 but went bankrupt five years later as cruder amusements and less aesthetic people invaded the neighborhood.

The first settler of Chelsea was Captain Thomas Clark, a veteran of the French and Indian wars, who had staked out a large estate for himself in 1750 between what are now Fourteenth and

Twenty-seventh streets, Seventh Avenue and the North River. Some said he named it for the London quarter of Chelsea, others that he named it for the Chelsea Hospital for soldiers. His grandson and heir, Clement C. Moore, built a house near Twenty-third Street and Ninth Avenue and lived in it from 1822 to 1853. Near by, the future site of Jim Fisk's Grand Opera House was in those years occupied by the stables of the Knickerbocker Stage Line. In those quiet surroundings, Moore wrote " 'Twas the Night Before Christmas," and donated the land between Twentieth and Twenty-first streets, Ninth and Tenth avenues, to the General Theological Seminary of the Episcopal Church, of which Moore became a faculty member.

Among the earliest of the working-class residents were Scottish weavers who established themselves in the block between Sixteenth and Seventeenth streets, Sixth and Seventh avenues, which soon was called Paisley Place. These Scots started out as crofters, as in their native Highlands, working at the looms in their own cottages. Soon, however, they were enticed by higher wages to the less imaginative looms of the Higgins carpet factory. Other nationalities soon followed the Scots, as Robert Hall wrote in *Valentine's Manual of Old New York.* "There was one peculiarity about Chelsea which did not, I think, exist in any other part of the city. Certain blocks seemed to be reserved for certain nationalities. Thus there was Scotch Row for the 'ladies from hell'; London Row for the blarsted Britisher; and Yankee Row for the native Americans who had the hardihood to intrude themselves among these foreigners. And oh! I forgot the Irish. . . ."

How times had changed for old Chelsea with its tree-shaded thoroughfares, its walled gardens and its suburban gentility was demonstrated with all finality on a sweltering summer's day in 1871 when more than fifty persons were killed in a street riot on the Chelsea-Hell's Kitchen border. The disturbance was caused by Old World political and religious differences all the more violent for being transplanted to American soil. Unfortunately these could not be surgically removed at Ellis Island. New York has had a long career as the retreat for displaced patriots of all

nations, a place for the losing side's leaders to regroup and re-
finance for another try at gaining the ascendancy. Its squares
have echoed to the oratory of a thousand obscure causes, and its
streets have been the scene of countless "sympathy parades." In
the 'seventies alone, there were reverberations of the hostilities
between the North and the South of Ireland, celebrations of the
Prussian victory over France, protests against the punishment of
Hungarian revolutionaries, public jubilation when Italy was uni-
fied. As Smith Hart wrote in *The New Yorkers,* a concise exposi-
tion of New York attitudes, "Whole sections of the people of
the city were getting further and further out of step with the people of America. Great economic upheavals sweeping over the
nation whipped up only a backwash of oratory in New York. . . ."

This time, on July twelfth of 1871, it was the Irish whose trans-
Atlantic grievances brought bloodshed to the streets—specifically
Eighth Avenue.

For days before there were rumors that the plans of the Orangemen for their usual celebration of the Battle of the Boyne, would
be violently opposed by the Fenians, Catholic Irish, mostly, who
were dedicated to overthrowing British rule in Ireland. The an-
niversary of the Boyne was July 12. That the battle had taken
place in 1690 only increased the potency of feeling on both sides.

On July 12 of the previous year, the Orangemen's picnic at
Elm Park had been attacked by the Irish of the opposite persuasion, but the only casualties were a few cracked heads and blackened eyes.

This year, the more belligerent Irish nationalists proclaimed,
the Orangemen would not get off so lightly. The newspapers
published rumors—and they were only that—that "10,000 Catholics
were arming in the city." The leaders of the Orange societies
warned that five thousand of their marchers "will be carrying
weapons," and declared that if their opponents had the right to
parade on St. Patrick's Day, "we have a perfect right to parade
on any other day."

In the hot, humid and temper-provoking July days, there were
pitifully few attempts to head off trouble. The attitude of the

largely Anglo-Saxon middle and upper classes was that the Irish Catholics, who were blamed for the Draft Riots of eight years before, needed another stern lesson and that it was up to the police and the militia to see that they got it. This attitude toward the Irish was expressed by Charles L. Brace: "Let but the Law lift its hand from them for a season, or let the civilizing influence of American life fail to reach them, and we should see an explosion from this class which might leave the city in ashes and blood."

Roman Catholic Archbishop McCloskey was one of the few restraining influences. He sent a letter to all parish priests in New York asking that Catholics "array themselves on the side of peace and order and allow the Orangemen to parade," with instructions that it be read from every pulpit the Sunday preceding Wednesday, July 12. Another calming voice was that of O'Donovan Rossa, a Fenian leader who had risked his life and spent years in British prisons for a free Ireland. Unpopular as he knew his sentiments to be, he told a meeting of the Irish organizations' leaders at Hibernia Hall in Prince Street, "Let the Orangemen have their celebration," and bluntly expressed the opinion that trying to interfere with the parade was "unworthy of Irishmen and Americans."

On Monday, July 10, Mayor A. Oakey Hall ordered Police Superintendent J. J. Kelso to cancel the police department's permit for the Orangemen's parade. The New York *Post* commented (with belated anti-Tweed bias) that "The Tammany Ring, which has the city in its clutches . . . has taken the part of the mob." Certainly there was little to be gained politically from upholding the right of the Orangemen to parade. Of the thousands of Protestant Irish in the city, fifteen hundred were members of the Orange societies. And of these fifteen hundred affiliated Orangemen, only 160, or slightly more than ten per cent, finally showed up for the parade.

There was such a storm of journalistic protest over the Mayor's proclamation that Governor John T. Hoffman, himself a Democrat, ordered it rescinded the following day. He also ordered out every available police and militia unit to protect the parade—no matter what the cost.

This on-again, off-again policy of high city and state officials, of course, only resulted in a further fraying of tempers.

Governor Hoffman rushed down from Albany to take charge of operations at New York police headquarters. Eight hundred police and twenty-three hundred militiamen in five regiments—many of them Irish Catholics—were mobilized to protect a parade of 160 Orangemen. It was patently a show of force organized to teach the "mob" a lesson.

The Ancient Order of Hibernians and other Irish societies, meanwhile, announced that all members who refused to join the "volunteer corps" and demonstrate against the Orangemen would be expelled.

On the morning of July 12, all parties were fully mobilized for the showdown. The eight hundred policemen and the Third Brigade of the New York National Guard, with Brigadier General Varian in command of the 6th, 7th, 9th, 22nd and 84th regiments, concentrated in the streets around the Orange societies' headquarters on Eighth Avenue.

The Irish were gathering their forces in Hell's Kitchen and at Hibernia Hall. A crowd of eight hundred, according to the New York *Times*, swarmed through Hell's Kitchen and Chelsea ordering shopkeepers to close up and join the demonstration. At Forty-sixth Street and Tenth Avenue the crowd surrounded a group of thirty workmen engaged in blasting rock and ordered them to lay down their tools and join the procession. Several who refused were badly beaten, the *Times* said.

A New York *Herald* reporter stationed at Hibernia Hall wrote that many German sympathizers showed up there with their Irish friends (a large percentage of the names on the casualty lists, in fact, were German).

One of the Germans, the owner of a lager-beer saloon, a round-faced and amiable Bavarian, was overheard by a New York *Sun* reporter asking his Irish friend, "What makes you Irishers all the time fight? What the devil difference does it make whether these Orangers parade?"

"Och, Schlosser, don't bother me," the Irishman said. "You wouldn't understand if I was talking from June to January. But I'll tell you one thing—those Orangemen are reptiles and we that know them well know that if we don't destroy them from the start, they'll ruin the country."

At the armory of the 9th Regiment Jim Fisk, railroad tycoon and fancier of gaudy uniforms, and his officers were assembling their companies under arms. Fisk had literally bought the colonelcy of this regiment with cash and favors. The year before the regiment had been badly in debt and could muster only three hundred men. Lieutenant Colonel Braine, a Civil War veteran, was its commander but agreed to step down to second-in-command if Fisk could be induced to rehabilitate the regiment. Fisk eagerly accepted, was elected colonel by the officers on April 7, 1870. With his "love of gold lace," Fisk soon filled out the regiment's ranks by handing out money to recruits and entertaining them with parties at the Grand Opera House. Now it was up to full peacetime strength of over five hundred enlisted men. The adjutant of the regiment was Henry S. Brooks, founder of the Brooks Brothers clothing firm.

Colonel Fisk showed up at the armory at seven o'clock that morning and, according to the New York *World*, "kept the men drilling in the science of street fighting," exhilarated by the prospect of leading "his men" into action.

Several hours before the parade was scheduled to start, the crowds began gathering around Lamertine Hall, headquarters of the Orange societies, at Twenty-ninth Street and Eighth Avenue. Many in the crowd were drunk. "Among these groups," the New York *Tribune* said the next day, "women were the most conspicuous by the vehemence with which they denounced Orangemen, police and soldiers alike."

Soldiers and police, too, were ducking in and out of the saloons or nipping from flasks. To the adjutant of the Third Brigade went a message on the police telegraph system: "Captain McDonald,

Police, reports that the commandant of A Company, 84th Regiment, was intoxicated when he left Police Headquarters." A number of enlisted men in the ranks of A Company, 84th Regiment, also were under the weather, reporters at the scene noted.

It was shortly after noon when the Orangemen, with justifiable apprehension, issued from the building and were swallowed up by the police and militia. The paraders were so hemmed in by their protectors—more than three thousand soldiers and policemen to 160 marchers—that only their banners could be seen. Inscribed on many of the placards carried by the marchers was: "Americans, Freemen, Fall In." No one was seen to accept the invitation.

The parade was to proceed down Eighth Avenue to Twenty-third Street, over Twenty-third to Fifth Avenue, down Fifth to Fourteenth Street, over Fourteenth Street to Fourth Avenue, disbanding at the Cooper Institute.

As the parade swung out, wrote a *Tribune* reporter, "a sullen stillness generally prevailed. The very air seemed oppressed with a sense of impending bloodshed. The Orangemen were pale, though determined."

The crowd was particularly enraged by the sight of the orange ribbons worn by the marchers, according to a *Times* reporter, who compared them to the "little red flag of the Spanish matador with which he enrages the bull in the arena." A roar of anger welled up from the throng, particularly when they caught sight of the portrait of Prince William of Orange borne aloft.

Part of the crowd's rage, undoubtedly, stemmed from sheer frustration. Their enemy marched smugly between hedgerows of bayoneted rifles and nightsticks. Captain George Walling, a veteran of the Draft Riots and commander of the police at the scene, divided his forces into two battalions, each protecting a flank of the parade. Outside the phalanx of police the five regiments of militia were deployed. The spearhead was formed by the 84th Regiment, with A Company, its drunken commander and its whiskey-inflamed rankers unfortunately in the vanguard. Down the line of march were the 7th and 22nd regiments, with the 6th and 9th regiments bringing up the rear. Colonel Jim Fisk, hatless and coatless, marched at the head of the 9th Regiment in his shirt sleeves and carrying a sword, which had been supplied him at the last moment by one of his officers. Many accounts had Fisk riding into battle on horseback and in full uniform, but ironically on this day, in his excitement, he had dashed out of the armory without his gold-laced tunic and plumed hat.

A bull-throated roar of rage swelled up from the crowd when the parade marshal's sword cane accidentally became unscrewed and the naked blade gleamed in the midday sun.

The murderous trouble broke out at the intersection of Twenty-fourth Street and Eighth Avenue.

The head of the parade had just passed that corner when bricks and stones showered down from the roofs of tenements overlooking Eighth Avenue. The militia officers later claimed that the barrage was followed by a shot from a tenement on the corner, but Captain Walling cited in his report "other accounts that the shot came from one of the soldier's rifles, which was accidentally discharged."

In any case, there was no doubt about what followed—a volley fired by the 84th Regiment, including the partly befuddled A Company, into the thick of the crowd, indiscriminately, mowing down women and children as well as men. A moment later, according to the *Tribune* account, "The 9th and 6th regiments in the rear of the Orangemen also began firing indiscriminately, sweeping 25th, 26th, 27th, 28th streets, the extreme rear of the 9th firing a few shots up Eighth Avenue into a platoon of policemen who were stationed at 29th Street. The firing was as wild as it was uncalled for, and wholly without order." Neither the 7th nor the 22nd regiments joined in the shooting.

"It was almost impossible to describe the scene at this point. Screams and groans, mingled with oaths and imprecations, rent the air," a *World* reporter wrote. "Children wailed and women shrieked in mortal terror, and men fled, trampling friend and foe, the weak, wounded and dying, beneath their cowardly feet."

With more than a hundred dead and wounded lying in the street, not even "the most desperate and drunken of the mob could be induced to resume the fight," the *Tribune* said, without indicating who was "inducing" them to attack the parade. "The mob sought safety in Seventh and Ninth avenues and not one of the cowardly scoundrels returned to aid their wounded."

Police Captain Walling, as honest a cop as could be found in those days, believed that the shooting was "reckless and wholesale," wholly unjustified by the shot supposedly fired from the tenement and the shower of bricks and stones, particularly since the militia fired without orders into crowds of people, most of whom were doing nothing more violent than shouting their disapproval of the parade. In his autobiography *(Recollections of a New York Chief of Police)* Walling wrote, "The sight which was disclosed when the smoke cleared away was heart-rending and terrible in the extreme. Dozens of bodies—men, women and children—lay upon the grounds; the shrieks and groans of the wounded rang out above the noise caused by the feet of the vast mob, now madly trampling upon the weaker of the fugitives in the wild rush to reach a place of safety.

Colonel Jim Fisk failed to cover himself with glory. When his regiment opened fire at Twenty-sixth Street and Eighth Avenue, there was a scattering of shots in reply. Of the five soldiers killed, three were from the 9th Regiment. One of the casualties was Private Henry C. Page of K Company, who was house manager of Fisk's Grand Opera House. Page was shot in the head and killed instantly. Unnerved by this gory sight, Fisk fled the scene. Later he claimed that he had been struck on the ankle by a piece of lead pipe and incapacitated for further duty, but it seems that he made remarkable time in removing himself from the riotous scene.

Tossing away his borrowed sword as so much unwanted baggage, he headed for a near-by saloon, "a bruised and weary pacifist." He tore through the saloon, vaulted over the courtyard wall, and clambered over a number of back-yard fences between Twenty-fifth and Twenty-sixth streets until he was well away from the scene of action. Then he headed for the North River—still making excellent time for an incapacitated warrior—and boarded one of his tugs. He landed at Sandy Hook and proceeded rapidly in the direction of Long Branch, New Jersey, where he finally halted his retreat at his summer home. By nightfall the *World* was able to ascertain that "the surgeons decided that the sea breeze at Long Branch might accelerate his recovery."

Behind him, in the city, was a shambles. Fifty-one persons were killed, 105 suffered gunshot wounds and many others with lesser injuries crawled away under their own power, and 169 were arrested. Caring for the dead posed a difficult problem for the authorities. The day before, on July 11, the Staten Island ferryboat *Westfield* sank in New York Harbor after its boilers exploded. The morgue was already overcrowded from that disaster. William Muldoon, the future New York boxing commissioner and famed physical culture expert, said the most horrible scene of his long life was watching the riot victims piled up on top of the torn bodies of those who had died on the *Westfield*.

The parade of the Orangemen proceeded without further incident to the Cooper Institute and was disbanded. People milled through the streets of Chelsea and Hell's Kitchen until late that night, but the only disorder reported was an unsuccessful attempt to storm the house of an Orangeman in West Twentieth Street. Rumors circulated throughout the city that the rifles of the militia were supposed to be loaded with blank cartridges but that live bullets had been inserted by mistake; that many bodies were being ferried over to Staten Island for secret burial by the authorities; that mobs were forming in the slums to take over the city. Few of the respectable citizenry slept soundly that night. But the trouble, so far as street fighting was concerned, was over.

The *Herald*, Bennett's raucous organ, exulted at the top of Page Three, its first news page, the next morning:

EXCELSIOR!
Law Triumphs—
Order Reigns
SIXTY ORANGE BRAVES
Ruffianly Riot and a
Remorseless Rebuke
BLOODY BOYNE ON THE BANKS OF THE HUDSON

The *World* editorialized that "New York has been disgraced by a street fight in 1871 over the merits of an Irish battle fought in 1690," and the London *Times* righteously blamed the trouble, not on British misrule in Ireland, but on the "combative temperament of the Irish manifesting itself in the New World." The *Tribune* printed a brief dispatch from Dublin at the bottom of its riot story to emphasize this point: "The Orange demonstrations throughout Ireland today were attended with little or no disorder."

It was Greeley's *Tribune* which pointed out one of the more far-reaching aspects of the riot—the loss of face incurred by Tammany Hall and the Tweed Ring which was its mainspring. Despite its claims to being the Protector of the Poor and the Defender of the Faith, Tammany had allowed the police and militia to cut loose at the crowds. It had weakly and belatedly sought to halt the parade, and had been overruled by a Democratic governor. Tammany, obviously, was losing its grip. The riot, Greeley wrote in the *Tribune*, "emphasized New York's misgovernment as nothing else could."

"Authority," old Horace thundered, "will always be respected so long as it is respectable."

The revelations by the New York *Times* and Nast's corrosive sketches of life among Tweed's fat cats began taking effect. An official audit estimated the Tweed Ring's loot at $30,000,000 for the thirty-month period ending July 31, 1871. Tweed himself was arrested eleven days before the election on a suit charging payment of $5,512,000 on fraudulent vouchers.

Despite the frantic efforts of Tammany wardheelers, the slum vote was split between Tammany and the Democratic reform slate, and a Republic state ticket was voted into office. Tweed, through the most prodigious trickery and fraud, was one of the few Tammany candidates who escaped the landslide. O'Donovan Rossa, quiet hero, was his opponent. He lost only because Tweed's lieutenants stuffed ballot boxes from morning to night. For Tweed, however, it was a mean and short-lived triumph.

The Boss was forced to flee the country, sojourning first in

Cuba and then in Spain. After years of dodging and maneuvering he was returned to the United States. He died in the Ludlow Street jail on April 12, 1878.

For Jim Fisk as well as Boss Tweed, the "Orange riot" was a personal calamity. He never lived down the charges of cowardice that followed his retreat from Eighth Avenue to Long Branch, New Jersey. The public could accept, even applaud and be amused by, the image of Jim Fisk as a jolly pirate, scuttling the ships of other financial buccaneers. But the picture of Fisk hurdling back-yard fences and fleeing the city in a tugboat, leaving windrows of dead and his own regiment behind him, was considerably less fetching. "Pif! Paf! Pouf!" jeered the New York *Herald* in its columns the day following the riot, "Colonel Fisk led the forlorn hope yesterday and, like General Boum, won his panache."

Fisk was no fool when it came to public relations, and he endeavored as quickly as possible to counteract the charges of poltroonery. He called a council of the 9th Regiment's senior officers at Long Branch, receiving them with his ankle massively bandaged and occasionally grimacing with pain. It was decided that for the honor of the regiment the reputation of its colonel must be rehabilitated. Lieutenant Colonel Braine, the long-suffering, was cast in the rôle of Fisk's public defender.

A squib appeared in the New York papers reading, "Lt. Col. Braine takes occasion to assert Col. Fisk did his full duty, was foremost in the fray, and there is no dissatisfaction in the regiment with the Colonel."

This bit of propaganda, of course, was greeted by a roar of disbelieving laughter.

His biographer (Robert H. Fuller in *Jubilee Jim*) quoted Fisk as saying in a less guarded moment, while "recuperating" at his New Jersey retreat, "I don't believe I was cut out for the military life. I ain't built for it, for one thing, because I can't run fast enough; and I haven't got the heart for it for another. We ought to leave all our home fighting to the Irish. They'd rather fight than eat any time, and the more of each other they can kill off, the better they feel about it."

Fisk's luck, from then on, was all on the miserable side. The fickle and vain Josie Mansfield, leading lady of his seraglio, was one of the first to turn against him. Fisk made the mistake of introducing her to a friend and protégé of his, Edward S. Stokes, a handsome rake who came from a wealthy Brooklyn family. When he learned that Josie was bestowing her favors on Stokes, Fisk cut off her allowance.

Josie and her new lover were desperate. Stokes had neither the inclination nor the ability to earn a living, and Josie was reluctant to return to the theater—she was more courtesan than actress, a firm believer in the easy way out.

The easy way out, in this case, it seemed to the luxury-loving pair, was to blackmail Jim Fisk, make the old lover support the new. Fisk, no craven when it came to assaults on his wealth, immediately charged them with trying to extort money from him in exchange for his love letters to Josie. In return, Josie and Stokes filed a libel suit against Fisk. On January 6, 1872, they were indicted for extortion.

That afternoon Fisk entered the Grand Central Hotel on Broadway just above Bleecker Street. Stokes was waiting for him, with a revolver in his hand, on the first landing. He fired twice and Fisk rolled back down the stairs. Next day he died. (Stokes was finally convicted of manslaughter after several trials in which money and influence played their mysterious rôles, and sentenced to a mere four years in Sing Sing. Josie lapsed into obscurity after a few years of notoriety. Stokes died in 1901, the same year Josie, a broken old woman, sought admittance to a Catholic home in South Dakota.)

Fisk died respectably enough, with his wife hurrying down from Boston to whisper a few words of forgiveness before he took his last breath. He lay in state at the Grand Opera House. Very few of the people of Hell's Kitchen, who now remembered him chiefly as the overly nimble colonel of the 9th Regiment, were among those who paid their respects.

The Flash Age, of which Fisk was a leading symbol, came to its inevitable end with the panic of 1873, which was brought on by the "mad speculation" and over-extension of the railroads in the post-Civil War years. The great Moody and Sankey revival of that year focused the minds of middle-class New Yorkers on less material matters. Down in the streets of Hell's Kitchen, it would have taken more than a pair of evangelists to rouse the people from their daily battle for survival.

3

The Rise of the Street Gangs

OUT of the spreading squalor and despair of Hell's
Kitchen in the post-Civil War years came the first gen-
eration of the street gangs which were to trouble the
Middle West Side for almost exactly half a century,
until they were smashed just before the First World
War by a combination of the New York Police Department and
a task force of special railroad police organized by the New York
Central.

Some of the gangs were dedicated to violence for its own sake.
Others were primarily concerned with loot, for which the pros-
pects were plentiful. The North River piers were moving up the
water front from lower Manhattan, and the great luxury liners
of Cunard, White Star, North German-Lloyd and Hamburg-Amer-
ican began discharging their passengers and their cargoes of silks,
wines, furs and other luxuries on the back doorstep of Chelsea
and Hell's Kitchen. Aside from this expensive cargo, the Thirtieth
Street yards of the Hudson River Railroad, subsequently part of
the New York Central system, presented another vast field of
temptation.

The first Hell's Kitchen gang which received any public notice was the Nineteenth Street Gang, whose members graduated from petty thievery to keep themselves alive to robbery, mayhem and extortion. Their principal haunts were Poverty Lane on Ninth Avenue between Seventeenth and Nineteenth streets and Misery Row on Tenth Avenue between the same streets. Even the police did not dare to invite a showdown with the score or more young thugs, who soon learned the law of the streets: what's yours is yours only as long as you're tough enough to hold on to it. The Nineteenth Street Gang was the counterpart of such juvenile terrorists as the Fourth Avenue Tunnel Gang, of which Richard Croker, the future Tammany boss, was a leading member; the Forty Little Thieves, led by Wild Maggie Carson, a twelve-year-old girl later adopted into a respectable family; the Little Dead Rabbits and the Little Plug Uglies in the Five Points section. Down in the Mulberry Bend district the Whyos, a slightly older group of hoodlums, were supreme. The Whyos, whom Herbert Asbury (*The Gangs of New York*) termed "as vicious a collection of thugs, murderers, and thieves as ever operated in the metropolis," often raided on the West Side, coursing through Greenwich Village and bashing citizens' heads. But they never ventured above Fourteenth Street into the territory of the Nineteenth Street Gang and its successors. Hell's Kitchen, in fact, was never invaded by outsiders, no matter how many troops they could muster, not even by the redoubtable Monk Eastman when he commanded upwards of a thousand henchmen.

Many of the Nineteenth Street gang graduated into the Tenth Avenue Gang, whose depredations were more extensive and better organized. Their leader was an intrepid lad named Ike Marsh. The Thirtieth Street railroad yards were their private hunting preserve, and they became expert at smashing in the doors of freight cars and disposing of the loot at cut-rate prices. When this enterprise palled, Marsh and several of his chief associates boarded a Hudson River Railroad express at Spuyten Duyvil, bound and gagged the express messenger and tossed overboard an iron box containing several thousand dollars in currency and government bonds, which they later recovered and divided among themselves.

The Tenth Avenue Gang was subsequently absorbed by the Hell's Kitchen Gang, which rapidly assumed power over the whole neighborhood from Twenty-third Street north to Forty-second. The new organization was stronger and bolder than any of its predecessors. It committed burglaries in the full light of day, made shopkeepers and manufacturers pay protection money, and systematically victimized the Hudson River Railroad. Strangers, especially those exuding any degree of prosperity, were held up at knife- or gunpoint almost the moment they set foot west of Eighth Avenue.

The hetman of the Hell's Kitchen Gang was a towheaded rascal named Dutch Heinrich, who first became notorious as a sort of early-day Willie Sutton, robbing banks and brokerages in various disguises. Heinrich was credited with having "just about the stickiest fingers in New York" by a New York *Herald* reporter. His depredations usually were accomplished without the pistol, knife and blackjack which most of his contemporaries regarded as essential in any criminal pursuit. Dutch's innocent blue eyes and bland manner, coupled with an amazing nonchalance, were more effective than any weapons.

Gustav Lening *(The Dark Side of New York Life)*, the chief chronicler of Heinrich's career, wrote that Heinrich had something approaching a magic eye for parcels containing large sums of money or bonds, which men in those days seemed to carry around rather casually like bundles of laundry. Lening told how Heinrich, late in 1871, stole a parcel containing $54,000 worth of bonds from a careless fellow named Blatchford, "which that wiseacre had laid down on a table in a fruiterer's shop while he was buying some fruit."

The following year Heinrich strolled one day into the Kennedy & Company brokerage at Cedar and William streets. A confederate engaged the broker in conversation while Heinrich's trained eye studied the confusion of documents and papers lying around the counter. Bankers and brokers in those days apparently conducted their businesses along Dickensian lines, with scrap paper and railroad bonds alike strewn around. While his confederate and the broker chatted away, Heinrich ferreted out a stack of bonds worth $33,000, sidled over, deftly slipped them into his pocket, and vanished a moment later. Often Dutch, a reasonable man to deal with, arranged for the return of the stolen bonds for a modest percentage of their face value, particularly if they were non-negotiable. Lening said he "frequently escaped prosecution," if he was recognized by his victims and picked up by the police, "either by restoring his plunder or by some arrangement."

Heinrich obviously was able to command an unusual amount of loyalty from his associates, a quality which later made him a natural gang leader. He and a man named Chauncey Johnson once snatched two bags of gold coins from the Bank of the State of New York. Each contained $5,000 in highly negotiable gold. Johnson made a successful escape with his share of the swag, but Dutch was captured with the sack of gold in his possession and appeared to have small chance of escaping a long term in prison. But the case against him was never brought to trial because, Lening wrote, "it is said that Johnson gave back the $5,000 in his possession on the condition that Dutch Heinrich should be set at liberty."

Occasionally, of course, Heinrich was spotted despite the disguises he affected and the skill with which he could work himself into a countinghouse background. Once, according to Lening, he was "discovered behind the counter in the Adams Express office among a number of valuable packages of money, for the removal of which he was certainly only waiting an opportunity. He wore a linen coat and carried a pen behind his ear, so that he was taken for one of the many clerks who are engaged in the office." Heinrich was heaved into the street before he could lay hands on the stacks of greenbacks all around him.

Not at all discouraged by this failure, Heinrich a short time later bluffed his way into the private office of the president of the Union Trust Company and made off with $99,000 worth of railroad bonds.

Successes of this sort brought him an unwelcome notoriety and he was soon being blamed for every sizable sum that disappeared down in the financial districts. Perhaps it was that notoriety, making it impossible for him to slip into a bank or brokerage without a cry for the police going up, which persuaded him to take over the captaincy of the Hell's Kitchen Gang. It was largely an executive post, concerned with disposing of the loot obtained by his henchmen and selecting the most promising places for them to plunder.

Heinrich might have risen to a considerable position as a "mastermind of crime"—the favorite newspaper expression—had it not been for a square-jawed and husky young cop named John H. McCullagh. At the time McCullagh was only a roundsman, or patrolman, but he subsequently became a police captain and thirty-odd years later chief of police. He was singularly incorruptible from his first days on the force, and lasted less than a year as police chief because of his uncompromising honesty.

His honesty, in fact, was matched only by his courage. One day he learned that two hogsheads of hams had been stolen from a freight car in the Thirtieth Street yards of the Hudson River Railroad. The usual police procedure was to take note of the theft, promise immediate pursuit of the culprits, and then forget the whole matter. Tracing stolen goods in Hell's Kitchen was regarded as a quixotic waste of energy.

McCullagh went alone to investigate the matter. This, too, was regarded as foolhardy. Any policemen having business to transact west of Eighth Avenue automatically summoned up at least three or four stouthearted comrades.

As McCullagh strode toward Tenth Avenue that day, word spread instantly that a lone cop was presuming to invade the district. Heinrich and his musclemen, hearing the news, let him nose around the railroad depot and yards for an hour or two. Then they pounced on him, Heinrich and two other members of the Hell's Kitchen Gang against Patrolman McCullagh.

It was one of the more notable brawls of a neighborhood famous for skull-cracking, rib-crunching, eye-gouging set-tos.

They battled over the cobblestones of Tenth Avenue for half an hour before McCullagh managed to lay each of the trio out with blows from his nightstick. The patrolman then stripped them of their belts and tied their arms behind their backs. He left them trussed up there on the street while he searched out a handcart. A short time later he toiled through the streets of Hell's Kitchen with his bruised and lumpy prisoners toward the West 37th Street station house. No one dared interfere with the cop who had subdued three of the toughest members of the reigning gang of the district. Heinrich's criminal career was ended with a five-year sentence in Sing Sing. Presumably he was so disheartened by his failure to cope with McCullagh, at odds of three to one, that he gave up criminal endeavors on his release. The Hell's Kitchen Gang soon faded into insignificance.

Another group of Hell's Kitchen buckos, better organized and more specialized in their vocational pursuits, had considerable success in safecracking. They spotted a likely site of operations at the intersection of Eighth Avenue and Fourteenth Street, where two banks were located in the same building. The New York Savings Bank was on the ground floor, the New York National in the basement.

The gang, a dozen strong, decided to tunnel their way into the bank building in hopes of striking gold twice. They rented an L-shaped house which enclosed the bank building on two sides and surreptitiously moved in with spades and pickaxes and explosives. The noise of their tunneling operations would be concealed, they assured themselves, by the racket from a dance hall and poolroom on the second floor of the bank building. The dance hall, furthermore, had a new-fangled "undulating" dance floor which swayed to the rhythm of the dancers and set up an enormous creaking which would drown out the noise of a major revolution.

The gang tunneled away for weeks, working only at night while the dance floor was undulating away and hauling out the dirt and rock as quietly as possible in the hours before dawn. They planned to blow the safes of both banks on the Fourth of

July when the noise of the fireworks would conceal their own less patriotic explosions.

The evening before the Fourth of July, however, a janitor was working overtime in one of the banks and heard the sound of a drill biting into the basement wall of the building. He dropped his broom and ran straight to the West Twentieth Street police station. The police surrounded the building and captured the whole gang at work in their tunnel, only a few hours away from a fortune in gold and currency.

Otherwise the police had little success in checking the depredations of the Hell's Kitchen gangsters. In that neighborhood there was only a vast contempt for the guardians of the law. There were probably more honest policemen than its residents were willing to admit. From their jaundiced viewpoint, however, it seemed that every time a cop was visible he was browbeating a saloonkeeper for a free drink, extorting money from streetwalkers who frequented his beat, running errands for the politicians. Police morale was naturally lowered by the fact that many of the department's higher ranking officers were unabashedly corrupt. The roundsmen were a slovenly lot, resembling a defeated Balkan army more than "New York's finest," and Hell's Kitchen saluted them by tipping chimney pots off the roofs and onto the constabulary skulls.

This regional contempt for the police force was vividly illustrated by the exploits of a tubercular but exceedingly competent street fighter named One Lung Curran. Cops walked wide circles around him. Particularly after the autumn day Curran's doxy complained that she did not have a winter coat. One Lung strode down the street and halted before the first cop he met. He drew out his blackjack and with one expert swipe of this weapon laid the officer low. One Lung stripped off the policeman's fine blue wool overcoat and presented it to his girl friend, who had it tailored into a smartly cut coat for herself.

A fashion trend developed immediately afterward, much to the sorrow of the police attached to the West Forty-seventh Street station. Every lass in the district demanded that her gallant procure a similar garment. And for weeks the desk sergeant at West Forty-seventh Street watched a succession of roundsmen stumbling into the station house with complaints that they had been waylaid and relieved of their coats. The police finally had to organize a strong-arm squad to conduct reprisals down in Hell's Kitchen and put a stop to the practice.

4

In the Days of
Good King Morrison

ONE September day in 1881 a reporter for the New York *Times* plunged into the depths of Hell's Kitchen with a police escort and returned to his office with a story that ran two columns in small, closely set type. The reporter was well acquainted with such civic pestholes as the Mulberry Bend district, the Bowery, Ragpickers' Alley, Cockroach Row and the Five Points, but he was inclined to regard Hell's Kitchen as the worst of the lot. "The entire locality is the lowest and filthiest in the city," he wrote. "The whole neighborhood is an eyesore to the respectable people who live or are compelled to do business in the vicinity, a source of terror to the honest poor, and an unmitigated nuisance to the police of the Twentieth Precinct, whose record books are filled to overflowing with the names of the residents of these tenement houses."

The anonymous reporter's guide was Patrolman John D. Frederick, who had walked his beat on West Thirty-ninth Street for seven years, during which he had made the total of 983 arrests for "every conceivable crime except murder." As the reporter and the policeman strolled down Thirty-ninth Street, the former noted that Officer Frederick was greeted with "curses alternated with obsequious how-d'ye-dos."

Newspaper attention had been attracted to the section a few days before by a particularly tragic shooting in a tenement house called The Barracks. A man named Andrew Wasbacher, one of the "honest poor" of the neighborhood, had been attacked by a gang of street fighters. In attempting to defend himself, he drew a revolver and fired with an inaccuracy that testified to his amateur status as a gunman. His first shot struck his daughter in the heart and killed her instantly and another in the fusillade fatally wounded Frederick Shebery, who was identified as Wasbacher's "hired hand." The New York *Times,* as a result, sent a reporter into the district to conduct a sort of sociological survey. His story in the *Times* of September 22, 1881, was the first of any consequence in the New York newspapers to describe conditions in Hell's Kitchen.

The reporter and his escort first visited The Barracks on the south side of West Thirty-eighth Street between Eleventh Avenue and the North River "in the midst of a collection of soap factories and fat-boiling establishments, the sickening odor from which is enough to create nausea in the strongest and healthiest." They called on the Wasbacher family and found a wake in progress. "Nailed over the entrance was a bow of white crepe, and in the front room was seated a party of women and children attempting to console the poor mother mourning for the death of her daughter and the incarceration of her husband. On the arrival of the visitors all but the mother joined in a wail of sympathy, touching and at the same time ludicrous, for there were evidences that copious draughts of villainous liquor had much to do with causing these demonstrations of grief. In the bedroom in the rear was a cheap pine coffin with the body of the girl. Poverty was plainly marked on every surrounding—but honest poverty, so far as the Wasbachers' apartment was concerned. Poverty resulting from idleness and the too frequent and too liberal use of liquor were the characteristics of most of the mourners, nearly all of whom lived in the wretched 'Barracks.'"

On the floor above was the room where Dr. Thomas Lookup Evans, an abortionist, "malpractitioner" and ex-convict, had committed suicide on a pile of rags a few years before. The present tenants, the *Times* reporter noted, had done little to improve the squalid conditions in which Dr. Evans died. "Two old women, who had closed the blinds of their rooms when the officer appeared, were the only occupants of the room. No carpet save one of filth covered the floor. . . . Furniture, fit to be called by that name, there was none. A bundle of rags and straw in a corner sufficed for a bed. Chairs with rickety legs were the rule in this and the other rooms of the building whose occupants rose to the dignity of chairs, while rough wooden benches and stools often answered every purpose. The thirteen families who occupy the building have not more than twenty beds between them, though the officer estimates the population of the house to be at least seventy-five souls. The families are those of men who drive carts used in the removal of manure, or of the vendors who eke out an existence by selling fruits, ice and the like on the streets. Generally they are of Irish descent, honest and industrious, whose principal fault seems to be a love for the intoxicating cup. 'The Barracks' are rather the abode of extreme poverty than of crime. Honest though the people may be, they are none the less repulsive to one accustomed to cleanliness." Two murders had occurred there in the past several years, the reporter was informed.

Next the reporter and the policeman visited the rookery known as Hell's Kitchen, whose overflow of violence gave the whole Middle West Side its sobriquet. It was located on the north side of West Thirty-ninth Street between Ninth and Tenth avenues, built on an outcropping of the rock which lies under most of Manhattan. The Hell's Kitchen tenement, they found, was even more reprehensible than The Barracks. Here "vice in its most repulsive form thrives . . . despite the efforts of the Police to root out the horde of vagrants, thieves, and utterly depraved prostitutes who make this locality their headquarters."

The visitors were greeted by a Mrs. Livingstone whose husband was then sojourning in the comparatively orderly and healthful surroundings of Sing Sing. Mrs. Livingstone was a harridan of formidable proportions, "filthy beyond description, with bleared eyes, bloated face, and a breath that rivaled the odor of the soap factories. She poured forth a volley of blasphemous and obscene epithets. Maudlin in speech, swaggering in action, there were left no traces of womanhood in her. A torn and dirty garment was all that covered her nakedness, and without shame she staggered about in her limited quarters, defying the Police and cursing Officer Frederick for being the means of sending her husband to prison."

An alley a few feet wide separated the Hell's Kitchen tenement from two neighboring rookeries so rickety they trembled with every breeze that stirred off the river. "There were two or three men about the premises, degraded, besotted, and devoid of ^ll manhood, who subsist upon whatever their wives or the women with whom they live can earn or steal. About the premises were a dozen women or more and a host of children as impudent as they were dirty. It was the same story as to furniture here as in 'The Barracks,' the only marked difference being that there was less, and what there was more decrepit. The crockery was cracked or broken, and probably had not been washed in years. Necessary household utensils were wanted except in one or two apartments. Vermin roamed about at will without a fear of bug poison. Neither men nor women, and more especially the latter, seemed to care for clothing, the possession of a solitary garment being, in two instances at least, all sufficient for the bleary-eyed wearers. The floor answered every purpose of a bed for the inmates. A young urchin who staggered into the alley with a basket laden with cold bits was the caterer for this delectable quarter. Doors and windows were closed to the visitors by such of the women as were sober enough to perform the act. One woman of about fifty even shrank from sight, probably less for shame than fear of arrest."

A few years before in that alleyway off Thirty-ninth Street a fourteen-year-old boy named Francis Farrell had been walloped over the head with a kettle by Thomas and Catharine Watson, the proprietors of the tenement next to Hell's Kitchen, and was robbed of his week's wages amounting to $4.50. Both the Wilsons were serving five-year terms in prison as a result, but they would return to their property with the assurance that nothing had changed—certainly not for the better.

Down toward the river on Thirty-ninth Street was a settlement of squatters living in shanties with their livestock. Among the settlers were a woman named Fitzpatrick and her daughter who had just been released from six months in jail. Mrs. Fitzpatrick's granddaughter had been found by the authorities with an ear missing and both eyes blinded by sores, and had died in Bellevue Hospital a short time later. Their shanty, the *Times* reporter wrote, was "too filthy to quarter dumb beasts in."

As they left the Hell's Kitchen rookeries, Officer Frederick mentioned the fact that during the year 1880-81, 287 persons had been hauled out of them and brought before the criminal courts of the city. The owner of the property, no better than his tenants for being a man of slightly more substance, was serving time in Sing Sing for highway robbery.

Around the block on the south side of West Fortieth Street, behind the Hell's Kitchen tenements but separated by another outcropping of rock, was the notorious House of Blazes. Shortly before the *Times* reporter's visit the principal amusement at the House of Blazes had been luring some unsuspecting vagrant onto the premises, filling him with whatever liquor was at hand, and then setting fire to him while the fun-loving residents roared with laughter and the victim tried—often unsuccessfully—to beat out the flames. More than one such unfortunate was reported to have died as a result of accepting the House of Blazes hospitality.

Arson was no longer the chief form of relaxation, but on Saturday nights, especially, it was no tamer around the House of Blazes. That was the night everyone got drunk and beat up his neighbors. Liquor in the neighborhood was exceedingly cheap and plentiful, with whiskey quoted at ten cents a gallon and brandy at five cents a quart. Presumably they were distilled from garbage. Every time a bottle of these potions were uncorked the flies fell dead from the walls and any outsider, unused to such beverages, was likely to be overcome by the fumes. Drinking was a required token of esteem around the House of Blazes. Anyone who refrained was immediately suspected of having notions of social superiority. One of the husbands was arrested for beating his wife to death. The arresting officers found him drinking amiably with his dead wife's sister and a twelve-year-old boy. The husband told the officers in an aggrieved tone that he had "licked" his wife because she refused to drink with him, and his fellow tenants were inclined to agree that he was acting within his rights.

One of the current interests of the House of Blazes was a not particularly romantic triangle involving "the woman who presides as the mistress of this place"; a New Englander who called himself "the renowned Buffalo Bill" and affected the frontiersman's shoulder-length hair, and a teamster known as Dutch John. The Yankee and Dutch John, the *Times* reporter was advised, "compete very fiercely for the honor of being known as the 'boss' of the place." They also competed for the woman, who "bestows her affections first upon one and then upon the other." This naturally led to hostilities between the two men. A few years before Buffalo Bill had stabbed Dutch John and almost killed him, but the latter refused to sign a complaint against his rival. (Despite his sportsmanlike refusal to eliminate Buffalo Bill via the criminal courts, Dutch John evidently lost out in his campaign for the woman. The tenements around the House of Blazes subsequently became known as "the ranches," apparently in honor of Buffalo Bill and his superior attainments as a brawler and lover.)

A sort of lean-to behind the House of Blazes shared in its notoriety. This ramshackle shed was occupied by the families of two men named Taylor and Kelly. Taylor was an Orangeman, Kelly a South of Ireland man—a combination guaranteed to set off fireworks. Whenever the mood was upon them, they flailed at each other with fists like sandbags, and "the quarrels between them have resulted in bringing the parties into both civil and

criminal courts for the settlement of their difficulties." Taylor
eventually was removed from the scene when he shot Sergeant
John H. McCullagh—the man who had cleaned up the Hell's
Kitchen Gang singlehanded—and was sentenced to Sing Sing.

Battle Row was a series of thirteen five-story tenements east of
the Hell's Kitchen on Thirty-ninth Street between Ninth and
Tenth avenues, and was occupied by 260 families with a total of
more than a thousand members. In September of 1881, eleven
of the residents were in Sing Sing, including a man named Mc-
Cabe who had thrown his wife from a fifth-floor window at the
climax of a domestic quarrel. Officer Frederick had arrested 183
persons in Battle Row alone during his tour of duty. The owners
of the Battle Row tenements, the *Times* reporter learned, were
making some effort to subdue the ruffianly element. "Seven of
the houses are owned by the Germania Fire Insurance Company,
whose agent co-operates with the Police in trying to rid the houses
of the hardest characters. The arrest of one of their tenants twice
results in his being dispossessed and compelled to seek other
quarters. This practice keeps the houses in a quasi-orderly condition. It was in this locality that three officers of the Twentieth
Precinct have been brutally assaulted. Officer McTaggert had
his teeth knocked out and was quite seriously injured by a notorious ruffian, one Mulligan, who is now serving a term of ten years
for a criminal assault upon his sister. Officer Stevens, who tried
to force a crowd of young ruffians to move on, had his head cut
open by a cart-rung wielded by one of the gang, and Officer De-
laney was badly injured by the same party."

The officer and the reporter inspected one of the flats in Battle
Row and were received by a drunken woman, "who sat in the
filth which covered the floor, holding in her arms a babe but a
few months old, which was apparently in a dying condition. In
a maudlin and hysterical way the mother weaved backward and
forward trying to quiet the babe. Both were dressed in rags, covered with dirt, and they presented a most pitiable sight. In another room, entirely bare of furniture, lay stupidly drunk a man
of forty. His wife, who was about the same age, was in that con-

dition known as 'jolly drunk.' Rags served to cover only part of their nakedness. The furniture had evidently gone to purchase liquor, for an empty flask lay on the floor near them. A little girl was trying with the few facilities at her command to get a meal for her drunken parents, and the mother amused herself in cursing the little one until the policeman entered, when she fell to cursing him and his companion, proclaiming with apparent pride in the intervals between her curses that she was the mother of five children. Two fat and lazy dogs completed the family, of which they were certainly the best looking members. On the sidewalk in front of the row, piled up ready for removal, was a lot of furniture guarded by the inevitable dog. They told their own story of dispossessment, and this story was intensified by the appearance of the owners, who sat on or near it, sullen, defiant, and apparently indifferent to the fact that they might have to pass the night in the street."

The last visit was to a tenement known in the neighborhood as Sebastopol for no discernible reason except that, like the Crimean city of the same name, it was under siege. The enemies here, the *Times* reporter said, were "crime, poverty, filth, vermin." As elsewhere in the district, the place swarmed with ragged children suffering from "the intolerable cruelty of their parents." The Sebastopol tenement was located on the north side of Fortieth Street and consisted of a row of six four-story brick buildings.

A police sergeant told the *Times* man, "Shy your hat anywhere in the neighborhood if you want a fight, and you'll be accommodated at any time after nine o'clock at night." A patrolman accompanying the sergeant added, "And you needn't be particular about waiting until night to do it, if you want the fight badly enough."

Other journalists, and later novelists, dramatists, short-story writers and artists in search of raw material, followed the intrepid *Times* man into Hell's Kitchen and brought the district a citywide notoriety. The reporters discovered other more or less picturesque haunts among the tenements, slaughterhouses and illuminating-gas works. There were Cockroach Row and Mulligan Alley in Forty-third Street, "which was no alley, but a row also, where one could count on at least one fight a night."

Soubrette Row was a favorite among reporters looking for feature stories. "Soubrette Row was segregated and unashamed," one reporter wrote; "it stood in close proximity to equally conspicuous landmarks with tables and waiters, and was handy to the station house. The row consisted of three houses in West 39th Street, and the houses had forty-five flats, of which as many as three were found, in at least one raid, to be occupied for other than disorderly purposes." What the reporter was trying to say, with the required Victorian circumlocution, was that Soubrette Row was one big whorehouse.

The other rows in Hell's Kitchen, the same reporter remarked, were much less interesting. "They were, despite the gangs, merely the tenement boiled down until the scum rose thick, and flavored in this locality by the customs of the sheep butchers, whose work lay near at hand."

Late in 1881 the section achieved a wider notoriety when *Harper's Weekly* ran an artist's sketch of the tenement called Hell's Kitchen, showing a sprawling wooden building with a long rickety flight of stairs leading to its perch on the outcropping of rock. "The policemen thereabouts," *Harper's* remarked, "are quite accustomed to panting up the stairs and could use steel helmets to advantage."

Of all the legends of Hell's Kitchen, the most durable, perhaps, is that of Martin "Bully" Morrison, a huge red-bearded Orangeman who lived in the original Hell's Kitchen tenement and terrorized the whole neighborhood, particularly those residents who were Irish Catholic. Acclaimed by his admirers as The King of Hell's Kitchen, he became a sort of Paul Bunyan in the district and was solemnly credited with being able to pluck a lamppost out of the sidewalk and wield it as a shillelagh on the skulls of Irishmen of the opposite persuasion. The sight of Bully Morrison and his two equally belligerent sons, Jock and Bull, roaring down

West Thirty-ninth Street when the mood and the liquor were upon them was said to be a blood-chilling spectacle indeed.

One habit particularly offensive to his Catholic neighbors was Bully's practice of guzzling beer from chalices stolen from Catholic churches.

Bully was described with something less than admiration in a New York *Times* story as "a noted blackguard and bully and common drunkard. He is an Orangeman and is cordially hated by the other residents, who, however, fear his personal strength. . . .

"When filled with the fiery liquor dispensed in the neighborhood, he roams about making the night hideous with his oaths and ribald songs and jests. He arms himself with a stave from a hay bale, and running amuck through the streets, declares he will 'kill all the Popish —— in the country.' "

Bully's wife was a fitting consort, the *Times* man said, "a receiver of stolen goods . . . the pigs, goats, geese and chickens find their way to her room in the rear of 'Hell's Kitchen' and thence to the markets, unless the police arrive in time to prevent this disposition of the property."

One reporter described Bully as "so ugly that he would make the hairy ape look like a canary bird." The renowned Detective Sergeant George "Boots" Trojan, a boy at the time of Bully Morrison's reign, told another reporter (in the New York *Evening Telegram*, September 4, 1921): "Morrison's red whiskers fairly bristled fire every time he got mad. He was of Scotch-Irish origin and could gulp a half pint of whiskey at one gulp. Then he was ready for action. . . ." Bully apparently quieted down when more and more of the Catholic Irish moved into Hell's Kitchen and the Orangemen became a minority. Like all bullies he shied away from adverse odds.

Another prominent ruffian who lived in the same block along West Thirty-ninth Street between Ninth and Tenth avenues was Pegleg Gordon, known as The Terror of Battle Row. When engaged in hostilities, Gordon would unscrew his detachable wooden leg and lay about him with a fearsome efficiency. A *Times* reporter who visited his family's lair in Battle Row wrote

an unflattering description of Pegleg and his surroundings. "A
tough, wiry and ugly fellow of about fifty, who makes his wooden
leg do more service in a fight than both his hands, it takes three
or four of the stoutest policemen to handle him. The mother,
daughter, and son, like the father, are hard drinkers and hard
fighters, and the latter has served a sentence for picking pockets.
Their house is in the portion of the block nearest Ninth Avenue,
and is one of the most wretched and filthy on the block. . . . The
only food in the house was some cold pieces, doubtless the fruits
of beggary, but there were two sleek-looking cur-dogs in the
room, by far the most respectable-looking beings in the apartment."

Equally outstanding in his method of dealing with opponents
was a character named Spitting William. Assault by expectora-
tion was William's way of defending himself. Unlike most of his
neighbors, William was a powder-puff puncher, inept at fighting
with his fists, feet or knees. In such a situation, it might have
been better if he had declared himself a pacifist or at least developed into a sprinter.

But William was made of sterner stuff. He worked in an Oriental spice factory, and apparently some of the pepper had
worked its way into his system. He took up chewing an odd and
exotic combination of plug tobacco, cloves and other pungent
spices.

One evening as William was lurching out of a Tenth Avenue
saloon a cop put the arm on him and announced he was going to
run William in on a charge of drunk-and-disorderly conduct.

William protested his innocence of this charge so violently that
he inadvertently squirted tobacco and spice juice into the officer's
eyes.

The patrolman, temporarily blinded, howled for medical attention while William capered down the street to his freedom. He
had discovered a foolproof method of dealing with anyone who
crossed him.

Three times, subsequently, the police tried to take him into custody on various charges, and each time Spitting William expectorated his way out of the embarrassment of arrest.

The police circulated a warning through the neighborhood that the next time William spit in a cop's eye he'd be shot right in his spicy mouth.

It turned out that a civilian saved the police the trouble of dispatching him. Somewhat overconfident of his powers of self-defense, William took to courting a formidable lass named Euchre Kate Burns, whom a New York *Herald* reporter characterized as the "champion heavyweight female brick hurler of the district." Up and down Eleventh Avenue Euchre Kate was regarded as the mightiest of female brawlers along the water front. Tampering with Kate's affections was dangerous enough, but she was also married to a jealous husband who, unlike most residents of the section, carried a revolver. Some friend of the family informed Burns that he was being cuckolded by Spitting William.

One Sunday morning Burns encountered William on Eleventh Avenue and shot him quite dead on the cobblestones. The exact sequence of events was never clearly established, but Spitting William's friends were certain that he never had a fair shot at the outraged husband. Either he had been caught without a quid of tobacco and spice in his mouth, or Burns had unsportingly stayed out of range while pumping bullets at William, or stark fear had dried up William's salivary glands and deprived him of the means of self-defense. In any case the police showed remarkably little interest in the killing and gratefully wrote it off as an unsolved murder.

A fair match for the bereaved Euchre Kate Burns, although it is not recorded that they ever engaged in a test of supremacy, was Battle Annie Welsh, the harridan-in-chief of Battle Row. Battle Annie, an Orangewoman full of brooding violence and with a shrewd eye for the main chance, was the leader of an organization which the newspapers playfully referred to as The Battle Row Ladies' Social and Athletic Club. Herbert Asbury says that Battle Annie was a practitioner of mayhem fully equal

to such viragoes of an earlier day as Sadie the Goat, Hell Cat
Maggie and Gallus Mag.

Some historians of the neighborhood have stated that Battle
Annie and her followers were also known as The Lady Gophers,
the female auxiliary of what was to be the most powerful of
Hell's Kitchen gangs. Actually, from all the evidence, Annie and
her cohorts were active along Battle Row many years before the
Gopher Gang came into existence. Likewise it was probably a
blot on the lady's reputation to assert that she was "the sweet-
heart of practically the entire Gopher Gang." A reporter who did
considerable research on the subject (Earl Sparling in the New
York *World-Telegram*, September 28, 1934) pointed out that the
Gophers came from below West Thirty-fourth Street. By the
time the Gophers came along Battle Annie had retired more or
less quietly to another part of town.

Still, she left her mark on Hell's Kitchen. In her salad days
Annie hung out in the back room of a saloon at West Fortieth
Street and Tenth Avenue. She would sit at a table with a tumbler
of whiskey cuddled in her paw and become more morose with
each application of the sauce. It would occur to her that some
female a block or two away had insulted her or failed to show
the proper respect. Out of the Family Entrance, all of a sudden,
would come Annie with the light of battle in her green eyes and
her mop of red hair flying in all directions. She would give a
marrow-freezing yell that sent strong men bolting for safety and
dogs scuttling for cover.

When Battle Annie went into action, it is recorded, she mus-
tered twenty-five to thirty bloodthirsty females and the whole
pack, Valkyries in tatters, went coursing through the streets looking for Annie's enemies. All of these followers had been instructed
by Annie in the art of gouging an eye and staving in a rib and
applying the knee to the groin.

Battle Annie reigned as queen of Battle Row for a good six
years. Toward the end of her regime she decided that there
ought to be a little drinking money to be made out of her organization. "When the practice of hiring gangsters was begun by

labor unions and employers," states the authoritative Mr. Asbury, "Battle Annie earned a handsome income by supplying female warriors to both sides in industrial disputes. For many years there was scarcely a strike in which women were engaged that did not find Battle Annie and her gangsters enthusiastically biting and scratching both pickets and strikebreakers."

Annie, for some unknown reason, finally drifted over to the East Side and out of the public eye. Apparently she had lost some of her old exuberance, for the last public record of her shows that a lone policeman managed to take her into custody for creating a disturbance of a minor sort, and he did not even have to resort to using his nightstick to persuade her to come along to the station house.

The favored watering hole along Battle Row was a saloon operated by one Mallet Murphy. It was by far the roughest joint in the neighborhood. Most saloonkeepers relied upon the modest bungstarter to maintain order among their patrons, but Murphy used a huge wooden mallet, heavy enough to stun an ox, to cool off obstreperous customers. Mallet Murphy's was the headquarters of the toughest street fighters in Hell's Kitchen, and naturally it served as their command post during an unusually bloody engagement with their enemies from San Juan Hill, which was located on Ninth Avenue in the upper Fifties.

One night the uptown gang sent word that they were massing their forces and would be marching upon Battle Row within the hour. Strategy, it was felt among the leaders of the Battle Row warriors, would be needed to offset the San Juan Hill gang's advantage in numbers.

The Battle Row Gang seized the high ground—always sound military doctrine—and when the enemy appeared on Eleventh Avenue an ambush had been arranged. The San Juan Hill hoodlums were literally buried "beneath tons of bricks neatly hurled from the cliffs running to the Eleventh Avenue corner," the New York *Herald* reported. In the barrage four of the invaders from San Juan Hill were killed and forty were injured. That discouraged any invasions from other sections of the city in the future. Members of other street gangs always requested permission to enter Hell's Kitchen from then on, even those belonging to the powerful Lower East Side gangs.

One of the least desirable jobs in New York City during the 'eighties undoubtedly was collecting rents in Hell's Kitchen. In the view of most residents a rent collector rated only a notch above a cop and several notches below a pimp on the social scale. The landlord's agent risked being thrown downstairs, having his eye blacked, being doused with pails of water as he made his unwelcome rounds of the tenements under his supervision.

Yet there were ways of dealing with the problem if the rent collector was sufficiently flexible in his methods. A young man who later became a prominent real-estate broker told a New York *Sun* reporter how he coped with the touchy clients of a twenty-family tenement house in Hell's Kitchen during the 'eighties. "The house was fairly well rented," he was quoted in the *Sun* of June 13, 1932, "but only half the tenants made any pretense of paying the landlord for the quarters they occupied. The others preferred to 'fight it out' each month to determine whether they were to pay rent or live rent free."

He decided to interview the tenant with the worst record of payment in the house. "Before me on the couch lay a huge man, bare-footed—the suspenders of his trousers dangling on the floor —wearing a brilliant red flannel shirt." Knotting his huge right fist, the tenant announced he had no intention of paying his rent—then or ever—and suggested that the young man get the hell out.

The collector spoke soothingly. "I haven't asked you for the rent. What I came to see you about was to ask you to do some work for me. You owe three months' rent. I'll cancel that and pay you the equivalent of an extra month, in cash, if you will introduce me to the other tenants and help me persuade them to pay the rent they owe. I want you to tell them in your own way why you think they ought to pay their rent."

The tenant sprang off his couch and said, "Come on, let's get to work."

Rent collecting from then on proved to be a cinch. "I won't attempt to describe his methods," the real-estate man told the *Sun*. "Suffice it to say that the other tenants understood his language and knew he meant what he said. 'Dis is me friend, de new landlord,' he would begin. 'He wants some more of dat dough you owe him—shell out.' Those who attempted to argue with him were literally roared into submission, as he added this threat: 'If ya don't come across now, I'll shake it out of your old man tonight.'

"They paid—and those who remained in the house paid regularly thereafter—that is, all but the ruffian I had hired to talk to them in their own language. He made a permanent job of it without consulting me—and I guess he was worth all he received. Six months later I handed the building back to my friends in much better renting condition than it had ever been before. But I have often wondered what happened to the owner or agent who tried to fire my burly 'persuader.'"

Another who learned how to deal with the rougher element of Hell's Kitchen, although in a much more direct manner, was the police captain who took over command of the West Forty-seventh Street station. He was Captain Tom Killilea, a County Galway man of considerable heft who had only the greatest contempt for street fighters. Killilea believed that the law was best administered with his larruping fists and heavy brogues, with a minimum of palaver in the courts. He came to the West Forty-seventh Street station with a reputation that should have given any sensible man pause—one of his feats was to seize four men and squeeze them in his unusually long arms until their bones cracked—but the thugs who lounged around the docks in his new precinct laughed it off. Five of them, in fact, sent a challenge to the station house three days after Captain Killilea took command.

Killilea advised their intermediary that he would meet all five of them, bare knuckles and no weapons, on West Forty-ninth Street just west of Eleventh Avenue.

The new captain strolled over to the impromptu arena, a twenty-foot section of the street closed off by carts and drays, after rejecting all offers of assistance from his brother officers. He squared off against the five hoodlums and in exactly twelve minutes he laid out all five of them. The only damage to Killilea was a few lacerations to his knuckles.

He despised any cop so effete as to use firearms in dealing with the citizenry, and once suspended a patrolman who fired his revolver to bring down a fleeing suspect instead of taking him into custody with his bare hands.

A certain amount of respect was accorded Captain Killilea in the northern end of Hell's Kitchen from then until he retired in 1892.

Killilea was in charge of the precinct when the first murder in that district which achieved prominence in the newspapers occurred, the so-called Hook Killing. The victim was Avery D. Putnam, a provision merchant with chivalrous instincts. While he was dismounting from an omnibus on West Forty-sixth Street, he noticed one William Foster leering at the ankles of Mabel Duval, the comely daughter of a French dressmaker. Putnam remonstrated with Foster, and the latter grabbed a car hook, which the newspapers reported was "a device for lifting the whiffletree." Foster slugged Putnam with the car hook and killed him.

Public sentiment against Foster grew wrathful, particularly after the New York *Tribune* fulminated against "Broadway beasts" and "fiends in human form who ride the stages."

A mob tried to lynch Foster as he was being taken downtown for arraignment, and only Captain Killilea's flailing fists saved him from being strung up to a lamppost. Foster grew so attached to his protector that when he was sentenced to the gallows in the courtyard of the Tombs his last and only request was that Captain Killilea walk beside him. The captain, a rather sentimental fellow when not dealing out summary punishment to hoodlums, gravely accepted the invitation.

5

The Tenderloin

UST to the east of Hell's Kitchen, between Seventh and Fifth avenues from Fourteenth Street almost to Forty-second, lay the district known for good and sufficient reasons as the Tenderloin or, as a crusading pastor named it, Satan's Circus. There was more wickedness here for many years, per square mile of redlight house and concert saloon, than in any other metropolis on earth. It flourished under the protection of the police and the patronage of Tammany Hall politicians, and might still be flourishing in the same old way, had not business and industry come marching uptown, on the heels of vice crusaders, and elbowed aside the madams, saloonkeepers, gamblers and other entrepreneurs.

In the days of the lobster palace and the private dining room with its red plush sofa, of the champagne supper with hot bird, cold bottle and lukewarm girl with hour-glass figure, the Tenderloin was the place where grandfather headed when in a sportive mood. A song of the period celebrated its attractions without, however, hinting at the consequences of a visit to the gaslit saturnalia in the shadow of the old Sixth Avenue El. The song had it that:

When the clock strikes two in the Tenderloin,
The wine and the wit are flowing high;
And every pretty girl that clinks a glass with you
Has a naughty little twinkle in her eye.

Your heart is as light as a butterfly,
Tho' your wife may be waiting up for you;
But you never borrow trouble in the Tenderloin
In the morning when the clock strikes two.

CHORUS

Lobsters! Rarebits! Plenty of Pilsener beer!
Plenty of girls to help you drink the best of cheer;
Dark girls, blonde girls, and never a one that's true;
You get them all in the Tenderloin when the clock
    strikes two.

For those New Yorkers who were inclined to avert their eyes
from such hellishness, the Reverend T. De Witt Talmage of the
Brooklyn Tabernacle, who christened the district Satan's Circus,
provided a less toothsome description of the Tenderloin. In his
sermons (collected in a best-selling work titled *The Masque Torn
Off*), the Reverend Talmage denounced, in particular, the respectable men who sought their pleasure in that district. "I believe,"
he said, antedating Billy Sunday, "in muscular Christianity." It
was also his opinion that dancing was the "first step to eternal
ruin for a great multitude of both sexes. You know, my friends,
what postures and attitudes and figures are suggested by the
devil."

The Reverend Talmage insisted that his congregation understand that his trips to the Tenderloin were strictly in the line of
his pastoral duty. "I went as a physician goes into a smallpox
hospital, or a fever lazaretto, to see what practical and useful
information I might get. . . . I shall not gild iniquities. I shall
play a dirge and not an anthem, and while I shall not put faintest
blush on fairest cheek, I will kindle the cheeks of many a man
into a conflagration, and I will make his ears tingle."

With a stern eye fixed on the males of his congregation, he launched into his celebrated denunciation of "The Lepers of High Life," saying:

"Call the roll of dissipation in the haunts of iniquity any night, and if the inmates answer, you will find there stockbrokers from Wall Street, large importers from Broadway, iron merchants, leather merchants, cotton merchants, hardware merchants, wholesale grocers, representatives from all the commercial and wealthy classes. Talk about the heathenism below Canal Street! There is worse heathenism above Canal Street. I prefer that kind of heathenism which wallows in filth and disgusts the beholder rather than that heathenism which covers up its putrefaction with camel's hair shawl and point lace, and rides in turnouts worth three thousand dollars, liveried driver ahead and rosetted flunky behind. . . . We want about five hundred Anthony Comstocks to go forth and explore the abominations of high life. . . .

"While there are men smoking their cigarettes, with their feet on Turkish divans, shocked that a minister of religion should explore and expose the iniquity of city life, there are raging underneath our great cities a Cotopaxi, a Stromboli, a Vesuvius, ready to bury us in ashes deeper than that which overwhelmed Pompeii and Herculaneum."

On Sunday after Sunday, the Reverend Talmage proceeded to bury his congregation under the ashes of rhetoric. The pastor was stronger on purplish adjectives than facts and figures. The complaisant authorities, however, were rather annoyed by the Reverend Talmage's suggestion, "Swear me in as a special police and give me two hundred police for two nights, and I would break up all the leading haunts of iniquity and arrest their leaders and send up such consternation in smaller places they would shut up of themselves." His offer, of course, was ignored.

At least one commentator, the anonymous author of *Snares of New York, or Tricks and Traps of the Great Metropolis*, believed that the "attractiveness of vice was too frequently exaggerated"— unwittingly, of course—by the fulminations of the Reverend Talmage and his fellow sin-killers. "Fired by passion or inflamed by wine, the visitor may, especially if he has been used to a plain country home, see these establishments in a false light, which lends a fictitious glory to very common things."

The same author agreed with the Reverend Talmage, however, that otherwise respectable citizens had a reprehensible interest in what went on in the Tenderloin. The out-of-town buyer, it seemed, was a menace in those days, too. "Drummers and salesmen whose business it is to wait upon country merchants visiting New York sometimes complain that these persons expect to be taken the 'grand rounds' before they will order goods or attend to business at all. The 'grand rounds' are simply a tour of fashionable houses of prostitution and gambling establishments. The salesmen are expected to know where these are located and to act as the escort of 'innocence' on this disgraceful journey. There may be city drummers to whom this is congenial employment—there are unquestionably others to whom it is repulsive."

The main thoroughfare of the Tenderloin was Sixth Avenue. The flashiest of the dance halls, theaters and cafés prospered in the flare of gaslight along this sooty Rialto, shaken and begrimed as they were by the steam trains rumbling on the El overhead. The parlor houses, houses of assignation and hotels where no questions were asked and no luggage was required were shunted to the side streets bisecting Sixth Avenue. Sheltered mostly in brownstone houses, the bagnios were thickest on Twenty-fourth, Twenty-fifth, Thirty-first, Thirty-second, Thirty-fifth streets between Seventh and Fifth avenues, thinning out as they approached the general respectability of Fifth.

Undoubtedly the fanciest establishments were those on Seven Sisters Row along West Twenty-fifth Street near Seventh Avenue. Here seven sisters who came from a small New England town, apparently with a single thought in mind, set up adjoining parlor houses and conducted their business with a Yankee sense of decorum. On certain nights no gentleman—all their patrons had to be genteel as well as wealthy—was permitted inside their portals unless he wore evening dress and brought a bouquet. He was expected to order expensive wine and to appreciate the soft-spoken refinement of his surroundings.

Patrons of the expensive Fifth Avenue hotels usually found in their morning mail shortly after arrival an elegantly engraved invitation to visit The Seven Sisters. If the invitation fell into the wrong hands, some uncouth character who insisted on behaving as though he were in a common bordello, he was immediately shown to the door.

Many of the girls recruited for The Seven Sisters, as well as other parlor houses in the Tenderloin, came from their native New England. They were mostly factory girls weary of long hours at the loom or bench, to whom a "life of shame" was preferable to what they had known. John H. Warren, Jr. (*Thirty Years' Battle with Crime, or The Crying Shame of New York, as Seen Under the Broad Glare of an Old Detective's Lantern*) explained these recruits from the land of the Pilgrim Fathers: "When it is considered that in former times the women and children of these New England hives of wealth and industry were once compelled to work from twelve to sixteen hours a day, what wonder that thousands of them freed themselves every year from the iron grasp of cupidity to find a home, or the semblance of it, at least, that presented the temptation, in exchange, of a few years of gilded misery."

The Seven Sisters were supposed to be the best madams in town, from the viewpoint of both patrons and inmates, yet even they made no pretense of running a philanthropy. When a girl lost her looks or her sense of decorum, out she went. The consequences were often tragic. One woman named Crazy Lou wandered the Tenderloin streets for years after she had lost her usefulness to the madams of the district. She was reputedly the daughter of a wealthy Boston merchant, and came to New York seeking the man who had seduced her. Instead she fell into the hands of a procurer who delivered her to The Seven Sisters for a fee, and she stayed there until she was no longer desirable enough for their choosy clientele. Her life story may have read like some very bad Victorian novel, but there was no doubt of the reality of the picture Crazy Lou presented as she begged for pennies, cadged her drinks, raided garbage pails, and otherwise reminded merrymakers that the "days of wine and roses" are sternly numbered. Crazy Lou, in the raddled flesh, was the moralists' best argument against sin and lightmindedness. Her end was exactly as the moral literature of the time would have predicted: she threw herself into the East River one night.

Even in houses of lesser elegance than The Seven Sisters', the patron was expected to buy champagne for everyone in the parlor and leave a minimum of a hundred dollars before taking his departure. Sin did not come cheaply in the Tenderloin, even in the more squalid houses. The badger game, the panel-house creeper, and a near-lethal dose of chloral hydrate awaited those who did not choose wisely among the brownstone bordellos. One way or another, the Tenderloin believed in taking a man for all he was worth.

In the panel house, the thieves literally came out of the woodwork. The victim was led to a room by his doxy, and while his attention was diverted, to put it delicately, a member of the staff crept through the honeycombed walls and opened a secret panel in the room. This operative, known as "the creeper," reached out of the panel and looted the victim's pockets. Sometimes, if the sucker caught on and was inclined to show fight, the creeper grabbed his trousers and threw them out a window to forestall pursuit. No man, deprived of his trousers, is likely to put up much of a fuss. The victim was usually wrapped in a burlap sack and sent home by cab, once he realized the hopelessness of his predicament.

The badger game—"What the Hell are you doing here with my wife?"—worked with infinite variations in the Tenderloin. An attractive young woman named Kate Phillips was regarded as the cleverest lure among the badger-game operators. One night she latched on to a wealthy St. Louis coffee and tea merchant, and before she and her co-workers were through with him he paid $15,000 for his indiscretion. One of her colleagues broke in on Kate and the merchant, announcing that he was an officer and was arresting the St. Louisan on charges of adultery. The merchant was taken before a fake judge and "arraigned," and released only after he paid a "fine" of $15,000.

The more respectable the victim, the merrier his welcome in the Tenderloin. One night the secretary to a prominent clergyman got into a fight with the creeper in a panel house. He was beaten almost to death, and most unwisely took his complaint to the police. Naturally the incident was widely reported in the newspapers.

"I was studying sociology at first hand," the clergyman's secretary explained.

The explanation was greeted with guffaws, and Henry Ward Beecher, no hairshirted celibate himself as it was later to be revealed, commented, "Men don't have to go through a sewer to find out that it's dirty."

Other humiliations awaited the unwary wanderer among the fleshpots of the Tenderloin. One was a sort of forerunner of the Coney Island skirt-blowing device. A naïve-appearing patron would be admitted to some of the parlor houses and informed that tonight everything was on the house. The delighted patsy would adjourn with the girl of his choice. What he didn't know, then, was that the ceiling and walls of the room were fitted with peepholes behind which he was observed by other patrons of the establishment. When he emerged, he would be greeted by bawdy shouts from the other patrons and offered critiques on his performance. This was a violation of the dictum, "Never wise up a sucker," but after all he could do little but protest the ethics of being exposed to the decadent gaze of voyeurs.

All through the district were the uproarious concert saloons, a sort of corruption of the English music hall. These dives offered music, singing and dancing, along with the dubious charms of the "waiter girls," who were expected to welcome the lickerish attentions of the customers. In the view of Mr. Warren, the waiter girls showed up rather poorly in the "broad glare of an old detective's lantern." He wrote:

"The waist of these fleshy beauties is the only part of them that boasts a covering of any sort, so that in their apparel there is no waste of material; indeed it is astonishing how little it takes to dress up one of these houris. . . . Huge-limbed and squabby, they show in their makeup the low breed of the human animal from which they spring, and on a closer inspection, their manners, habits, language, and tastes will be found in perfect harmony with their exterior charms."

In defiance of the much-flouted Sunday-closing laws, the dives along the east side of Eighth Avenue gave what they called "sacred concerts" on Sunday evenings. Liquor, of course, was served at these devotions. The vesper services consisted largely of a buxom blonde in a tight and abbreviated costume singing:

> "George, Georgie, pray give over,
> Georgie, Georgie, you're too free.
> Stop your palaver, else I'll tell Father,
> Georgie, give over and let me be."

The chief allurement of the Tenderloin, however, was the dance hall. A man with time and money on his hands might seek out a parlor house or a house of assignation in the small hours, but first he dipped into the lively and raucous pleasures of the Haymarket, the Sans Souçi, the Cremorne, the Egyptian Hall or Sailors Hall. A New York *Sun* reporter wrote of these resorts, "A band played dance music better than any other dance orchestra in town. Once inside the place you never lacked a partner to either dance or drink with. Girls were everywhere. Waltzes were the rage and the visitor far from home with no one to report him found pleasant hours there."

Of all the Tenderloin dance halls, the Haymarket on Sixth Avenue south of Thirtieth Street was the most notorious. It was the place most male visitors to New York demanded to see their first night on the town. Many of the girls who frequented the place were beautiful, and the men were likely to be dangerous. "It was a motley crowd with a few good suckers mixed in for the easy picking of the thieves." But no red-blooded man liked to admit to his friends back home that he had not explored the Haymarket and possibly a few of the auxiliary amusements of the Tenderloin. Diamond Jim Brady often brought out-of-towners to the Haymarket, but it was remarked that he always left his gaudier sets of diamonds at home on such visits.

The Haymarket was indisputably New York's most celebrated center of low life for thirty-odd years until just before the First World War. (After the turn of the century it was still reporting one hundred thousand paid admissions annually, and closed its doors in 1913 only after its license was revoked.) The dance hall had been built in 1860 as a public bath. During the Civil War it served as a variety theater but was unable to withstand the competition from Tony Pastor's and the Tivoli downtown. Subsequently it housed Worth's Museum, with fire and sword eaters, Siamese twins, two-headed calves, the pickled head of President Garfield's assassin, and other curiosa on display. William McMahon took a long-term lease on the three-story building in 1872, remodeled it and reopened as the Argyle dance hall. Inside a year he changed its name to the Haymarket, after a similarly wicked resort in London. Under McMahon, it was a rough joint, with pickpockets, lush-rollers and thugs operating out in the open. The police received so many complaints they could hardly look the other way. Some of the capers pulled by its customers even appalled the other divekeepers of the Tenderloin.

No doubt these gentry were relieved when McMahon sold out to Eddie Corey, whose father and uncle were policemen, and his more or less silent partner, Charlie Noonan, who operated the cigar stand at the Hoffman House. Corey remodeled the character of the place as well as its interior. He announced that he was there to make money, not enemies, and that rowdies would be booted out onto the Sixth Avenue streetcar tracks.

Men were charged twenty-five cents admission to the Haymarket—that was to weed out the cheap toughs—and the women who frequented the place were admitted free (except that the doorman ran a private racket and made them tip him two-bits on entering). Corey wanted no out-and-out harpies around the place, and the women were forbidden to smoke, drink to excess or dip their fingers into wallets. Dick Butler, the Hell's Kitchen political figure, wrote in his memoir (*Dock Walloper*, written with Joseph Driscoll) that the girls had to pass "a sort of civil service examination" before they were recognized as habituées in good standing, and observe two rules of conduct regarding the men they met in the place. "Rule No. 1 was that no man who fell for them was to be robbed on the premises. Rule No. 2 was that if they stole from a patron after taking him elsewhere, and the man put a rap in against them with the police, then they had to pay the money back to calm the patron and save the police from undue embarrassment."

This fitted in, of course, with the police department's policy regarding the Haymarket and similar resorts. "All that the police asked, aside from a little carfare now and then, was that outward order and decency should be preserved. A man's morals, or a woman's morals either for that matter, were his or her private business, just as long as nobody was held up under a street lamp or cracked over the skull."

Aside from these safeguards, the man venturing into the Haymarket for a glimpse of metropolitan wickedness could expect to be taken to the cleaners. A man had to spend $50 to a $100 at a sitting to permit his female companion to show an adequate profit for the night. That meant he had to drink champagne, and make a good job of it. The girls mostly confined themselves to ginger ale or white crème de menthe, for they needed their wits about them and drunken women were not regarded as glamorous. "No cheapskates were tolerated," Butler recalled. "Wines were featured on the menu and if a tightwad ordered beer he got a skimpy mug with '5¢' painted on its side so everyone could see that he was a nickel-nurser. His girl would get up and leave him as if signaled, and pretty soon the penny pincher would be led outside and told not to come back."

During the day, when Sixth Avenue was a drab street indeed and its denizens were all sleeping the sleep of confirmed night hawks, the Haymarket was shuttered and lifeless. It looked like the premises of a business recently gone into bankruptcy, and was painted a repulsive shade of yellow. When night came, however, gaslight shone from every window and the razzmatazz of its bands drew in the crowds from Sixth Avenue, now swarming with life and color and movement. The high-rollers and low-lifers of Satan's Circus strolled through its doors. Hundreds of heads bobbed on the dance floor to the strenuous patterns of the waltz and the two-step. The Haymarket's sign, proclaiming Parisian titillations inside, swung from its iron hooks:

GRAND SOIREE DANSANT!

Tables surrounded the dance floor on three sides, and above them were boxes and more tables in the gallery. Behind them, lining the walls were cubicles where a man could be entertained in private after selecting one of the comely, bustle-swinging girls from shoals of femininity drifting through the establishment. "Beautiful adventuresses," wrote Dick Butler, perhaps with an excess of nostalgia over youthful revelries, "who came from big cities and small towns all over the world, were to be seen there, patiently waiting for some rich prize to fall in their laps." In the cubicles the girls gave private recitals of the can-can, the hoochy-cooch and other non-aesthetic dances. Some of them, according to Herbert Asbury, "gave exhibitions similar to the French peep shows. The descriptive title of 'circus,' which is now generally applied to such displays in this country, is said to have originated in the Haymarket."

When a patron staggered into the dawn—despite Corey's insistence on a "clean house"—he still faced various perils to his purse.

Not the least voracious of the vultures waiting outside was Weeping Willie Graham, the Haymarket's chief bouncer, a burly fellow who could grab an obstreperous or otherwise undesirable patron by the scruff of the neck and the seat of the pants and hurl him into the middle of Sixth Avenue. Willie Graham, according to Dick Butler, "would make a great to-do over some rich sap and then, after the sucker got silly on wine, Willie would break into tears. His wife was dying, his sister was in a hospital too, and he didn't know what to do or where to turn for financial assistance. He sprung it five to ten times a night on as many simps. It was usually good for ten or a hundred dollars."

The wine-fuddled patron might also be taken by the girl with whom he had whiled away the night in the Haymarket, or robbed by her accomplice waiting up a dark alley. One Long Island potato grower, tossing away the proceeds of his crop, left the Haymarket in bad company, was robbed and killed, and his body was stuffed in a furnace. A seafaring man named Captain Craft was another big spender who came to a sorry end, also in a furnace. He left the Haymarket early one morning, a trifle unsteady from "wealthy water," as champagne was called in the Tenderloin. Seeking still less wholesome company, he wandered into one of the dives along West Twenty-eighth Street. He ordered up champagne for the habitués a number of times, but finally got a clear look at the greedy faces around him and declined to buy any more wine. His drinking companions were incensed, but Captain Craft insisted that "I'll spend my money as I like." The drabs and barflies who had been sponging off him swarmed over him, knocked him senseless and hauled him down to the cellar. They cut his head off with a cleaver and stuffed his torso into the furnace. An expensive wake was held upstairs while the cremation proceeded in the cellar.

Favored customers of the Haymarket were often hoisted into a hack and sent home under escort of a "caretaker" by Proprietor Corey, who realized it was only good business to protect his patrons from outside thuggery and chicanery. Evidently the policy paid off handsomely, for when Corey retired and sold out to his partner, Noonan, he was able to buy a ninety-two-ton yacht, build a fine home on Long Island and become commodore of the Jamaica Bay Yacht Club. A sardonic newspaper writer said Corey was even "credited with having once spent a few minutes inside the Larchmont Yacht Club."

Raffish as it was, the Haymarket was the "class joint" of the

Tenderloin, "lily white compared with some of the dives that existed in 28th and adjoining streets." Twenty-eighth was generally regarded as the toughest street in the Tenderloin. At the old Alhambra they averaged a fight every ten minutes. The Broadway Gardens, running from Broadway to Sixth Avenue, was another dance hall for Quakers and pacifists to avoid. There most of the brawls revolved around the favors of the chorus girls who performed in the show. Still, in those days, anyone suffering a black eye in a difference of opinion found succor close at hand: all the drugstores of the district featured leeches, which attached themselves to the bruise and reduced the swelling, a sovereign remedy much preferred to the beefsteak cure. (West Twenty-eighth Street became somewhat more respectable, although not much quieter, after the turn of the century. Music publishers lined both sides of the street between Broadway and Sixth Avenue, and the racket made by aspiring composers and song pluggers soon gave the block the name of "Tin Pan Alley.")

Another famous resort in the Tenderloin was Charlie Ackron's Tivoli, on West Thirty-fifth Street near Broadway. Unwary customers of the Tivoli were clipped by some of the nimblest short-change artists in the business, the management holding that anyone too stupid to count his money deserved to be cheated. One night, however, they clipped the wrong man. State Senator John Ford rolled into the place in a frolicsome mood, but soon was objecting to the sticky fingers of his waiter. The management supported the waiter, and the senator was heaved into the night before he could reveal his identity. That bum's rush turned into a most expensive gesture so far as Charlie Ackron was concerned. Senator Ford bent all his energies toward having the Tivoli closed, and succeeded. Ackron went to prison several times in later years on swindling charges.

The Bohemia in West Twenty-ninth Street, the Heart of Maryland near by, the Cairo and the Tuxedo, the Buckingham Palace in West Twenty-seventh, the Star and Garter at Thirtieth and Sixth Avenue, across from the Haymarket, Sailors Hall in Thirtieth Street, the Stag Café operated by Dan the Dude, Paddy the

Pig's, McElroy's Pig's Head, and the Burnt Rag, also were rivals of the Haymarket when the Tenderloin was in its heyday.

The Star and Garter acquired a certain celebrity through its chief bartender, Billy Patterson, who was reputed to be the most talented mixer of cocktails, cobblers, toddies and punches in New York. It was his proudest boast, however, that he didn't have an enemy in the world. In this, he was apparently mistaken. One night a "mysterious assailant" sapped him as he left the Star and Garter and left him near death in the gutter. The incident gave rise to the Cock-Robinish query that echoed around the Tenderloin for years, "Who struck Billy Patterson?"

Another famous deadfall was the French Madame's in West Thirtieth Street off Sixth Avenue. The hefty proprietress was respected throughout the district for her skill in cooling off a rambunctious patron with the bludgeon she kept close at hand in the cashier's cage and for her efficiency in grabbing a troublesome female by the hair and propelling her into the street. The chief attraction at the French Madame's was a series of cubicles in which the girls danced the can-can nude for a dollar and performed more esoteric rites for a small additional fee.

The Cremorne, located in the cellar of a building in West Thirty-second Street, was one of the bawdiest resorts in the Tenderloin. It bore the name of an equally notorious London dance hall. The women who frequented the place were given brass checks for the whiskey or mixed drinks they induced the men to buy and saved the corks from the wine bottles brought to their tables, exchanging them later for their commissions in cash. The Cremorne was one of the cheaper places—providing one didn't get rolled by the girls and their male confederates—with drinks selling for fifteen cents each or two for a quarter. The manager of the Cremorne was given the sobriquet of Don Whiskerandos in recognition of his luxuriant beard and mustache. He also affected a grandee's manner, looking with disdain on the antics of his patrons and holding himself aloof from even the most generous of wine buyers.

Next door was an establishment that also called itself the Cre-

morne. Actually the sign was only a lure, baited for out-of-towners and other innocents who thought they were walking into *the*
Cremorne. It was a mission operated by a reformed drunk named
Jerry McAuley. This tricky evangelist locked the doors on those
who wandered into his mission by mistake, and harangued them
on the evils of drink and dissipation until they were too weary
and dispirited to continue their search for entertainment.

The Tenderloin operated without much interference for a good
twenty years before a really determined crusading minister
aroused the city to a consciousness of the evil existing unabashedly in its midst. There were occasional demands for reform, for
a severance of the mercenary relations between the politicians,
the police and the divekeepers. On such occasions Superintendent
of Police Thomas F. Byrnes, who pursued criminals with vigor
but turned a blind eye toward commercial vice, would transfer
the captains of various precincts and make a great show of "cleaning up the Tenderloin." All that meant was that the new captain
visited each madam with a demand for the customary $500 "in-
itiation fee," which his predecessors had also received. The police also conducted periodic raids to convince the public they
were guardians of morality. "Notwithstanding regular monthly
payments for protection," it was noted, "Police Headquarters
sometimes put the bee on the precinct captain. He would then
have to raid the brothels of many of his protégés, merely as a
public demonstration of official vigilance. The madams learned
that such raids always occurred just after the first of the month—
the date when ward men called to collect protection payments.
Raids had a depressing effect on business. And the harassed
champions of free enterprise found them costly, for bail had to
be secured not only for the madam but for every girl in the establishment." The bail monopoly was in the hands of William
R. Nelson, the Tammany district leader in the Tenderloin, who
charged five dollars for every prostitute bailed out.

The man who first called it the Tenderloin was Captain Alexander S. Williams, more familiarly known as Clubber Williams

for his dictum, "There is more law in the end of a policeman's nightstick than in a decision of the Supreme Court"—a slogan to which Williams devoted himself with all his bullish energy. Williams was transferred to the Tenderloin precinct after long years of service on the gang-ridden East Side. He held down the Tenderloin precinct's captaincy from 1876 to 1879, when he became superintendent of the Bureau of Street Cleaning for two years, and from 1881 to 1887.

On first taking command of the precinct, he told a friend, "I've had nothing but chuck steak for a long time, and now I'm going to get a little of the Tenderloin."

And so he did, retiring after those nine meaty years to Connecticut with several hundred thousand dollars which could hardly have been saved out of a police captain's pay.

Williams' prowess with the nightstick had been proven on countless occasions before he was transferred to the West Side. A bull-shouldered former seaman, he had made the toughs of the Houston Street area respect him while he was still a rookie. He knocked out the two leading thugs with his nightstick and threw them through the plate-glass window of a saloon, then in succession battered the daylights out of a half-dozen of their friends as they closed in to attack. Later, while captain of the East Thirty-fifth Street station, he decided to break the notorious Gas House Gang, organized a strong-arm squad, and dealt out beatings every time a member of the gang showed himself on the streets. There were protests against such strenuous measures, but Williams demonstrated for a group of police reporters just how they worked. Williams hung his watch on a lamppost at Third Avenue and Thirty-fifth Street, then strolled around the block with the reporters. When they returned to the lamppost, the watch was still hanging there. Clubber Williams was brought before the police commissioners eighteen times on charges of brutality but always acquitted. No such complaints buzzed around him while he ran the Tenderloin precinct. Clubber was too busy seeing to it that he got a choice cut.

Big Bill Devery, the chief of police, thoroughly approved of his precinct captains looking after their own interests—provided, of course, they didn't forget the overriding claims of headquarters for a share in the boodle. There was nothing Big Bill hated worse than a nosy self-righteous cop who wanted to close down brothels and afterhour saloons, unless it was a loud-mouthed reformer going around and upsetting people. He was a genial and hearty fellow, weighed 260 pounds, had a jolly red face and a thick black mustache. Big Bill liked to hold seminars around the pump at Twenty-eighth Street and Eighth Avenue, and was known as the Philosopher of the Pump. His advice to cops:

"Hear, see and say nothin',
"Eat, drink and pay nothin'."

Devery believed it was the police department's job to protect the lives and property of the citizens. The citizens, in return, "shouldn't worry about what they don't see." *Laissez faire* was his policy. Crooks went unmolested as long as they pulled their jobs out of town and laid low in New York. He boasted that only one safe was cracked in New York during his regime and that was a mistake. "Two days later the safecrackers sent a note of apology to the Chief, saying they were from out of town and meant no disrespect." Devery believed vice should be segregated and often rebuked clergymen for "breaking up the old East Side brothels and driving the habitués in among respectable people in the better parts of town."

Big Bill kept a close watch over everything that happened in the Tenderloin. No one could work there without his imprimatur. At the Haymarket, according to Dick Butler, the Hell's Kitchen politician and saloonkeeper, Devery was virtually the personnel manager. "Most of the hiring was done on the recommendation of Big Bill. Without his say-so, nobody could connect; with his O.K., even a cripple could get a job. I remember that Devery, who had a swell sense of humor, once recommended a waiter with a wooden leg, and the fellow was put to work right away. His artificial prop squeaked, especially in damp weather, and another waiter was assigned to oil the leg every night at the knee joint."

Chief Devery's considerable services to the Tenderloin did not go unrewarded. He collected his pay for favors through his tailor. Anyone who wanted Devery's help on a project went to the tailor and ordered a suit. "No matter what he charged, you paid," Butler recalled, "even if it was one thousand dollars for an ordinary one-pants suit. Devery would come to the tailor shop later and collect. . . ."

They might have all gone on feeding juicily off the Tenderloin, except that one of those jeremiads from the pulpit finally, in 1892, touched off an outburst of civic morality.

6

The Reverend Dr. Parkhurst
Goes out on the Town

THE Tenderloin and other centers of depravity were never quite the same after the Sunday of February 14, 1892. That was the day that the Reverend Dr. Charles H. Parkhurst ascended to the pulpit of the Madison Square Presbyterian Church and denounced the "polluted harpies that, under the pretense of governing this city, are feeding day and night on its quivering vitals . . . a lying, perjured, rum-soaked and libidinous lot."

The Reverend Parkhurst's charges, which were made in the same lurid generalities that New York had come to expect of its crusading pastors and to find more interesting as a study in rhetoric than as solid evidence of municipal corruption, were hardly startling to any knowledgeable New Yorker. What shocked his auditors was the use of such strong language from the pulpit; the less worldly among his parishioners rolled their eyes heavenward at his intemperate choice of expletives.

Dr. Parkhurst's venture into public affairs was at least a bold and thunderous one. His attack on Richard Croker, the current boss of Tammany, and his figurehead, Mayor Hugh J. Grant, and their associates was a series of broadsides delivered in the manner of an Old Testament prophet:

". . . Every effort to make men respectable, honest, temperate, and sexually clean is a direct blow between the eyes of the Mayor and his whole gang of drunken and lecherous subordinates, in this sense that while we fight iniquity they shield or patronize it; while we try to convert criminals, they manufacture them; and they have a hundred dollars invested in manufacturing machinery to our one invested in converting machinery. . . .

"Sin never gets tired, never is low-spirited, has the courage of its convictions, never fritters away its power and its genius pettifogging over side issues. . . . Neither the Devil nor any of his minions can be caught in a trap. You can hammer him, but you cannot snare him. Cajolery only lubricates the machinery of his iniquity. Petting him oils the bearings, minimizes the squeak, and maximizes the velocity. . . . Say all you please about the might of the Holy Ghost, every step in the history of an ameliorated civilization has cost just so much personal push."

He concentrated his attack on the protection given gambling, prostitution and racketeering of all kinds by the police and the politicians, charging them with establishing a scale for their services "carefully graded and as thoroughly systematized as any that obtains in the assessment of personal property or real estate." Tammany Hall, he said, was "a form under which the Devil disguises himself."

Much more striking evidence of the affinity between New York's underworld and the police department, however, had been provided only a week earlier by the New York *Mail and Express*, the city's most vigorous anti-Tammany organ, which was published by Colonel Elliott F. Shepherd. Colonel Shepherd's paper charged that there were 250 faro banks, 720 policy games, and uncounted hundreds of houses of prostitution operating in the city, as well as six hundred saloons which were violating the excise law by staying open after 1 A.M. week nights and admitting patrons through their side doors on Sundays, when they were

supposed to be closed up tight as a bung in a barrel. The *Mail
and Express* gave the names and addresses of these resorts. It
also charged that thieves of all kinds had a working agreement
with the police whereby they turned over eighty per cent of their
loot to the police; that gambling houses were paying fifty per
cent of their profits for protection and disorderly houses were
"taxed" $100 a month by the police. It cited the fact that to be-
come a patrolman in the New York Police Department, one had
to pay $300 to high police officials, to obtain a sergeancy cost
$1,400 and promotion to a captaincy, with its superior advantages
of sharing in the graft, was a $14,000 assessment.

Possibly the *Mail and Express*'s coldly factual articles helped
to inspire Dr. Parkhurst's sermon of February 14, although he
does not mention them in his memoirs. He had come to loathe
Tammany Hall and the police department after joining the New
York Society for the Prevention of Crime, of which he was elected
president in 1891. This was an organization of lawyers and merchants, with a sprinkling of civic-conscious clergymen, which
had not achieved anything like the fame of the Society for the
Prevention of Vice whose president was the ubiquitous Anthony
Comstock.

Until his outburst of February 14, Dr. Parkhurst had avoided
comment on mundane matters and confined himself to spiritual
themes, recognizing that his congregation preferred being lulled
to being aroused, harassed and harangued from the pulpit. Dis-
cussing this preference of his parishioners, he later told a meeting
of the alumni of the Union Theological Seminary: "We can ma-
lign David for his vices, and pour canister shot into poor Solomon
for his irregularities; and his being a back number and having no
extant relatives to pound you with a libel suit, the whole performance reduces to an elegant sedative, just warm enough to stimu-
late the blood if the church is cold, and cold enough to discourage
perspiration if it is July."

Dr. Parkhurst was not, in fact, the crusading type. He preferred the quiet of his study to brawling in the market place, had
a taste for an ironic detachment from contemporary affairs, and

favored the joys of scholarship above the fame sought by certain evangelistic colleagues. He was a frail, myopic man of fifty who grew a scraggly crop of whiskers to protect his throat from colds. He was born in Framingham, Massachusetts, and attended Amherst after being rejected for service in the Union Army because of his poor eyesight. He had planned to devote his life to teaching school, until one of his preceptors recommended a spell of preaching to aid his emotional development. After becoming the pastor of a church in Lenox, he decided to make the ministry his life's work. In 1880 he came to New York on being appointed pastor of the brownstone "American Gothic" church in Madison Square. It was his subsequent work with the Society for the Prevention of Crime that convinced him that the church had "lost touch with life" and must concern itself and accept responsibility for the state of the community—ugly and sordid as it might be.

Among the members of his congregation who thoroughly approved of the sermon was Thomas Collier Platt, the Republican boss of New York State, although ordinarily, he once told Theodore Roosevelt, he liked his theology "wholly divorced from moral implications." Until quite recently, Boss Platt had had an amicable working agreement with his Democratic opposite number, Boss Croker of Tammany Hall, but they had fallen out over Croker's failure to keep his promises regarding a split of the local patronage. Physically fragile as a dry stick but mentally tough as rawhide, Platt made his headquarters across the square from Dr. Parkhurst's church in the Fifth Avenue Hotel, where he received his subjects in the Amen Corner of the lobby. He has been characterized by M. R. Werner (in *Tammany Hall*, a painstaking history of that institution) as a "listless but energetic, polite but firm, cautious but essentially dishonest Republican politician . . . who, more than any one man in the history of America, was responsible for the corrupt alliance between millionaires and their corporations and those whose business was supposed to be the government of the state." He had no great love for conventional morality, his political enemies having once climbed to the window of his room in an Albany hotel and caught him in a "compromising situation." Presumably he was aware, in advance, of the context of Dr. Parkhurst's sermon, which admirably suited his purposes in revenging himself on Dick Croker for reneging on a political deal.

Another member of Dr. Parkhurst's audience that Sunday morning was W. E. Carson, a reporter for the New York *World*. Carson was present on orders from his city editor, who had been tipped off that Dr. Parkhurst's sermon would have a volatile effect on city politics. The *World*, under Joseph Pulitzer, was now anti-Tammany, although not quite so violently as the *Mail and Express*.

Carson's story in Monday morning's *World* caused even more of an uproar than Dr. Parkhurst had anticipated and provoked a counterattack which must have dismayed him. His ministerial colleagues and many of his parishioners deplored the "sensationalism" of his sermon. The Tammany bigwigs denounced him as a follower of "St. Billingsgate." Even the *World*, which should have been grateful for the exclusive story, criticized him in its editorial columns for "so violent an outburst of vituperation," and suggested that he ponder the commandment against bearing false witness. Charles A. Dana's *Sun*, a wholehearted supporter of Tammany and all its works, proposed that Dr. Parkhurst be relieved of his pastorate.

"The air was full of feathers and fur," Dr. Parkhurst later reminisced, "indicating that a variety of flying fowl and creeping beast had been hit. I had waked up a whole jungle full of teeth-gnashing brutes, and it was a question whether the hunter was going to bag the game or the game make prey of the hunter."

Chief of the "teeth-gnashing brutes," of course, was Dick Croker, boss of Tammany and a most formidable adversary to have "waked up." Croker had managed to restore Tammany Hall to the powerful position it had held during Tweed's reign. Croker, a leading light of the Fourth Avenue Tunnel Gang in his youth, slugged and gouged his way to political supremacy. In 1874, while holding down the post of county coroner, he became involved in an election-day brawl with John McKenna, an anti-

Tammany Democrat, at East Thirty-fourth Street and Second Avenue, in which McKenna was shot to death. While awaiting trial in the Tombs—he was subsequently released after a jury failed to agree—Croker met Edward S. Stokes, who had just slain Jim Fisk and also was awaiting trial, and became friendly with him. They were an odd combination, one a street fighter with political aspirations, the other the son of a genteel Brooklyn family, but the friendship endured. After Stokes served his remarkably light sentence in Sing Sing, he took over the management of the Hoffman House. Croker made the Hoffman House Tammany's headquarters during election campaigns. In less than twenty years following his arrest on murder charges, Croker became "the most powerful leader New York politics had ever known," according to M. R. Werner (*Tammany Hall*). Financially as well as politically, his fortunes prospered amazingly. He lived in a Fifth Avenue mansion, maintained a racing stable worth more than $100,000 and invested another quarter of a million in a stock farm for breeding race horses.

Dick Croker was able to maintain himself in the style of a nabob simply because he was taking a good share of the graft accumulating from police protection of every form of vice and crime, which the foreman of the 1894 Grand Jury estimated at $7,000,000 a year. "During the 1890's in New York City police bribery was so open and generally accepted," M. R. Werner has written, "that the particular motion of the hand behind the back and the palm turned up in the shape of a cup was used on the vaudeville stage then and later as the symbol denoting policeman. Like all good burlesque, it was based firmly on truth, for it was the traditional way in which large policemen really did take money from small Italian fruit vendors and portly German saloonkeepers."

To protect this juiciest of rackets, Croker obviously could be counted on to fight with a violent determination.

Tammany's strategy, undoubtedly concocted by Croker, was a brazen denial of all the charges leveled against it and the police by Dr. Parkhurst. It would demand that the reverend gentleman "put up or shut up," and doubtless he would lapse into a mumbling and humiliated confusion. It seemed a safe bet that Dr. Parkhurst had no real evidence of the corruption against which he had blazed out in the pulpit. Reformers never seemed to learn that sweeping generalities would not stand up in court. With all the confidence in the world, Croker and his friends had him summoned before the Grand Jury. De Lancey Nicoll, the district attorney, was a good Tammany man and could be counted upon to place Dr. Parkhurst in the worst possible light.

Dr. Parkhurst's appearance before the Grand Jury on February 23, nine days after his celebrated sermon, was the fiasco that Tammany's leaders predicted it would be. The day of his appearance the *Sun* directed one of its editorial harpoons at Dr. Parkhurst: "The good name of the whole community . . . has been assailed by him with violence, and the public dignity demands that he should be compelled to fortify his words with proof in order that the accused may be brought to punishment, or, failing in that duty, that he himself should be proceeded against criminally." Dr. Parkhurst was unable to offer the Grand Jury any legal proof of the existence of a conspiracy between Tammany and the police to protect organized vice and crime. A week later the jurors handed down a statement criticizing him for making such sweeping charges without any evidence to back them up.

Tammany and its supporters celebrated an illusory victory. Underestimating Dr. Parkhurst's courage and determination, they were quite certain that the crusader had been put in his place. They should have been warned that he would not give up so easily by the fact that on March 1, just before the Grand Jury rebuked him, he went to District Attorney De Lancey Nicoll's office with evidence against nine East Side saloons, which he charged with having violated the excise laws by staying open on Sunday. Dr. Parkhurst was coldly rebuffed by Nicoll, who informed him, "Dr. Parkhurst, I refuse to have any official communication with you until you have withdrawn the falsehoods that you spoke against me from your pulpit."

Fortified by the Grand Jury's reprimand, the *Sun* began flaying

Dr. Parkhurst in the best pamphleteering style of nineteenth century journalism. "It was a flagrant offense," the *Sun* said of his sermon of two weeks before. "It was made the more wicked and flagrant because of the place wherein it was committed, and because it was accompanied by other and more general charges against public officers, for which also he can furnish no facts in substantiation. The grand jury accordingly has done right to present this clerical slanderer to the Court and to the public in his true colors. But it should go further and District Attorney Nicoll should not allow his case to be passed by with simple exposure and reprimand. Dr. Parkhurst should be indicted, tried and convicted as the slanderer he is." Next day, March 3, the *Sun* grew even more vituperative:

"The best employment to which the Rev. Dr. Parkhurst can now devote himself is prolonged prayer and repentance to atone for the grievous sin of which he has been guilty. An appropriate place wherein to give him the opportunity to subject himself to such spiritual mortification would be a penitentiary cell."

The *Tammany Times* was even more contemptuous, and suggested that sheer lunacy was responsible for Dr. Parkhurst's charges. "A loose idea in a man's head is a serious thing," the Tammany house organ editorialized. "Every once in a while an idea probably forms in Doctor Parkhurst's head, and then it gets loose and rattles around at such a great rate that it drives the poor man crazy. It keeps rattling around until the next idea forms and drops off, and that is the reason he seems to be crazy all the while."

Dr. Parkhurst's only supporters were his fellow members of the Society for the Prevention of Crime, a few parishioners and several of the city's newspapers, including the *Mail and Express*, the *Evening Post*, and the *Times*. A short time later the *World*, too, came around to his support. Joseph Pulitzer, editor and publisher of the *World*, invited the clergyman to his offices in Park Row and told him, "I am now beginning to understand what it is exactly you are aiming to accomplish; that it is not the social evil that you are combating, but the collusion between the police and the criminal classes." Dr. Parkhurst recalled in his autobiography (*My Forty Years in New York*) that Pulitzer also offered him the services of a *World* reporter to obtain evidence of the collusion.

Dr. Parkhurst, however, had resolved to engage more professional help in his fight against City Hall. Near-sighted and professorial though he was, ill-suited to the rôle of undercover investigator, he had decided to get the evidence needed to topple the Tammany wigwam down on Fourteenth Street. The *Sun* and the Tammany mouthpieces had gone a little too far in heaping scorn and ridicule on the frail little pastor. On the advice of his associates in the Society for the Prevention of Crime, Dr. Parkhurst engaged the services, at six dollars a night, of an oversized young private detective named Charles W. Gardner. Gardner knew his way around the city's deadfalls—all too well as events showed. As another companion and witness, Dr. Parkhurst was to be accompanied on his clandestine rounds by a wealthy young member of his congregation named John Langdon Erving. So radiant was Erving's sense of virtue that he was known to his friends, playfully perhaps, as Sunbeam.

On the night of March 5, the three men set forth on what became the most celebrated rubberneck tour in New York's history. The liveliest account of Dr. Parkhurst's several nights on the town was written by Gardner (*The Doctor and the Devil, or Midnight Adventures of Dr. Parkhurst*, a paperback volume issued in 1894). When the minister and Erving showed up at Gardner's quarters that night, the private detective decided their attempts at costuming themselves as ruffians on a spree were amateurishly inadequate. Dr. Parkhurst, he later wrote, wore "a passé suit of broadcloth . . . cut in ministerial fashion," Erving looked "like a costume plate of a dead year, just a bit run to seed." Dr. Parkhurst readily agreed to let an expert redesign his costume, and Gardner fussed away at the job until he was satisfied his companion would pass as a roisterer, at least in a dimly lit dive full of drunks. "He is a very jovial man," Gardner wrote of Dr. Parkhurst, "and appreciates a joke. I must say that as a companion no 'rounder' is better company than the celebrated apostle of reform."

The first night the odd-looking trio visited a resort on Cherry Street, where Dr. Parkhurst manfully swallowed a wicked dose of the local approximation of whiskey. "He acted as though he had swallowed a whole political parade—torchlights and all," Gardner noted.

After visiting some of the lower depths of the East Side, Dr. Parkhurst burst out in a tirade on a water-front street corner. "Here is a city which is now waking up to begin its daily toil for millions of dollars. Just one tithe of the money and energy to be thrown away today in this race for wealth would turn this hellhole we were in into a decent place. How many of these seekers of wealth know, or care, that the excise laws of this city, the laws of moral health—all laws, in fact—are broken right here in this part of town? And, mind you, this saturnalia of crime tonight is going on right under the eyes of the police. They are cognizant of it; their superior officers at police headquarters are aware of it, yet they dare to say that I am guilty of bearing false witness against my neighbors because I put my finger on the sore and say to the police, 'Cure this spot and you are doing your city the duty you owe it as its servants.'" It was just as well no one was sober enough to take notice of this harangue or the undercover investigation would have been quickly ended.

As it was, on subsequent nights, the Reverend Dr. Parkhurst's disguise was almost penetrated on several occasions. In a Third Avenue saloon the trio ran into an Amherst classmate of Dr. Parkhurst's who could not be shaken off or shushed up. The bartender became suspicious and chased Dr. Parkhurst, Gardner and Erving into the street.

"Show me something worse," Dr. Parkhurst kept telling Gardner.

And the detective was able to produce some shocking sights. In one house of prostitution, the staff consisted of a German woman, the madam, and her five daughters. In Chinatown they watched a small family group including a Chinese, his Caucasian

wife and their eight-year-old son smoking opium. At the Golden
Rule Pleasure Club in West Fourth Street they found a basement
resort catering to homosexuals. The place was divided into cubicles. "In each room," Gardner recalled, "sat a youth whose face
was painted, eyebrows blackened, and whose airs were those of
a young girl. Each person talked in a high falsetto voice and
called the others by women's names."

Dr. Parkhurst was bewildered. Gardner was required to explain homosexuality, and the minister was so shocked he ran
straight out of the dive, saying, "Why, I wouldn't stay in that
house for all the money in the world!"

Generally, however, Dr. Parkhurst was able to master his re-
pugnance and observed, calmly enough, the most lurid scenes.
At Hattie Adams' brothel in Twenty-seventh Street Gardner engaged five of the girls to dance the can-can in the nude and play
leapfrog, with Gardner acting as the frog. Dr. Parkhurst, Gardner
wrote, watched "with an unmoved face . . . slowly sipping a glass
of beer." The proprietress was rather suspicious of the minister,
who did not seem to be enjoying himself as a man should at such
revels. Gardner assured her that Dr. Parkhurst was "a gay boy
from the West," but Hattie was bemused by her guest's inappro-
priate solemnity. "Then Hattie tried to pull Dr. Parkhurst's whiskers, but the Doctor straightened out with such an air of dignity
that she did not attempt any further familiarities." (During the
subsequent trial of Hattie Adams, a *World* reporter asked one of
Hattie's girls how Dr. Parkhurst had impressed her. "I thought he
was a pickpocket," she was quoted as saying. "He sat there solemn and his eyes were rolling everywhere as if he had some
scheme.") Later, at Marie Andrea's in West Fourth Street, Dr.
Parkhurst and his companions witnessed a much more depraved
exhibition called a "French circus" by the habitués. Gardner
wrote that he was sickened by the performance but Dr. Parkhurst
"sat in a corner with his feet curled under his chair and blandly
smiled." It seemed to Gardner that Dr. Parkhurst was "getting
past the shocking point."

The investigation, however, had come to an end. Dr. Parkhurst and his two companions swore out affidavits on what they had seen, and a squad of private detectives engaged by Gardner to conduct a simultaneous investigation of law-breaking saloons, 254 of which were observed selling liquor on Sunday with many policemen among their patrons, also drew up their reports. On Sunday, March 13, Dr. Parkhurst delivered his second sermon on the subject of organized and protected vice, told his congregation he now had the evidence the law demanded, and flourished a list of thirty houses of prostitution operating in the precinct in which the Madison Square Presbyterian Church was located, that list having also been compiled by his private detectives. Referring to Hattie Adams' establishment only three blocks from the church, he told the jam-packed audience that he felt the necessity of leaving town for a month to "bleach the memory of it out of my mind."

Of "Tammany-debauched" New York, he declared, "It is rotten with a rottenness that is unspeakable and indescribable, and a rottenness that would be absolutely impossible except by the connivance, not to say the purchased sympathy, of the men whose one obligation before God, men and their own conscience is to shield virtue and make vice difficult. Now *that* I stand by, because before Almighty God I know it, and I will stand by it though buried beneath presentments as thick as autumn leaves in Vallombrosa or snowflakes in a March blizzard."

In one day less than a month, Dr. Parkhurst had stirred up more controversy, more recrimination and denunciation over commercialized vice than any of his crusading predecessors in the past thirty years. Many people were affronted at the thought of a clergyman "wallowing" in dives and brothels. They were inclined to agree with the *Sun's* insinuations that swilling beer and paying the inmates of whorehouses to participate in depraved exhibitions constituted evidence of Dr. Parkhurst's own inclinations, that Dr. Parkhurst had not only betrayed his ministry but bragged about it from the pulpit. Not unexpectedly, Robert G. Ingersoll, who toured the country preaching agnosticism, condemned Dr. Parkhurst's "skulking methods and decoy tricks."

Tammany's supporters tried to becloud the issue as best they could. "The attempt was made, especially by Dana's paper [the *Sun*]," wrote Dr. Parkhurst in his memoirs, "to prejudice me in the public mind by charging me with persecuting the unfortunate inmates of houses of evil resort, and the police chimed in with Dana to the same purpose."

But Dr. Parkhurst's second sermon, and his offer of evidence to support his charges, had put Tammany on the defensive. It had to make a show, at least, of cleaning up the Tenderloin and other districts where vice prevailed. Hattie Adams and Marie Andrea were indicted on charges of operating houses of prostitution. Police Superintendent Thomas F. Byrnes ordered his precinct captains to see to it—for the time being—that saloons observed the legal closing hours. The police and the district attorney's office were disposed to make a few gestures in the direction of law enforcement, then settle back and wait for the blathering about reform to blow itself out.

Meanwhile, the authorities did all they could to embarrass and harass Dr. Parkhurst. One night, for instance, they conducted a raid in the Tenderloin to demonstrate how stern they could be with prostitutes. The police raiders broke into the parlor house in West Thirty-first Street and forced the lightly clad women out of the establishment and into a late snowfall.

When the women protested against this needless cruelty, the officers laughed and said, "We're doing this on old Parkhurst's orders."

Forty bedraggled prostitutes marched over to Dr. Parkhurst's house in East Thirty-fifth Street, "all of them howling mad," as he recalled in *My Forty Years in New York*. They all managed to crowd into his parlor and "made a unanimous and clamorous charge of cruelty, which Mrs. Parkhurst and myself listened to quietly till they had exhausted themselves." The women were mad enough to string up the minister to the lamppost outside his door, but the moment they quieted down Dr. Parkhurst was able to convince them that he was the last person in New York to have his "orders" obeyed by the police, that he had nothing to do with their brutal expulsion, and that he regarded them as the victims of a system he was trying to destroy.

Mrs. Parkhurst brought out clothing for the less adequately clothed young women, and then served tea and toast while her husband continued to explain his attitude toward prostitution. By the time his guests left, hours later, "they went away loving Mrs. Parkhurst and myself as sincerely as they hated the police and the city government."

Even more heartening to the beleaguered minister was a mass meeting held in the Cooper Institute, which served as a rallying point for hundreds of his supporters. Judge Noah Davis told the assemblage, "Most men tell us that the President of this Society [for the Prevention of Crime] should never have done what he has done; that a minister of the Gospel should spend his whole life persuading mankind to make some atonement for the sin of Adam . . . but if I had been brought face to face with the situation that confronted Dr. Parkhurst, if my charges had been denied, if a district attorney had laughed at me, if a grand jury had pointed the finger of scorn at me, I would have dived to the bottom of hell, if need be, to prove that I had spoken the truth. . . ." The meeting and the great ovation given him, Dr. Parkhurst believed, "rather marked the turning of the tide and was the first popular expression of sympathy."

But there was still the ordeal of testifying in court against Hattie Adams and Marie Andrea, which would be a predictably nasty business. Dr. Parkhurst knew that the district attorney's office, prosecuting the cases against the two madams, would afford him the least possible protection as a witness; that the unscrupulous gentlemen employed by the Tenderloin would give him a merciless battering in cross-examination and in the summation before the jury. The law firm representing Hattie Adams at her trial on May 4 was that of William F. Howe and Abe Hummel, the city's top criminal lawyers. Howe, a brilliant if sometimes maudlin performer before the bar, almost invariably succeeded in overcoming a jury, partly by the blaze of his diamond accessories and partly by his blandishments, which made the state's witnesses seem to be the real culprits rather than his clients. Hummel was a great legal brain who left the talking to his stentorian partner. He came to court each day dressed in black, a somber background for Howe's jewelry display, and carrying a large Bible. Other members of the defense staff were three attractive girls, coached by Howe and Hummel to sit up front in the courtroom and keep their gaze fastened on Dr. Parkhurst while he testified, giggling or gasping at the more sensational parts of his testimony.

When Dr. Parkhurst was summoned to the witness stand, he was heard to murmur to Sunbeam Erving, still at his pastor's side, "Would that the chalice should be taken from my lips."

Howe tried to force an admission from Dr. Parkhurst that salacious intentions had propelled him into Hattie Adams' house. The Tenderloin's leading advocate had a poor case, but hoped to distract the jury by insinuations that Dr. Parkhurst was twice as evil as his client. Howe, according to the biographer of Howe and Hummel, had been sold on the idea of having Hattie stand trial by Police Superintendent Byrnes. The usual procedure was to have an accused madam plead guilty in General Sessions and pay a $50 fine at most. Inspector Byrnes, however, reasoned that Dr. Parkhurst, rather than testify in open court to what he witnessed in Hattie Adams' place of business, would back down on his charges. "They figured that sooner than testify he would head back to Massachusetts, which was just where they wanted him to head," a member of District Attorney Nicoll's staff at the time later recalled. Dr. Parkhurst, once again underestimated, confounded his adversaries by standing up to their oblique attacks on his character.

Howe, in despair over his failure to crack Dr. Parkhurst on the witness stand, declared that young Erving's morals had been corrupted by the fact he was allowed to accompany the minister on his rounds of the redlight districts. Howe insisted that Erving show the jury how he danced with a naked inmate of one of the brothels they visited. Sunbeam's performance was anything but titillating. One of the reporters wrote that Erving looked "like a timid man removing a mouse from a chimney corner with a pair of tongs."

In his summation, Howe excoriated Dr. Parkhurst as a lecher who concealed himself in ministerial broadcloth. "In the words of M. Thiers," Howe roared at the jury, "I cannot elevate him to the level of my contempt. Speak as you will of her, Hattie Adams is worth a thousand of his kind."

"Truly the devil's advocate," moaned Dr. Parkhurst to his supporters.

The jury ignored Howe's charges against the leading prosecution witness and found Hattie Adams guilty. She was sentenced to six months in jail.

Two days later Dr. Parkhurst and Erving were subjected to a similar ordeal at the trial of Marie Andrea. Her attorney, Charles W. Brooke, also a leading light of the criminal bar, took the same line as Howe. His questions regarding the orgy staged in Madam Andrea's house so unnerved Erving that the young man collapsed on the witness stand. The court was informed the next day that Erving could testify only at the risk of losing his sanity. Dr. Parkhurst stood up quite well against Brooke's leering cross-examination, calmly turning aside Brooke's thesis that it wasn't necessary to witness exhibitions in *two* whorehouses in the same evening to establish the fact that prostitution existed in New York. Again the jury was more impressed by Dr. Parkhurst's calm sincerity than the defense lawyer's snide accusations. The jurors deliberated for only a few minutes before voting Marie Andrea guilty.

For months after those two trials, Dr. Parkhurst kept speaking out in his pulpit and through newspaper interviews against the official protection of vice and crime. Almost a year and a half passed before the public was thoroughly aroused from its apathy —and then not so much by moral indignation as by the depression of 1893 and the sobering thoughts encouraged by economic distress. Through 1892 and 1893, Dr. Parkhurst continued to collect evidence against the procurers, madams and divekeepers of the Tenderloin, and their protectors, for the day of judgment he was confident would come. His adversaries in the underworld and the city government were equally confident they could survive any reform movement. They did, however, operate more clandestinely—and therefore less profitably—than before Dr. Parkhurst first assailed them from his pulpit in Madison Square.

7

"A Free and Easy Life in a Free and Easy Town"

SOMETHING of the tenacity and arrogance with which the police officials preserved the houses of prostitution and assignation in their precincts from the interference of decent people living in their vicinity was clearly illustrated in one of the departmental trials to which Captain (later Inspector) Alexander S. Williams was subjected. The records of the proceedings against Clubber Williams were read into the transcript of the first of the investigations which turned the New York Police Department upside down and shook out some of the bigger clinkers. Under considerable pressure, the Clubber's superiors brought him to trial before the Board of Police Commissioners on charges of conduct unbecoming an officer.

Williams was then captain in charge of the Tenderloin precinct, with its station house in West Thirtieth Street. The record of his trial showed that many residents of the neighborhood complained about the scores of disorderly houses operating with the encouragement and protection of the police. One man almost tearfully pleaded with Captain Williams to clean up the block in

117

which he lived because the foul-mouthed pimps and their loud
and bawdy whores were corrupting the children who played in
the streets around them. Captain Williams contemptuously dismissed him, and went back into conference with his ward man,
the civilian entrusted with collecting a precinct captain's share
of the proceeds. Many others tried to sway Williams toward doing his duty and all were shown the door. If they didn't like the
neighborhood, why didn't they move? Williams' family was established at Cos Cob, Connecticut, well beyond the range of a
drunken trollop's obscene raging against the world; that was one
of the advantages of having exchanged the rump for the tenderloin.

Even the pleas of a parish priest had no visible effect on Clubber Williams. The record of his trial showed that the Reverend
Cornelius Praetoni, pastor of St. Francis Catholic Church on West
Thirty-first Street between Sixth and Seventh avenues, protested
against the fact that "immoral houses and lewd women are, and
for a long time have been, close to his church; that the women
continually insult and solicit him as he passes through the street—
priest though he be—and have even done so without clothing upon
them . . . and that the young ladies of his church are especially
subjected to insult and indignities by the men who come to patronize these houses."

When Father Praetoni asked Captain Williams to close down
the bawdyhouses, he received a mock-pious reply: "Oh, it would
be too bad to drive the inmates out in the cold of winter."

Anticipating the Reverend Dr. Parkhurst by five years—this
was in 1887—Father Praetoni took action against the madams
operating in the vicinity of his church and made citizen's arrests
of thirteen of them. Naturally this aroused a certain amount of
public comment, and Clubber Williams' superiors evidently urged
him to bestir himself. His officers made a great show of arresting
ten women who kept houses of assignation and brothels.

The only record of Captain Williams' trial before the Board of
Police Commissioners was kept by a stern soldierly man named
Fitz-John Porter, a member of the board. The other three com-

missioners did not commit themselves to paper and ink. Porter had a strong sense of justice, and little wonder, for he had long suffered from injustice. During the Civil War, he had been a major general commanding a corps in the Army of the Potomac; he was General George B. McClellan's right hand in the campaigns in northern Virginia, and had saved the line during the crisis of the Seven Days' Battles. He was abruptly cashiered in 1863, a victim of wartime political intrigues. He was a friend of General McClellan's and made no secret of the fact even after McClellan was relieved just before Second Bull Run. McClellan's successor, the vainglorious John Pope, charged him with disloyalty and disobeying orders in the face of the enemy, and made the charges stick. Porter had to wait twenty-three years, until 1886, the year before Williams' trial, before the government got around to clearing him. As a police commissioner, therefore, Porter was meticulous about putting himself on the record when another man's career and reputation were at stake.

Despite his passion for justice and a natural sympathy for any accused man, Porter could not stomach Clubber Williams' claim before the commissioners that he was being persecuted. Williams procured expensive counsel for his trial, the starchy Elihu Root, a future Republican statesman. Neither Williams nor Root could convince General Porter that the former had not been guilty of "a spasmodic application of the power of the law," as he sardonically phrased it in his report. Porter and one other commissioner voted for Williams' conviction, which would have ended his brutal and rapacious career, but the other two members of the board voted the Clubber to be innocent of the charges. The vote being tied, Williams was free to return smugly to his "piece of the Tenderloin."

Father Praetoni's concern for the welfare of the children of his parish, being raised in streets where the pimp and the whore engaged in their open and unabashed commerce, was not merely a moralistic outburst. The children of his parish, and others like it, often became recruits for the system of commercialized vice.

The boys became cadets or pimps—there was a difference, to be defined below—and the girls were their victims.

A report of the Committee of Fourteen, which was subsequently organized to stamp out prostitution and allied rackets, gave the composite history of the origin and progress of a typical cadet. "Usually he is the boy who first became acquainted with immoral women as he played about the steps or in the street in front of his tenement home. As the acquaintance grew, the women engaged him to run errands, in return for which they gave him presents of candy, fruit or pennies. As the boy grew older he found that these women were sought by different men who gave him dimes and quarters to carry messages to them or take them to apartments where they lived.

"As time goes on, the boy becomes a member of the street gangs of his neighborhood. Often some of the more adventuresome girls of the same age in the district are taken into the gang and enjoy the benefits of the petty thieving carried on. The boy and girl chums soon become very intimate and the strange loyalty begins which astounds judges when they seek to secure evidence against the boys appearing before them as cadets. The boys in these street gangs who develop fearlessness and physical strength later attach themselves to political leaders and become members of district clubs, associations and athletic clubs. It is not long before they become invaluable to the politicians in certain districts through their aid as repeaters and strong-arm men at the polls on election day. In the meantime, they have acquired a taste for good clothes and idleness. . . ."

The nineteenth century spiv, to satisfy his longing for flashy clothes and jewelry, usually persuaded his former "girl chum" to enter prostitution, and then went looking for other susceptible girls to recruit for the same purpose, the Committee of Fourteen report said. "The height of his ambition, to have a house, is now often gratified, and the combined earnings of a number of women make him a rich and dangerous member of the community."

It was that group's successor, the Committee of Fifteen, also organized to investigate vice conditions, which offered an explanation of the difference between the cadet and the pimp. The two terms are often used interchangeably. The cadet, the committee said, procures girls for houses of prostitution, is paid his fee by the madam, and then goes hunting for other recruits. The pimp takes over from the cadet after the girl enters prostitution, becomes the girl's protector and shares in her earnings, and maintains his relationship with her as long as it is profitable.

Regarding the cadet, the committee said, "His occupation is professional seduction. By occasional visits he succeeds in securing the friendship of some attractive shopgirl. By apparently kind and generous treatment, and by giving the young girl glimpses of a standard of living which she had never dared to hope to attain, this friendship rapidly ripens into infatuation. The Raines Law hotel or the 'furnished room house,' with its café on the ground floor, is soon visited for refreshments. After a drugged drink, the girl wakens and finds herself at the mercy of her supposed friend. Through fear and through promises of marriage she casts her fortunes with her companion and goes to live with him. The companion disappears; and the shopgirl finds herself an inmate of a house of prostitution. She is forced to receive visitors of the house. For each visitor the girl receives a brass or pasteboard check from the cashier of the house entitling her to twenty-five cents. . . ."

To protect the millions of dollars in annual income from the whoring industry and its brass-check system, the politicians in power and their collaborators in the police department, through 1892 and 1893, struggled with every means at their command to stifle the demands for reform.

The police conducted sporadic raids in the Tenderloin, for which they sought the widest possible publicity. On one occasion Police Captain Max Schmittberger, Clubber Williams' successor in command of the Tenderloin precinct, raided a dozen brothels and brought sixty inmates to Jefferson Market Court.

"Now," the doughty Schmittberger remarked to reporters in aggrieved tones, "I'd be glad to know just what Dr. Parkhurst would like me to do. I've cleaned out the Tenderloin until it looks like a Connecticut village."

Schmittberger did not specify which Connecticut village he meant, but it must have been a bawdy place indeed, for the Tenderloin was still in business, though not so brazenly as before Dr. Parkhurst began his cannonades from the pulpit.

Tammany and its creatures managed to damage the Parkhurst crusade through its one vulnerable member—Charles Gardner, the hulking private detective who had accompanied Dr. Parkhurst and Sunbeam Erving on their tour of the redlight districts—before the first year was out. Somehow Police Superintendent Byrnes and his sleuths learned that Gardner's past was not quite lily-white, that his first wife was rumored to have left him when he tried to induce her to become a prostitute. On December 4, 1892, they arrested him on charges of extortion. The complainant was Lillie Clifton, madam of a house in West Fifty-fourth Street. At the trial two months later, Mrs. Clifton, three other madams and a saloonkeeper all testified that Gardner had tried to shake them down. They paid him various sums of money to protect their establishments from being raided by the police, they told the court.

Gardner was defended by John W. Goff, a waspish, reform-minded former assistant district attorney, William Travers Jerome, a future district attorney and one of New York's most tenacious prosecutors, and Frank Moss, another enthusiast for reform. All three men were to play prominent rôles in the investigations which broke the power of the boodlers in the New York Police Department. They put up a vigorous defense for Gardner, claiming that he had been framed by the police and the testimony against him was entirely perjured. They even accused Recorder Frederick Smyth, who tried the case, of prompting Mrs. Clifton when she took the witness stand. There was a rank odor about the whole proceedings against Gardner, not at all dispelled when he was found guilty and sentenced to two years in jail.

The State Supreme Court reversed his conviction and ordered him released from the Tombs eleven months later. Mrs. Clifton confessed that she had lied to the court on orders from Big Bill Devery, then a police captain, who subsequently was made chief of police despite his unsavory rôle in the rigging of an extortion case against Gardner. The Gardner case served to show very clearly the character of the men who were fighting to preserve their corrupt administration of the New York Police Department.

These men managed to keep the lid on the town until the fall of 1893, largely through the refusal of Governor Roswell P. Flower, a Democrat, to entertain any notions of an investigation of law enforcement, and the equally adamant stand of the Democratic majority in the state legislature. That autumn, however, the electorate turned the Democrats out of office, and legislative control passed to the Republicans.

Practically the first order of business in Albany when the legislature reconvened in January, 1894, was to order the appointment of a committee to investigate the New York Police Department and its connections with Tammany Hall, organized crime and commercialized vice. State Senator Clarence E. Lexow was named chairman of the investigating committee.

Before the Lexow Committee finished taking evidence and published its report in five fat volumes totaling almost six thousand pages, the most vicious system of corrupting a city in American history was exposed. It would be impossible to outline the findings of that committee in a few pages, but the testimony concerning the operations of a few leading figures in the Tenderloin will indicate their nature.

The committee went into action with great speed and efficiency. On February 2, less than a month after it came into being, the committee arrived in New York to begin taking evidence. John Goff, who had defended Gardner so vigorously, took over the job of committee counsel with even more zeal. De Lancey Nicoll, the Tammany district attorney, acted as counsel for the police department.

Hundreds of subpoenas went out, and a large number of the Tenderloin's leading citizens scattered like quail before the coming storm. A whole "colony of the keepers of disreputable resorts" migrated to Chicago to escape service of the subpoenas, the Lexow Committee later noted in its report. Mrs. Mathilda Hermann, known as the French Madam, proved to be particularly difficult to land as a witness for the very good reason that she had more grievances against her police protectors than any of the other proprietors. Mrs. Hermann, said the committee, was "provided with a considerable sum of money, placed under an escort and sent first to Canada, then to Chicago." An investigator for the committee located Mrs. Hermann and induced her to return to New York. In Jersey City, the committee reported, "attempts were made to take her from the custody of our officers," but the hoodlums hired by Mrs. Hermann's former associates were repulsed in a battle in the railroad station. Her testimony, as will be seen below, proved to be worth the effort.

The most prominent of those who fled rather than face John Goff's searing cross-examination was Dick Croker himself. The walls of Tammany were being breached, and he had no intention of being caught in the debacle. He could always deny what others testified against him, but could not risk testifying against himself under oath. Off to England he went with his racing stable, to settle down in a peaceful shire while his followers were scourged by Goff and the Lexow Committee. He left with a blazing hatred of reformers, saying of the Reverend Dr. Parkhurst, "There is not a man in New York whose tongue is more vicious, whose example is more dangerous or who has scattered more that is bad all over the city. And he poses as a preacher of the gospel and then villifies his fellow man. And he poses as a preacher of virtues. Is this one of the lessons he wishes the people to follow? Are these the instructions he wishes the people to follow? Are these the instructions he wants to give his fellow man and to children? His attacks are not worth analysis, not worth serious attention except to call attention to the damage he is doing by the example he is setting."

Dr. Parkhurst, meanwhile, was disavowing any Comstock-like urge to purify human nature. His aim simply was to break the links between Tammany, the police and the underworld. "No," he said, "I was not and am not a reformer. I do not believe in moral reform applied externally. They have a genuine itch to make the world better, all the reformers I have met; but they irritate more souls than they heal and purify. They try to relieve a moral itch under their own skins by scratching their neighbors. They work on the principle that you can pump goodness into a man if you will first pump out the badness to make room for it. A saint, according to them, is a deflated sinner. For such a doctrine I cannot pump up any enthusiasm."

Despite all their former protectors' efforts to prevent them from talking, some of the Tenderloin madams were giving the Lexow Committee a graphic picture of how police officials ruled that district as a private fief. One of the star witnesses was Mrs. Mathilda Hermann, who had operated two adjoining houses with electric lamps on the stoops to guide customers to her parlors.

Mrs. Hermann, wearing a huge plumed hat that almost hid her pug-nosed face, appeared before the committee with a strong sense of grievance.

Counsel Goff was so delighted to have arranged her appearance there that he made an unusual attempt at geniality. "Well, Mrs. Hermann, I am glad to meet you," he said.

"I am very sorry to meet you, Mr. Goff," said Mrs. Hermann.

But the French Madam—whom police had called their "French gold mine"—gave an angrily forthright account of how the police had leeched on her business. She admitted her profits had been running between $1,000 to $1,500 a month just before she was forced to close and flee to Canada, but the police had been increasing their demands for protection money, and enforcing those demands with their fists. Her establishment catered to foreigners and sent its envoys to the West Side docks to meet all the ships.

She estimated that she had paid the police $30,000 in the past six years, $20,000 of it in the past two years. Even so, any cop felt at liberty, apparently, to mistreat the "French gold mine." In her thick French accent, she told the committee how a drunken policeman met her on the street near her house and "called me evil names, and I was ashamed and I crossed the street to go to my house, and the policeman followed me, and he took the pitcher out of my hands and threw the beer over me, and commenced to lick me, and called me a 'French bitch' and from that commenced to lick me."

"With his fists?" Goff asked.

"No, with his club . . . then I was awful ashamed, and lots of people outside, and he licked me, and I begged him to let me alone, and then he said, 'You will suffer for that; you doing something against my friends,' and he told me he would lick me some more, and then he took me to the station house, and I had a wrapper on, and I was all wet, and when I got to the station house, I felt my diamond earrings were out."

"Your diamond earrings were gone?"

"Yes, sir, then the matron was there, and I told my earrings is lost, and I said the policeman licked me awful bad, and she said, who do you want, and I send for somebody there, and I said—"

"The matron asked you how much you wanted to give, and she will send somebody there?"

"Yes, sir; then about ten minutes after—"

"You said you would give her $15?"

"Yes, then fifteen minutes afterwards she came back and told me the man did not find the earrings. . . ." Mrs. Hermann finally recovered her jewelry, she testified, on payment of $30. But that was the least of the expenses she incurred as a result of the beating. Surgery was required, she said, to mend the internal injuries she suffered at the hands of the drunken patrolman.

When she balked at further increases of the fees she was paying for protection, the police arrested her and charged her with being a common prostitute. This charge offended her deeply, she told the committee, because she was proud of being "a business-woman" whose only interest in prostitution was the proceeds, not the sordid physical details. Not only that, she was accused of selling herself to three policemen and a bootblack for a dollar apiece. "Never a man in New York or a Frenchman," she said vehemently, "can say they stayed with me for a dollar."

A much less willing witness was Maud Harvey, who had operated a house of assignation in West Twenty-fourth Street.
Counsel Goff knew he was in for a difficult time when she argued
about which Bible was suitable for oath-taking, and refused to be
sworn in until the committee guaranteed it was a Catholic Bible
on which she placed her hand.

Mrs. Harvey was willing to discuss certain details of her business, such as the fact that she charged two dollars for the use of
one of her rooms on the understanding that her clients had to
clear out by midnight. She admitted that, after operating the
place for ten years, she was able to pay $17,000 for another house
and install a maid servant, even though the Lexow investigation
had caused her to cease operating.

Although the police raided her establishment only once in ten
years, she insisted that "I never gave up a cent" in protection
money. "The only money I ever paid was to the Sisters of Charity."

Goff trapped her into admitting that she closed down only
when the committee began its investigations, then shot the purely
rhetorical question at her:

"Do you mean the mere appointment of this committee had
more terrors for you than the 3,800 policemen in the city of New
York?"

More revelatory of her attitude toward law enforcement was
the testimony of the committee investigator who had served the
subpoena on her the night before. He quoted her as saying,
"Why is it that they take me when the street is full of such houses
as mine?" He also recounted the following bit of dialogue:

Mrs. Harvey: "I must go to see somebody."

The Investigator: "The police?"

Mrs. Harvey: "What, those God damned sons of bitches? No,
the stinkin' bastards, I wouldn't go to them."

Some of the houses in the Tenderloin were under the direct
protection of Tammany and police officials. Captain Schmittberger, a bulky man with the standard "constabulary mustache"
and heavy-duty brogans, a man who knew his way around the

profitable West Side precincts, appeared as a more or less friendly witness. By that time other cops had spilled the story of how they bribed the police commissioners to obtain promotions, and the evidence that precinct captains served as funnels for all the bribery and corruption was firmly established. Now was the time for a policeman to appreciate the virtues of frankness. Schmittberger blandly admitted taking about $1,000 a month in protection money from brothels, gambling houses and saloons, and that $200 of this went to his immediate superior, Clubber Williams, now an inspector.

Captain Schmittberger also told of a "very quiet house" operated by Mrs. Georgianna Hastings which was patronized by wealthy and respected citizens, judges, city officials and other men with a need for discretion. When the Lexow Committee tried to serve Mrs. Hastings with a warrant demanding her appearance, in fact, a judge of the criminal courts happened to be in the establishment and prevented execution of the warrant.

Asked why Mrs. Hastings was exempt from paying the usual assessment to the police, Schmittberger replied, "Georgianna Hastings is a very peculiar character, and some of the gentlemen who visit her house probably would not like to see their names in print, and I presumed when I went to the precinct there, that that was the reason she was never interfered with; in fact, she keeps a very quiet house, and I was given the tip, so to say, if I didn't want to burn my fingers not to have anything to do with her, and I didn't; I never saw the woman, and I wouldn't know her now if she stood before me."

Schmittberger quickly learned what it meant to burn his fingers on a house protected by the higher-ups. He sent one of his patrolmen to a house operated by Mrs. Sadie West in West Fifty-first Street to warn her that the neighbors were complaining about her, even though Police Commissioner James J. Martin had warned him not to bother Mrs. West under any conditions. Schmittberger testified:

"I sent Casey there to find out what kind of house it was, and he rang the bell, and the woman was very reluctant to give him any information; and she asked him if he knew Commissioner Martin; he said, 'Yes'; this woman said, 'Commissioner Martin is a friend of mine, and don't do anything until you hear from him.' That same evening I received a message . . . to be at Commissioner Martin's office the next day, and he said, 'Did you send an officer around to such and such a house?' giving the number; I said, 'Yes, sir; the officer did it at my direction'; he said, 'Well, you send that man back there and make him apologize, say he made a mistake.' I said, 'Hold on, commissioner, this originates from a complaint of citizens.' 'Well, I don't care; I want you to do what you are told'; so I had to send that officer back and he had to apologize, beg the woman's pardon, that he was sent there to make an investigation. . . ."

Later Schmittberger complained before the committee that the Tenderloin precinct now was good for only $200 a month as a police captain's share of the graft.

"What is the world coming to?" said Counsel Goff in mock consternation. "Only $200 a month in the Tenderloin? The golden days have passed?"

"Yes, sir," was Schmittberger's solemn reply.

Other witnesses, terrified by threats they had received, avoided testimony before the committee by extreme measures, up to and including suicide. There was, for example, Mrs. Evelyn Bell, a rather pallid and genteel figure of a woman who affected flowing lavender gowns, in striking contrast to the blowsy and defiant creatures who dominated her sisterhood. Mrs. Bell had been the proprietor of a bordello in West Thirty-sixth Street, and was one of the few outstanding madams of the Tenderloin who had not joined the exodus to Chicago.

Mrs. Bell testified willingly enough that she had paid $50 a month for police protection. That particular session ended, and she was to return and resume her testimony. She never returned, however, taking flight from the city that night. Where she went or why she had fled in sudden terror, no one ever determined, but few doubted that the men who had been her protectors in business advised her that she was risking a knife across the throat or acid dashed into her face.

The soft-spoken Mrs. Bell returned to New York several months later, shortly before the eleven-month hearings of the Lexow Committee were scheduled to end. A newspaper reporter found her in bed, stupefied with whiskey and morphine.

A Lexow Committee investigator served a subpoena on Mrs. Bell, and she promptly slashed her throat with a razor and took a large quantity of morphine. She was removed to a New Jersey sanatorium, safe at last from the underworld and the committee.

One phase of the investigation which aroused considerable public outrage was the testimony of citizens who had been brutally clubbed by various officers with sadistic instincts. Many of the victims came forward to exhibit broken ribs and battered faces. One man had been so mercilessly belabored over the head with a patrolman's nightstick that his eye was left hanging on his cheek by a thread of flesh. Another victim was a fifteen-year-old girl who had been clubbed while walking down Broadway with her father. Patrolman Thomas Coleman was charged with sixteen unprovoked assaults on various persons, including the girl. His excuse was that, just before attacking the girl with his nightstick, he had taken five quinine pills and a glass of lemonade, which unhinged him.

"And under the influence of these terrible and powerful narcotics and stimulants, you knocked down this little girl on Broadway?" Council Goff acidly inquired.

Patrolman Coleman could make no reply.

"Now," Goff said, "I think we will excuse you that you may pursue your brilliant and meritorious career on the force."

"Much obliged to you," said Coleman, stepping down from the witness stand and strolling out of the courtroom.

The foremost exponent of the nightstick, Clubber Williams, was summoned as the next to the last witness before the committee. Even Goff could not dent his tremendous self-assurance. The inspector steadfastly denied charges that he had accumulated half a million dollars, although he was forced to admit that he owned a seventeen-room mansion at Cos Cob, a large stable, a dock and boathouse, and a fifty-three-foot yacht. He denied ever having received any form of tribute from brothelkeepers in the districts under his command.

"Why did you leave them [the brothels] there?" demanded Goff.

"Because they were kind of fashionable at the time," Inspector Williams replied.

When Goff remarked that he had no intention of becoming involved in a personal altercation with Williams, the brawny inspector growled in reply, "You better not, either." His superior, Police Superintendent Byrnes, fared less fortunately under Goff's questioning, was cornered into admitting he was worth $350,000. His explanation: Jay Gould and other financiers, grateful for the measures he had taken to protect the Wall Street area from criminals, had shown him how to invest his savings. Byrnes admitted that the police department was honeycombed with venality and corruption, but placed the blame on the police commissioners, who controlled the appointments. Byrnes was the last witness before the Lexow Committee.

In November of 1894, before the committee finished its inquiry, Tammany was voted out of power; a reform administration headed by Mayor William L. Strong took over the City Hall, and Theodore Roosevelt became the dominant member of the Board of Police Commissioners, relentlessly pursuing every cop suspected of misconduct until he turned in his badge or mended his ways. Clubber Williams was retired "for the good of the service." Superintendent Byrnes also retired, subsequently prospering as an insurance company executive. Captain Schmittberger, having been a friendly witness before the Lexow Committee, was permitted to remain on the force and ended his career as a chief inspector. Goff was elected recorder (a judicial post subsequently eliminated) and later served on the State Supreme Court, not unexpectedly gaining renown as a "hanging judge."

The Tenderloin settled down patiently to wait out the electorate's flirtation with reform, watched with amusement as Mayor Strong took after the street cleaning department and made the workers wear white suits so everybody could see when one of them loafed against his broom or slipped into a saloon for a fast one. Perhaps they were less amused at the Strong administration's program of building new schools, parks and playgrounds, which was popular with the voters. But they could afford to be patient. "These reform movements are like queen hornets," an East Side politician philosophized. "They sting you once, and then they die." Sydney Brooks, an Englishman who studied American municipal politics, observed that New Yorkers were hedonists who preferred "a free and easy life in a free and easy town."

"The reformers," Brooks said, "were unable to conquer that social distrust of 'gentlemen' which one encounters so often and so unexpectedly in Americans, and especially in city politics."

Then, too, there was much resentment against the Strong administration's strict enforcement of the liquor and gambling laws. The poorest citizen liked to feel free to wager a few cents daily in the policy games, and the workingman wanted to be able to buy a drink on Sunday, his only day off. The Sunday closing of saloons was especially resented, and thus the Raines Law came into effect. It provided that any hotel could sell liquor on Sunday. As a result, hundreds of saloons leased the floors above them, proclaimed themselves hotels and threw open their doors on Sunday. The Raines Law hotel, quickly converted into a house of assignation, soon became a tawdry monument to the moralists.

By the time the next election for mayor came around, in 1897, the citizenry was restive, Tammany quietly exultant, and the Tenderloin ready to spring back to its pre-Parkhurst liveliness. After all, as Dr. Parkhurst said in his famous sermon, "sin never gets tired, never is low-spirited." Dick Croker announced he was giving up his estate in England to lead Tammany to victory again; "The Return from Elba" was how newspaper cartoonists styled this proclamation.

All was forgiven. Tammany's candidate for mayor, Robert Van

Wyck, was elected mayor on November 2, 1897, and crowds danced in the streets of the Tenderloin singing:

> "Well, well, well
> Reform has gone to Hell."

Dr. Parkhurst concluded that "you cannot legislate the human race into heaven," and went on to live an extraordinarily long and useful life, which was terminated in 1933, at the age of ninety-one, when he fell off his porch roof at his summer home while walking in his sleep. He never led another crusade. Tammany, of course, returned to its old way of doing business. The New York *Times* reported to its unshocked readership on March 9, 1900, that a Tammany "commission," consisting of one city official, two state senators and the dictator of the city's poolroom syndicate, was collecting $3,095,000 monthly in graft from gambling sources alone.

New York once again was a "free and easy town," and the Tenderloin, a little tamer than before 1892, was doing business at the same old stand.

8

Crime of Passion, All-German Cast

ALTHOUGH they were separated only by the width of Eighth Avenue, Hell's Kitchen and the Tenderloin were different worlds. Crime and violence in the Tenderloin were simply commercial transactions; in Hell's Kitchen, however, the laws were broken for different reasons, revenge, hatred, passion, racial or national pride, desperate poverty. The Tenderloin, to most of the people of Hell's Kitchen, was a contemptible place, and there was nothing lower than a pimp, procurer, madam or anyone else who lived on the proceeds of prostitution.

Of all the races mingling in Hell's Kitchen before the turn of the century, the Teutonic was regarded as the most orderly, least inclined to express itself with fist, club, knife or revolver. The Germans devoted themselves to work and the consumption of vast amounts of wurst and lager.

The crime of passion, which delighted the then-burgeoning and wildly imaginative Sunday supplements, seemed least likely of all to overtake a German. He appeared to his neighbors to be

135

too stolid, too unemotional for illicit passion. Whatever frivolity
existed in the dim recesses of the Teutonic soul was satisfied by
listening to the blare and thump of the Bavarian bands in the
beer gardens of Yorkville. Yet it was an all-German triangle that
provided New York with one of its most sensational murder cases
in the 'nineties.

It was a kind of Mauve Decade version of the Snyder-Gray case
of thirty years later, it has been suggested, and like the crime of
Ruth Snyder and Judd Gray was concocted to eliminate the third
party to a triangle. In many ways, though, Hell's Kitchen's murder, to the connoisseur of such matters, was a much lustier and
bloodier affair. It was executed with a certain excess of violence,
a Teutonic flair for thoroughness, that made the later sashweight
murder comparatively pallid.

The three persons directly involved in the affair were Mrs.
Augusta Nack, a sort of Mademoiselle Bovary of Ninth Avenue;
Willie Guldensuppe, a muscle-bulging masseur at the Murray Hill
Baths, and Martin Thorn, a dapper and dashing Ninth Avenue
barber. The legal consort of Mrs. Nack was a negligible quan-
tity, a drab fellow unsuited for any heroic rôle in the proceedings.

Yet it was Mr. Nack's ineffectuality, in a sense, that set the
drama in motion. Herman Nack lived with his wife for several
years at 439 Ninth Avenue (near Thirty-fourth Street). Augusta
was a midwife. Herman operated a sausage store on Tenth Avenue and, bored with bologna, developed a "Tenth Avenue
thirst." Herman soon drank himself out of business—a process
given impetus by Augusta's outspoken contempt for his performance in the marital bed. A few days after he lost his sausage
business, and his sole usefulness in Augusta's eyes, his wife booted
him out of the house. She had decided to take in boarders who
could take over certain husbandly functions in addition to providing income.

The first boarder to make his appearance was Guldensuppe,
who was thirty-five years old and had plenty of energy left over
from rubbing down drunks and potbellies in the Turkish baths on
Forty-second Street. In addition to a Lionel Strongfort build,

Willie flaunted a mass of wavy blond hair and a gaudy mural tattooed on his chest. Much admired at first, that tattoo was to vex Mrs. Nack in the climax of their association.

For two years Willie Guldensuppe reigned supreme in Augusta's somewhat changeable affections. Then came a second boarder, Martin Thorn, who was Willie's opposite in physique and temperament. Martin had dark curly hair and mercurial black eyes. Willie was muscular, Martin poetic; Willie smelled of sweat, Martin of eau de cologne; Willie beat hell out of Augusta when irritated, Martin was gentle and gallant. Under the circumstances Willie really didn't have a chance against the newcomer. No longer bedazzled by his muscles, Augusta saw clearly now that Willie was simply a brawny lout.

Martin Thorn made it plain almost immediately that he would like to step into Willie's shoes, not to mention the departed Mr. Nack's.

Augusta was agreeable, but Willie entered boorish objections to being displaced. The atmosphere around Mrs. Nack's ménage was growing unbearable.

As for the mistress of this establishment, her neighbors were quite unable to understand how she was able to attract two such prepossessing men. The newspapers later described her as a handsome blonde with the contours of a Wagnerian soprano, a fitting vessel for volcanic passions. A study of police photographs is disillusioning in this respect. Her figure was constructed along Percheron lines, and there was a rather baleful look in her eyes (possibly the photographer reminded her of Herman Nack). One newspaper writer provided a fairly accurate description of her: "Her skin is smooth and clear, her features forceful, the nose straight and prominent, the eyes shrewd, burning, deep set and very close together. It is a face full of determination. . . ."

In February of 1897, Mrs. Nack and Martin Thorn decided to eliminate Guldensuppe. One night when Willie came home from the Murray Hill Baths, Thorn confronted him with a revolver, but before Thorn could pull the trigger the masseur pounced on him and disarmed him. Guldensuppe then proceeded to whale the stuffing out of Mrs. Nack and her new favorite. On a number of subsequent occasions Willie, with a cold ferocity, beat up the pair. It didn't occur to Willie to remove his unwanted self from the scene. Nor did it occur to Thorn and Mrs. Nack to move elsewhere. The discordant trio seemed to be bound to 439 Ninth Avenue by a stubborn pride—or perhaps it was only a fateful lethargy. Willie was certain that sheer muscularity would prevail over such an epicene rival as the soft-handed Thorn.

By the middle of June, Thorn and Mrs. Nack convinced themselves that only murder, more carefully planned this time, would permit them to enjoy each other in peace. First Mrs. Nack found an untenanted and fairly isolated cottage in the Woodside section of Queens, which could serve as their private abattoir. Then they stocked the place with an array of weapons that would have delighted any homicidal doge of Venice.

Item: one dagger with a poisoned tip.

Item: one revolver.

Item: one bottle of carbolic acid.

Item: one carving knife for post-morten surgery.

Item: one hammer for the *coup de grâce*.

Item: one rope for hanging, just in case Willie died as hard as he lived.

Mrs. Nack also purchased a large square of oilcloth in a store in Astoria and a quantity of plaster of Paris in a drugstore. Thorn arranged for rental of a surrey from a Tenth Avenue undertaker. All was in readiness.

On June 24, Mrs. Nack telephoned Guldensuppe at the Murray Hill Baths and asked him to meet her the next day at the cottage in Woodside. From the honeyed tone of her conversation, Willie gathered that she had wearied of his rival and was eager for a tryst. He agreed to the meeting.

On June 25, Thorn waited in a second-floor bedroom while Augusta Nack prepared to receive Willie in the parlor downstairs. A moment after the gullible masseur strutted into the Woodside cottage, Thorn dashed downstairs with revolver, dagger and knife. It was all over in a few seconds. Thorn shot Guldensuppe three times, then planted the poisoned dagger in his heart. Before he had stopped thrashing around, Thorn decapitated him with the carving knife. Then Augusta went to work with a brisk efficiency. She carved up Guldensuppe's headless corpse, then left the torso and limbs to drain in the bathtub. The head was encased in plaster of Paris. It was their belief that if the torso and legs were recovered but the head never found, a *corpus delicti* could not be established and no one could be tried for murder—a fairly common misconception of laymen. Nevertheless, Thorn and Mrs. Nack did not want to take a chance on the torso's being identified, since they would be immediately suspected in any presumed foul play involving Willie Guldensuppe. As a finishing touch they peeled the tattoo off Willie's chest.

Thorn brought the surrey over from Tenth Avenue and that night they dumped Willie's head, which sank to the bottom and was never recovered, and the other parts of him, neatly packaged in oilcloth, in the East River. Then they decided to separate until it was determined whether Willie's murder would out.

If they hoped that the inevitable discovery of Willie's torso in the East River would be a mild sensation for a day or two, and then written off as just another unsolved murder, they were terribly mistaken. What they may have failed to take into consideration was the all-out circulation war among the New York newspapers. William Randolph Hearst's *Journal* was shouldering its way through the competition and challenging Joseph Pulitzer's *World*—a contest which would reach its climax next year in the coverage of the Spanish-American War.

Guldensuppe's torso was found in the East River at the foot of East Eleventh Street the day after the murder, a Saturday, just in time to create a sensation for the Sunday papers.

"It is a murder," Coroner O'Hanlon announced with the air of having presided over a masterpiece of deduction, "most foul, deliberate, mysterious and terrible."

The police proceeded with their investigation in their customary plodding and methodical manner, but the *Journal's* editors had decided to convert the murder into a Hearstian triumph and turned the whole staff loose on the story.

The *Journal* engaged tugboats and dragged the East and Harlem rivers for the rest of the headless and legless corpse. It offered a $1,000 reward for information leading to the solution of the "Unique Murder Mystery of the East River." Two famous palmists were hired to make a study of the victim's hands. An expert in tattooing was called in to examine the mutilated chest, someone having guessed that a tattoo had been removed. Julian Hawthorne, billed as a "noted writer of detective stories," delivered himself of the somewhat erroneous opinion, "The victim is a peddler—two men took him unawares and stabbed him to death." The *Journal* also announced that it had summoned into consultation on the case a psychometrist, explaining that psychometry was the "art of determining the relations of mental phenomena."

All these trained seals performed dutifully, but it was the *Journal*'s crack reportorial staff which outdistanced the police and ran circles around the *World*'s legmen.

In the days immediately following discovery of the torso, the *Journal* and the police managed to identify the corpse as Willie Guldensuppe. A *Journal* reporter was lucky enough to drop into the Third Avenue saloon kept by Martin Cowan, not far from the Murray Hill Baths, and while refreshing himself heard Cowan mention that one of his customers seemed to have disappeared. The customer was a rubber at the baths. The reporter then learned from fellow employes at the baths that Guldensuppe had been missing since the day before the murder. Also that Guldensuppe had a tattoo corresponding to the place on the corpse's chest where the skin had been stripped. And another masseur told the reporter of overhearing Guldensuppe's telephone conversation with Mrs. Nack the day before the murder.

A squad of girl reporters was dispatched from the *Journal* to interview Mrs. Nack, who denied knowing anything about Guldensuppe's disappearance, and kept her under a constant twittering surveillance, which must have been almost as nerve-racking as the knowledge of her guilt.

The police, meanwhile, located an Astoria storekeeper who remembered selling oilcloth to a "stout German woman."

Now the *Journal* was hot on the scent and marveling in front-page editorials at "how vast was its service to Justice." Its reporters hired bloodhounds to search Ogden Woods not far from the murder cottage. They located residents of Woodside who told of a couple identifying themselves as "Mr. and Mrs. Braun" and claiming that they had been engaged to clean the unoccupied cottage. The neighbors' suspicions were aroused, they said, because "Mrs. Braun" neglected to open the doors and windows while cleaning. Bursting into the cottage itself, the *Journal* reporters could find no signs that a murder had been committed there. But the village lamplighter told of having seen blood in a pool near the house and a duckling waddling out of it with his feathers crimsoned. It developed that in draining the blood from Willie's corpse the long-unused pipes from the bathtub had burst between the house and the connection with the sewer. In all their thoroughness, Mr. Thorn and Mrs. Nack had made the fatal error of failing to check the plumbing.

Mrs. Nack was arrested immediately, Thorn several days later when a fellow barber betrayed him.

The murder story in the next few days shoved a far more important matter—the discovery of vast gold deposits in the Klondike—off the front pages of the New York papers. The *Journal* crowed lustily over its devotion to justice. The other papers were inclined to deprecate the Hearst organ's work on the case. The *World* insinuated the Hearst people were persecuting an innocent woman and engaged an attorney for Mrs. Nack. The *Herald* snidely gave all the credit to the police, whose efficiency indeed had increased since the Lexow investigation, the iron-broom tactics of Police Commissioner Theodore Roosevelt and the appointment of the capable Captain Stephen O'Brien to head the detective bureau.

Both Mrs. Nack and Thorn insisted on their innocence under

constant questioning. The evidence against them, they realized, was all circumstantial. The state's case was by no means watertight, should the accused pair stand firm in their denials of guilt.

Thorn, furthermore, had engaged the law firm of Howe and Hummel, which had appeared with amazing success on behalf of more than six hundred persons charged with murder or manslaughter. Howe was not only the leading forensic actor of the New York Bar—he often delivered hours-long summations before the jury on bended knee—but one of the city's gaudiest dressers. His suits, according to his biographer Richard Rovere (*Howe and Hummel: Their True and Scandalous History*) were "something from the dreams of an English bookie; and his oratory, as purple as anything from his wardrobe . . . was so overpowering that it brought tears not only to the eyes of the jurors but to his own as well. Howe's defenses were such good theater that very often in the 'nineties the old Bowery Playhouse would contrive an evening's entertainment by acting them out straight from the court records." David Graham Phillips, the novelist who once covered Hell's Kitchen precincts as a police reporter, described Howe as a "gaily bedecked elephant careening across the sky." He was now sixty-nine years old and ailing, and his last famous case was to be the defense of Martin Thorn.

During the trial, the defendants continued to protest their innocence and even denied knowing each other very well. To the consternation of the Hearst editors, and moralists everywhere, it appeared that Thorn and his paramour might escape punishment. The *Journal* and the *World* devoted several full pages every day to the trial, describing every blink of Mrs. Nack's baleful eyes and every organ tone of Counselor Howe's mellifluous voice. Pitched battles were fought between *Journal* and *World* reporters for the few available telephone lines into New York from the Long Island City courthouse. There were rumors along Park Row that heads would roll if the Hearst forces did not secure a conviction and cap their triumph in tracking down the accused pair.

Howe was performing splendidly as Thorn's advocate. He hammered at the *corpus delicti* theme for all it was worth, poured scorn on the state's contention that it was, indeed, the remains of Willie Guldensuppe. With Willie's head safely at the bottom of the East River, he was able to pursue this argument with confidence.

Mockingly, to the jury, Howe pretended that Willie Guldensuppe was a fictitious character who had existed only in the malicious minds of Mrs. Nack's neighbors and her official prosecutors.

Eyes rolling, Howe mocked the whole idea that such a preposterous creature could ever have drawn breath.

"This asserted victim Goldensoup . . ." he would say, turning confidentially to the jury as though he and they understood the chicanery behind the state's plot to pin the murder of a mythical victim on the defendants.

"This man they call Goldylocks, or Silverslippers, or whatever . . ."

"The alleged victim Gildersleeve . . ."

"This creature of fantasy known to the gentlemen of the prosecution as Gludensop, or is it Gildenglub . . ."

Willie Guldensuppe, he roared across the courtroom, was "a creature as imaginary [sic] as Rosencrantz's friend Guildenstern."

Unknown to Howe, who was justifiably confident that he was going to win an acquittal for both defendants, Mrs. Nack had been in consultation with a Reverend Miles. The Reverend Miles was not the prison chaplain, merely an evangelist, scenting publicity, who came to visit the accused woman in her cell. Occasionally the reverend gentleman brought along his winsome young son on the visits.

One day, according to the *Journal's* recreation of the event, the boy climbed into Mrs. Nack's lap and lispingly beseeched her to confess the murder in the name of God and the Reverend Miles. The *Journal* later quoted her as saying:

"When that adorable child pleaded with me for the truth, I could do no other than tell it to him."

Howe's carefully fabricated defense went down the drain.

Mrs. Nack turned state's evidence and got off with nine years in prison. Thorn went up for life. The *Journal* published the news of the confession a good twelve hours ahead of its rivals, upon which the *World* and the *Herald* insinuated it was all a plot between the *Journal*, the Reverend Miles and the prosecution to get Augusta off the hook at Thorn's expense. To most unbiased parties connected with the case, including many of the detectives who worked on it, the murder may have been executed by Thorn but it was undoubtedly proposed, planned and pushed through by the strong-minded Augusta.

"I had the prettiest case," Howe wrote his partner, "and here is all my work shattered. I can still prove that they couldn't identify Willie's body and that it wasn't cut up in the Woodside cottage. Now all my roses are frosted in a night and my grapes withered on the vine. . . ."

Some years later the newspapers reported Mrs. Nack's release from prison, "chastened and repentant," and her return to obscurity in Hell's Kitchen.

9

Slaughter on Tenth Avenue

AROUND the turn of the century, with reform discredited and the police again directed by the favorite sons of Tammany, the streets of Hell's Kitchen were once more ruled by gangs. Sometimes it was the Gophers, five hundred strong and perhaps the toughest if not the largest street gang in New York; sometimes it was a gang of policemen, clubbing their way through the streets on an extra-legal mission of revenge; sometimes it was a lynch-minded mob full of fury at men of another race, and sometimes it was a corps of mercenaries hired by a private corporation to conduct mass reprisals against the gangs preying on its property. Nightsticks and paving stones, chimney pots and blackjacks were always bouncing off someone's skull. Larry Hart's later musical salute to mayhem, *Slaughter on Tenth Avenue*, had a solid foundation in fact in those days. Mob action and street fighting made New York's thoroughfares unsafe, on the East Side as well as the West, just at the time the nation was proclaiming its determination to bring law and order to Cuba, Puerto Rico and the Philippines.

The most serious disturbances were those directed—on at least one occasion by high police officials—against the Negroes, who subsequently moved in great numbers into the formerly sedate and exclusive residential sections of Harlem. The Negroes had started colonizing in the area at the northern end of Hell's Kitchen, west of Columbus Circle, that became known as San Juan Hill to the great resentment of many whites. San Juan Hill was so named in honor of the 10th (Negro) Cavalry which stormed up the Spanish-held heights in Cuba and, despite the highly publicized claims of ex-Police Commissioner Theodore Roosevelt and his Rough Riders, seemed to have broken the enemy position first. The heroic action of the 10th Cavalry gave the Negroes of New York a great deal of self-confidence—too much for their white neighbors, who preferred to think of them as servile, bobbing and bowing darkies.

The inter-racial tensions reached a climax one summer's night in 1900, but before that there had been several serious incidents involving white and Negro mobs.

Tenth Avenue was riotous the night of July 20, 1899, after two white men fought with a Negro woman, for some undisclosed reason, in West Thirty-ninth Street near Tenth. Several Negroes came to the woman's assistance. Soon whites and Negroes were both being reinforced from all directions. A Negro on a bicycle led his cohorts in driving the whites up Tenth Avenue to West Fortieth Street, where the retreat was quickly halted, a white mob having gathered there. The Negroes were chased up the side streets, and the cyclist found himself surrounded by whites brandishing clubs and paving stones and yelling, "Lynch him, kill the nigger."

The Negro, James Harris, drew a revolver, fired twice into the crowd, and wounded two white men.

A precinct detective named Pitts, according to a newspaper account (New York *Herald*, July 21, 1899), saw the mass of howling men about to overwhelm the Negro, and jumped off the Belt Line streetcar he had been riding. He fought his way to the Negro's side and placed him under arrest. All the way to the West Thirty-seventh Street station the crowd kept trying to snatch the prisoner away from Pitts, but several blocks from the station house he was joined by two patrolmen whose nightsticks helped fend off the enraged whites. Police reinforcements were summoned to guard Harris in the station house and keep order in the streets outside, throngs of whites and Negroes having gathered to mill around outside and threaten a major race riot. A dozen billy-swinging cops finally charged shoulder-to-shoulder and dispersed them before any serious casualties could occur.

The most serious outbreak came a year later. On August 15 and 16, 1900, police-aided and police-directed mobs ruled the West Side streets and brought back vivid memories to the older residents of 1863 and 1871. A cop-killing incident touched off the rioting and was responsible for the police participation.

The evening of August 12, at Forty-first Street and Eighth Avenue, a Negro named Arthur Harris, whom police later identified as a Tenderloin pimp, stepped into a cigar store at the intersection. He left on the sidewalk a woman the newspapers said was his "paramour." When Harris left the store, he found his woman struggling with a man in civilian clothes. Harris tried to free her, and the white man struck him over the head with a club. Harris' opponent was Robert J. Thorpe, a Twentieth Precinct officer on vice-squad patrol. The woman, he said in a deathbed statement, was "soliciting." Whether Thorpe managed to announce himself as a police officer to Harris was never learned. Harris, at any rate, plunged a knife into Thorpe's heart and fled. Thorpe died a few hours later.

The whole West Side, especially the Tenderloin and Hell's Kitchen districts, and most especially the police, were enraged over the killing. Had Harris surrendered or been captured immediately, no further trouble might have ensued, for their fury would have been directed at the cop-killer himself. But as any young police reporter knows, a great shock wave goes through a police department when any officer is killed; such a killing must be avenged immediately, and an unremitting tension exists until the killer is taken into custody.

The police, too, had been annoyed with the raffish type of Negro who had migrated from the South and settled in the Tenderloin. One reason may well have been that the newcomers evaded payment of protection money, but even the New York *Herald*, which was liberal in its attitude toward the Negroes and harsh toward high-ranking police officials, agreed that the police had a point in claiming that New York "has become a Mecca for dissolute and worthless Negroes from the Southern cities." A *Herald* editorial (August 17, 1900) further stated: "That the Tenderloin is infested with depraved and vicious Negroes is obvious to pedestrians who by day note the groups of flashily dressed colored men who swagger idly about the street corners, or who by night are accosted or even held up by the female associates of these loathsome wretches. . . . But the whites are equally degraded and even more numerous. Why does Chief Devery permit this? Why are the dives allowed to exist that are the rendezvous of these creatures and the nursery of infamy?"

For several days the West Side seethed with unrest, fight talk in the saloons, threats of violence, discussions of how to "clean the niggers out." The trouble finally broke out the evening of August 15, the night before Officer Thorpe's funeral, for which the police had laid elaborate plans. A wake was being held in the home of Thorpe's sister at 481 Ninth Avenue, where the body reposed. According to the police account—there was no other testimony on this point—the disorders started outside the Thorpe home. Two elderly white women were assaulted by a Negro who overheard their remarks as they left the wake; a group of whites quickly collected and surrounded the Negro; and the Negro drew a revolver and fired wildly into the crowd. No one was wounded, and the Negro was taken into custody. That was shortly before 10 P.M. In less than half an hour the whole West Side erupted.

Charges were later made, and circumstantial evidence certainly supports them, that the police fomented the outbreak. The people of Hell's Kitchen were not so fond of the police that a cop-killing would drive them to excesses of grief and rage. But, it was charged, many gangs in the district were "hostile to the Negroes and friendly with the unofficial powers that are now potent in police affairs."

Much of the evidence against the police was gathered by Frank Moss, the attorney who had been a member of Parkhurst's crusading forces. His charges were contained in a pamphlet titled "The Story of the Riot," published several months later by the Citizens' Protective League, numbering five thousand persons and organized at St. Mark's Church, West Fifty-third Street and Eighth Avenue, to protect the rights of Negroes in New York. Prefacing the mass of affidavits he had collected from riot victims, Moss charged that "many policemen were seized with a desire of vengeance on Negroes generally. During the day before the funeral there were rumors of coming trouble, and those colored people who have illicit dealings with the police—keepers of gambling, disorderly and badger houses—seeing signs of coming trouble, closed their places and kept off the streets. Several officers told informants of mine that they were going to punish the Negroes that night."

Certainly the rioting broke out with a speed and violence that indicated skillful organization behind the scenes.

From Broadway west to Ninth Avenue, and in all the side streets between Thirty-fourth and Forty-second, mobs of whites assaulted with fist, club and boot every Negro they could catch—women as well as men, and even a few children. Obviously respectable Negroes on their way home from long hours of work outside of Manhattan were dragged off streetcars and beaten within an inch of their lives. The police, regulars and reserves, were everywhere and encouraged the rioters by example. The police, Moss charged, "ran with the crowds in pursuit of their prey; they took defenseless men who ran to them for protection and threw them to the rioters, and in many cases they beat and clubbed men and women more brutally than the mob did. They were absolutely unrestrained by their superior officers." The West Thirty-seventh Street station, where most of the victims were taken for further beatings and booked on trumped-up charges, looked like a "field hospital in the midst of battle." The only instances in which the rioting mobs were restrained, Moss said, were when they invaded the Broadway hotels in pursuit of

Negroes and might have inflicted property damage. The police were determined to confine the rioting west of Broadway, out of sight of respectable and easily shocked citizens.

It soon became apparent that the rioting was getting out of hand. The police wanted to avenge Thorpe's murder, on the innocent and defenseless, but they couldn't afford to let the mobs get out of hand. The riots of '63 and '71 were a constant reminder of the uncontrollable rages that seethed below the surface of the metropolitan slums. Police reserves were summoned from every station between Charles Street and 125th Street, and finally from four East Side precincts. At 11 P.M. police officials ordered all saloons west of Broadway closed, but a *Herald* reporter observed that this only "threw hundreds of half-intoxicated men into the streets who hastened to swell the ranks of the rioters. . . . In the heart of New York a race war was on between whites and blacks —as fierce if not as fatal as those that have taken place in the South."

"Negroes had been baited wherever found," another reporter observed. "They were pursued, beaten and kicked by young men, and the usual attitude of the police was to push their way through to the victims, use their clubs on them and then carry them to the police station, where the brutality was continued."

North of Forty-second Street—outside the precinct where Thorpe's brother officers were taking their misdirected revenge— the situation was quite different. Captain Brennan of the West Forty-seventh Street station "cleared his streets of white and black turbulents impartially, and trouble was averted."

The affidavits gathered by Frank Moss showed conclusively that the police encouraged and supported the mobs—until, that is, the mobs got out of hand and police officials ordered that both races be clubbed impartially to halt the rioting. A Dr. P. A. Johnson told of seeing a Negro cornered in a saloon on Seventh Avenue near Thirty-third Street. Three cops drove him out of the saloon with their nightsticks while the crowd yelled, "Bring him out, we'll lynch him." The physician said the crowd paid no attention to his appeal, "For God's sake, don't kill me, I have a wife and children," and swarmed around him with "murderous cries." Somehow the Negro fought his way clear of the crowd and was about to make his escape when two policemen chased him down the street and clubbed him senseless.

Police stopped all the streetcars running on Eighth Avenue and threw all Negroes to the crowds, most of them younger men, while people, watching from the windows overlooking the violent scene, "yelled 'shame' at the mobs," wept, and pleaded with police to stop the mayhem. Oscar Slaughter, a Negro who swore out an affidavit for Moss, told how several policemen dragged him off a streetcar at Thirty-sixth Street and Eighth Avenue and knocked him senseless with their nightsticks. Slaughter hid in a hallway in Thirty-second Street all the rest of the night with a number of other terrified Negroes.

Adolphus Cooks, a longshoreman employed by the Anchor Steamship Company at their pier at the foot of West Twenty-fourth Street, was walking home after having worked for thirty-nine and a half consecutive hours unloading a ship. A cop ran up to him in Twenty-eighth Street and began raining blows on his head and body. Cooks somehow escaped, hid in a cellar all night and reported for work at the usual time the next morning.

Other Negroes told of being forced to run a gauntlet of nightsticks wielded by "six or eight" officers in Eighth Avenue. A Negro servant employed by Major General O. O. Howard, "the Christian general" of Civil War fame, was beaten senseless and badly injured, an incident that enraged the general more than the whole high command of the Confederacy. A Negro woman told how her brother became delirious after being beaten by the police and was sent to the "insane pavilion" at Bellevue Hospital shouting, "Devery did it! Devery did it! Here they come." Charles Bennett, a waiter in a Coney Island saloon, affirmed that he was clubbed off an Eighth Avenue streetcar, taken in a patrol wagon and "beaten all the way to the 20th Precinct station house." Inside the station Bennett heard Police Inspector Thompson shouting at the other officers, "Club every damned nigger you see—kill them—shoot them—be brave, same as I was."

It was shortly before midnight when the police decided to halt the rioting. Eighth Avenue from Thirty-fourth Street down to Twenty-eighth Street was a mass of rioters, black and white, and the Negroes were beginning to band together to defend themselves. Several cops were slashed with razors and nicked with knives. The whites, too, were getting out of hand and smashing shop windows. Big Bill Devery, political-minded and shrewd enough to realize that property damage would arouse the citizenry if nothing else would, conferred with Inspector Thompson and Captain Cooney, the commander of the Twentieth Precinct, on the scene at Eighth Avenue. The rioting had to be stopped, Chief Devery ordained, although until now he had watched with a benign and proprietary eye. All available police were to form up behind Captain Cooney and charge straight down Eighth Avenue. The avenue by now was thronged with curiosity-seekers from all over the city, but they'd have to take their chances.

Captain Cooney led the "magnificent charge," a *Herald* reporter observed, "thwacking heads in the finished style of an ordinary policeman." The police "clubbed everyone in sight who refused or delayed in getting off the avenue." Women and children fell under police nightsticks and brogans as the cops went flailing down the avenue. No one was given a chance to explain himself. A policeman in civilian clothing who had just arrived on the scene in answer to the general riot call got a taste of the nightstick himself. He started to protest, to reach for his shield and identify himself. This was only interpreted as an attempt to draw a concealed weapon and several of the unfortunate's brother officers ganged up on him, and almost knocked him senseless. When the victim pulled himself together and staggered into the West Thirty-seventh Street station to complain of the inhospitality of this precinct, he found Big Bill Devery, Inspector Thompson and Captain Cooney still in an excited condition, the heat of battle still upon them. The officer tried to explain himself, but Chief Devery snatched away his shield and ordered that he be held on a charge of carrying a concealed weapon. It took a day or two for the officer to clear himself and recover his shield, but it is doubtful whether he ever again looked on his duties—or his superiors—with the same devotion.

By midnight, a reporter for the *Herald* noted, "the cry was no longer 'Down with the Negroes!' It was changed to 'Damn the police!'" Many a young tough had cheerfully joined the cops in waging war on the Negroes. A temporary alliance, to be sure, but who would have thought that the cops would turn on them so quickly? The Negroes, too, quickly realized that the police were their principal enemies. "All the colored persons with whom I talked last night said that they were in no fear of the citizens, but that they were in constant terror of the police, who were merciless in their treatment of all men and women with dark skins."

One of the most damning affidavits concerning police brutality, published by Frank Moss in his pamphlet, was that of a Negro named Elliott. He was injured in the rioting on Eighth Avenue and taken to the West Thirty-seventh Street station house. After being booked, Elliott was shoved into the back room and clubbed some more by various policemen apparently stationed there for the purpose. His screams eventually brought Captain Cooney into the room. "Don't kill that man in here," Elliott quoted Captain Cooney as telling his men. "The reporters are out there." Elliott was then kicked out of the muster room and into a cell. His cries, however, had been overheard by a *Herald* reporter, whose account the next morning supported Elliott's subsequent affidavit: "From my position outside the door I heard the prisoner screaming at the top of his voice and begging for mercy."

Next day the Twentieth Precinct was swarming with reporters from all the newspapers, and police officials knew that their excesses of the day before must not be repeated. That day, too, Thorpe's slayer was captured in Washington, D. C.—just about the time Thorpe's funeral was being held. Ninth Avenue was blocked off and ten thousand police attended the services and marched behind his body. The emotionalism which touched off the rioting was drained away.

Yet, as with all excesses, there was a hangover. The Grand Jury refused to indict anyone in connection with the riot, and

Mayor Van Wyck tried to pretend it never happened. As for the Board of Police Commissioners, now relieved of the abrasive presence of Theodore Roosevelt, the *Herald* said it "has not hesitated to write another page of its damning history." Neither the police commissioners nor anyone else in the city administration could answer Frank Moss' charge: "Humble citizens of all races today are in more danger from policemen's clubs than they are from the assaults of criminals."

The Negroes moved uptown to populate Harlem, but Hell's Kitchen's attitude toward any Johnny-come-lately was still hostile. In subsequent years the Greeks, moving into the neighborhood around Forty-second Street and Eighth Avenue, were rather roughly handled until a display of the *evzone* spirit established their right to settle down in their coffeehouses and second-floor anisette parlors.

The prejudice against a commingling of the races was confirmed in many minds by the murder committed above what was then called a "chop suey parlor" in Eighth Avenue. An entry on the blotter of the West Forty-seventh Street station, on June 18, 1909, told the story in its barest essentials: "At 4:45 P.M. an unknown woman, white, about 33 years, five feet, 130 pounds, dark complexion and hair, partly dressed with white cotton underwear, was found dead in the room occupied by Leon Ling, in a trunk on the fourth floor, rear hall room at 728 Eighth Ave., with a sash cord tied about the neck. Body in badly decomposed condition."

It was quickly established—to the satisfaction of the authorities, at least—that the body was that of Miss Elsie Sigel, the granddaughter of a Civil War general. Her grandfather was Major General Franz Sigel, a gentleman more renowned, as were so many of his colleagues, for dash and courage than for talent and ability. Next to Carl Schurz, however, he was the ranking German-American hero of the Civil War. As a firebrand of twenty-four, he led four thousand other revolutionists in the unsuccessful anti-Prussian uprisings of 1848, and was forced to flee to Switzerland and then to the United States. He became a teacher in St.

Louis, organized the 3rd Missouri Infantry at the outbreak of the Civil War and helped save the city and its arsenal for the Union. By the time of the battle of Pea Ridge, down in Arkansas, he was a major general commanding two divisions at that Union victory. Transferred to northern Virginia, he commanded I Corps during the Second Bull Run campaign. Later, given an independent command in the Valley of the Shenandoah, he was defeated at the battle of New Market and relieved. His last chance at glory came when Jubal Early threatened Washington in 1864; Sigel occupied Maryland Heights with a hastily collected force and fought a creditable delaying action. It was not a brilliant career but he was credited with being "a great factor uniting the German population of the North behind the Union." After the war General Sigel was active in New York politics, became Collector of Internal Revenue and edited a German-language newspaper until his death in 1902, seven years before his granddaughter's body was found in a Chinese waiter's room in Hell's Kitchen.

Elsie Sigel's family was inclined, at first, to disown her in death. Her father, Paul Sigel, when called to identify the body at the morgue, told reporters, "I do not know her." Her strong-minded aunt, Mrs. Franz Sigel, said, "My niece was a faithful member of the Audubon Society and would not wear a bird on her hat as this poor creature did. . . . We do not recognize the body in the morgue as Elsie Sigel, and will not bury it. We are convinced she has wandered away in a temporary fit of mental aberration."

The young woman's mother, however, was much less concerned with family pride and the fact that her late father-in-law was eminent enough to have a statue erected at Riverside Drive and 106th Street. She promptly identified the jewelry found on the victim when police brought it to her, and Mrs. Franz Sigel immediately announced that she had been removed to a Connecticut sanatorium. "Mrs. Sigel is a raving lunatic," her sister-in-law told the press, "and we doubt that she will ever recover."

Elsie's father, however, broke down three days after the body was found and admitted the victim was his daughter.

Scores of detectives were turned loose on the case because of the prominence of the victim's family and the extraordinary interest shown in the case by the newspapers, an interest which grew with every revelation of the victim's fascination with Oriental men. Elsie Sigel, a Salvation Nell type to begin with, had gone down into Chinatown as a missionary to distribute Bibles, religious tracts and girlish appeals to foreswear heathen gods.

It was immediately apparent to the police that Ling, the waiter in whose room her body was found, had strangled her in a jealous rage. Both he and the man occupying an adjoining room over Sun Leung's chop suey restaurant, another waiter named Chon Sing, had disappeared. Thirty-five of Elsie's love letters to Ling were also found in his room. The New York *World* disclosed that it had uncovered the fact that Ling had met Elsie at a Chinatown mission two years before and "made no secret among his companions of his infatuation for her."

New York was shocked at the thought of a liaison between a well-bred Caucasian girl and a Chinese waiter. A co-worker of Elsie's was quoted as warning against the "strong fascination of the Oriental character for young American girls." The *World* published a front-page cartoon titled "The Real Yellow Peril," showing young white women staring into a Chinatown mission and about to enter. A preacher was quoted in the newspapers as warning, "The number of mission workers ruined by their pupils would shock the country."

The police investigators learned that the week before her body was found in the waiter's room Elsie had sent a telegram from Washington saying she would be home in a few days. When she did not appear, her father asked police to put her name on the "confidential list" and make discreet inquiries as to her whereabouts. The investigators also turned up a letter in broken English from the missing Ling to the murdered girl, which read in part, "I hope you do not get mad with me, because all the trouble comes from me. Hope some day the happiness come to us both."

Several days after the body was found, Chon Sing, the other waiter missing from Sun Leung's restaurant, was arrested in an upstate New York town and brought back for questioning. "Me talk now," police quoted him as saying, and he kept his word. Sing told of seeing Ling strangle the girl in a jealous rage. Elsie had been a fickle creature, judging from the letters she wrote. The police revealed on June 25 that Elsie, in one day, wrote Ling, "Don't think that I will ever give you up," and his rival, Chu Gain, the owner of a Mott Street restaurant, "I don't want you to feel too bad because Willie [her name for Ling] was here tonight. You know that I love you, and you only and always."

The police never managed to lay their hands on Leon Ling. The police property clerk, however, is still holding Ling's trunk to be used as evidence against him in the event he is ever brought to trial, which seems dubious after the passage of almost half a century. One of the qualities of the constabulary mind is never to give up hope.

10

The Decline of the Street Gangs

O MANY New Yorkers who were not directly menaced by the activities of the street gangs, the Gophers, the Parlor Mob, the Gorillas and the Rhodes Gang of Hell's Kitchen, and their counterparts in other sections of the city, were merely the picturesque descendants of the old Five Points hoodlums and part of the local color. Mostly the gangs frequented, fought and committed their depredations within their own districts, and any respectable citizen strolling down those streets after dark should have known the risks he was taking. The city as a whole, however, was less complacent when it was revealed in the newspapers that the youthful gangsters were making themselves available on an individual contract basis, with murder retailing at $100 or less. For lesser crimes there was a sliding scale: throwing a bomb, $5 to $50; shooting a man in the arm, $5 to $25; shooting a man in the leg, $1 to $25, and a non-fatal knifing, $1 to $10. That human life and suffering could be held so cheaply provided a shocking insight into the conditions which nurtured such desperate young men.

Despite the various waves of reform, there had been little real improvement in Hell's Kitchen. Few of the Civil War-era tenements had been replaced, nor had anything been done about the sewage (most tenements still had outside privies), the hardy species of rats and cockroaches which roamed the cold-water flats, the minimal heat in the wintertime, the garbage-strewn hallways, the dim flicker of gas fixtures which passed for lighting, the falling plaster and the leaking roofs. Jacob A. Riis, the Danish-born journalist who began a crusade for better housing after years of observing slum life as a reporter at New York police headquarters, tried his best to convince the more privileged classes that the street gangster, whose activities had enough of the anarchical spirit to frighten them, was the end-product of such living conditions. Riis wrote:

"The gang is the ripe fruit of tenement house growth. It was born there, endowed with a heritage of instinctive hostility to restraint by a generation that sacrificed home to freedom, or left its country for its country's good. The tenement received and nursed the seed. The intensity of the American temper stood sponsor to the murderer in what would have been a common 'bruiser' in a more temperate clime. New York's tough represents the essence of reaction against the old and the new oppression, nursed in the rank soil of its slums. Its gangs are made up of the American-born sons of English, Irish and German parents. They reflect exactly the conditions of the tenements from which they sprang. Murder is as congenial to . . . Battle Row as quiet and order to Murray Hill. The 'assimilation' of Europe's oppressed hordes, upon which our Fourth of July orators are fond of dwelling, is perfect. The product is our own."

In his celebrated work, *How the Other Half Lives*, Riis exhibited a perfect example of what would be called, thirty-odd years later, social consciousness. He became aware of some of the grimmer aspects of poverty in his native town of Ribe, Denmark, at the age of thirteen. A schoolteacher's son, Riis was horrified by a tenement which had been built over a sewer and was infested by rats. He used his Christmas money to exterminate the rats and buy soap and whitewash to clean the place up, watched, no doubt, by the uncomprehending or noncommittal eyes of the inhabitants. He came to the United States in the post-Civil War years, worked as a reporter on the New York *Tribune,* Horace Greeley's paper, and the *Evening Sun.* Even before the first of his books and the enthusiastic support of Theodore Roosevelt made him nationally famous, Riis exercised considerable influence and aroused the wrath of the slum landlords and the politicians with whom they were allied. He exposed the contamination of the city's water supply and caused the purchase of the Croton watershed.

It was the children and the youth of the slums who aroused the greatest measure of Riis' concern. He thought it preposterous that the "overflow from the tenements of our home-heathen that are growing up in New York's streets today" were largely ignored, "while tenderhearted men and women are busying themselves with the socks and the hereafter of well-fed little Hottentots thousands of miles away. According to Canon Taylor, of York, 109 missionaries in the four fields of Persia, Palestine, Arabia and Egypt spent one year and sixty thousand dollars in converting one little heathen girl. If there is nothing the matter with these missionaries they might come to New York with a good deal better prospect of success." Riis cited the fact that these same "tenderhearted" people were able to tolerate in their midst the existence of baby farms, where illegitimate and unwanted children were sent even at the beginning of the enlightened twentieth century and where, according to Elbridge T. Gerry of the children's society which bore his name, "they feed them on sour milk, and give them paregoric [a tincture of opium] to keep them quiet." Baby-farming, Riis said, "means starving babies to death." Those children who escaped the baby farms and were brought up by their parents were not much more fortunate, in his opinion, because most of them were brutalized in childhood by the conditions of the homes and streets in which they lived, by employers of child labor, by the law itself when they were flung into reformatories for expressing their resentment of the world they inherited.

Membership in the street gangs—then as now—gave them a

warped pride, a sense of identity, a feeling of belonging. Some of the gangs amounted to private armies, who ruled large sections of Manhattan and were led by young men of genuine if misdirected executive ability. Alfred Henry Lewis, the leading authority on the gangs of that time *(The Apaches of New York)*, credited Paul Kelly's Five Points Gang with being able to muster fifteen hundred young thugs in an emergency. They were supreme in the area between Broadway and the Bowery, Fourteenth Street and City Hall Park. Monk Eastman's gang had a thousand members and reigned between Fourteenth and Monroe streets, the Bowery and the East River. Once when police raided Eastman's headquarters in Chrystie Street they removed two wagon-loads of guns, knives and bludgeons of all sorts. Occasionally Eastman's and Kelly's gangs, in a dispute over territorial rights, would clash in the streets with hundreds of members fighting on each side; there was nothing the police could do on such occasions but wait for the hostilities to end and haul off the bodies. The Gas House Gang, whose domain was Third Avenue between Eleventh and Eighteenth streets, could muster a mere two hundred troops, according to Lewis. The Hudson Dusters were in control of Manhattan's West Side below Fourteenth Street, and were a formidable lot until most of their leaders succumbed to the cocaine habit.

Hell's Kitchen, particularly the area from Seventh Avenue to the North River and from Twenty-third Street to Forty-second, was the fief of the Gophers, so named because originally they lurked in basements. Five hundred of them could be rallied on occasion, and qualitatively speaking, the contemporary experts agreed, they were the toughest of all the New York street gangs. "The Gophers," Alfred Henry Lewis said, "owned a rock-bottom fame for their fighting qualities, and, speaking in the sense militant, neither the Eastmans nor the Five Points would care to mingle with them on slighter terms than two to one." Lewis quoted Whitey Dutch of the Five Pointers as saying, "Them Gophers are as tough a bunch as ever comes down the pike."

Between these various gangs, Riis said, there was a "species of ruffianly Freemasonry," which was suspended only when local feuding broke out.

The Gophers and other street gangsters, according to Lewis, were fierce enough fighters en masse but individually they were unimpressive, a "stunted litter." For all their collective prowess, they "seldom stand taller than five feet four. Their weight wouldn't average 120 pounds. They are apt to run from the onslaught of an outsider. This is not perhaps from cowardice; but they dislike exertion, even the exertion of fighting, and unless it be to gain money or spoils, or a point of honor is involved—as in their duels and gang wars—they back away from trouble. In their gang battles, or when fighting the police, their strategy is to lie flat on the ground and shoot. Thus they save themselves a clubbing, and the chances from hostile lead are reduced."

(Some of Lewis' contempt for the average gangster may have resulted from the fact that his companion on his rounds of the city's dives often was one William Barclay Masterson, sports editor of the *Morning Telegraph*. In the old West, Masterson was better known as Bat, sheriff at Dodge City during its most uproarious years, gunfighter, gambler, Indian scout and buffalo hunter. The toughs of the West Side knew all about Bat Masterson. His newspaper office was located in the old carbarns at Eighth Avenue and Fiftieth Street. Then a bald and dumpy middle-aged man, with "killer-gray" eyes visible under the brim of his black derby, Masterson commanded respect whenever he strolled into a Hell's Kitchen saloon with Lewis at his side. A New York *Sun* writer described how a barroom full of young thugs, noisy with brag and bluster, would become still as a church when the retired gunfighter, who was still known to carry his old Dodge City equalizer on occasion, made his way to the brass rail.)

To Riis, more sociologist than journalist, the gangster was a "queer bundle of contradictions. . . . Fighting his battles with the coward's weapons, the brass knuckles and the deadly sandbag, or with brickbats from the housetops, he is still in all seriousness a lover of fair play, and as likely as not, when his gang has downed a policeman in a battle that has cost a dozen broken heads, he is to be found next saving a drowning child or a woman at the peril of his own life." Whatever the social worker, the policeman or the respectable citizen thought of him, the gangster had the loyalty and support of his neighborhood behind him, particularly when the district was invaded by the police in search of a culprit or under orders from the station house to put down a disturbance that was nobody's business but the parties' involved. "The entire neighborhood," Riis observed, "takes a hand on these occasions, the women in the front rank, partly from sheer love of the 'fun,' but chiefly because husbands, brothers and sweethearts are in the fight to a man and need their help. Chimney-tops form the staple of ammunition then, and stacks of loose brick and paving stones, carefully hoarded in upper rooms as a prudent provision against emergencies. Regular patrol posts are established by the police on the housetops in times of trouble in these localities, but even they do not escape whole-skinned, if, indeed, with their lives; neither does the gang. The policeman knows of but one cure for the tough, the club, and he lays it on without stint whenever and wherever he gets the chance. . . ." The rôle of the woman in the guerrilla fighting of Hell's Kitchen was somewhat similar to that of a pioneer woman in a besieged fort: she was expected to carry ammunition and minister to the wounded.

Riis, however, could see nothing romantic or picturesque about the street gangs. "Bravado and robbery," he wrote, "are the real purposes of the gangs; the former prompts the attack on the policeman, the latter that upon the citizen."

The Gophers, however they were known to the police and the press, always were and still are called the Goofers on the West Side. No one in Hell's Kitchen can explain the discrepancy, but it is still apparent that the word Goofers was not used in any comic or derogatory respect. The Gophers are now semi-legendary in Hell's Kitchen; such names as Newburgh Gallagher, Marty Brennan, Stumpy Mallarkey and Happy Jack Mullraney have passed into a sort of pantheon of heroes, and the only reliable information about them, in colorless officialese, has to be gathered from the police records. But there's no doubt that, as Herbert Asbury wrote, these buckoes made Hell's Kitchen "one of the most dangerous areas on the American continent." The Gophers, reigning over Hell's Kitchen for twenty-odd years, actually absorbed several generations of street fighters. Many landed in prison, but many others outgrew the need of belonging to a gang and became respectable wage earners.

One Lung Curran, who started the fad of converting policemen's coats into ladies' wear, was a leading figure during the early days of the Gophers' domination of the water-front streets. So was Happy Jack Mullraney; a partial paralysis of his face made him appear to be laughing all the time—no matter what his mood, which was seldom cheerful—and thus his sobriquet. He was very sensitive about his twisted face. One night he irked Paddy the Priest, the proprietor of a saloon on Tenth Avenue, and Paddy sneered, "Why don't you try laughing out the other side of your face, Happy Jack?" Mullraney's riposte was devastating. He pulled out a revolver and put a bullet through Paddy's skull. And he still wore that happy, artificial smile when the judge sent him to Sing Sing for life.

The Gophers never produced any outstanding gang leaders like Monk Eastman of the Lower East Side or Paul Kelly of the Five Points Gang.

But, as might be expected with a largely Celtic roster, the gang could boast its own bard, although his efforts were more suitable for accompaniment by a mouth organ, perhaps, than harp or flute. It was the same One Lung Curran, whose occasional withdrawals to the tubercular ward at Bellevue gave him time for reflection and creation.

His finest hour, poetically speaking, came when the Hudson Dusters finally managed to even the score with a particularly bothersome cop. Patrolman Dennis Sullivan had announced that he intended, singlehanded, to wipe out the Hudson Dusters, whose arrogance in the district below Fourteenth Street and along the water front was becoming unbearable. A saloonkeeper who refused them a half-dozen barrels of beer for one of their routs had his establishment wrecked and all his liquor carted off, and there were many similar depredations. Patrolman Sullivan arrested Red Farrell, the leader of the gang, and nine of his henchmen.

In retaliation, the Dusters, who had been waiting for their chance, pounced on Sullivan one night while he was about to arrest one of the gang on a merchant's complaint. His prisoner scuttled away as ten or twelve fellow Dusters swarmed all over Patrolman Sullivan. They stripped off his uniform blouse, snatched his revolver, nightstick and shield. They belabored him with blackjacks until he finally sank unconscious to the paving stones of Greenwich Street. That still wasn't enough, they reckoned, to teach the cop a lesson. Sullivan was rolled over on his back, and four Dusters stomped their iron-shod heels into his face. By the time the Dusters fled Sullivan was hardly recognizable to the police reserves who were summoned from the Charles Street station to rescue him.

It was in honor of this brutal occasion that Curran wrote:

> "Says Dinny, 'Here's me only chance
> To gain meself a name;
> I'll clean up the Hudson Dusters,
> And reach the Hall of Fame.'

> "He lost his stick and cannon,
> And his shield they took away,
> It was then that he remembered
> Every dog has got his day."

This modest effort, along with half a dozen other verses celebrating the Dusters' exploit in all its grisly detail, was so highly regarded by the Dusters that they had it set up in type and distributed copies throughout the West Side.

Aside from the Hudson Dusters, who were careful to bow tamely to the Gophers on the infrequent occasions they met along the boundary line on West Fourteenth Street, no other gangs were permitted to trespass on Gopher territory. Single members of other gangs, if they sent word that they wished to enter Hell's Kitchen on some strictly social errand, would be given passports.

Shooting sometimes broke out when such amenities among the gangs were not observed. In 1906, for instance, one James Keenan was attacked by the Haymarket Gang, an affiliated branch of the Gopher tribe, in a saloon at Thirty-fourth Street and Twelfth Avenue for not having observed the diplomatic courtesies. The proprietor intervened, allowing Keenan to escape unharmed. Less than an hour later Keenan returned with a revolver and opened fire on the Haymarket Gang's patrol, which was still lounging in the saloon. The gangsters fled, but a waiter was shot by mistake. Later that night, unable to locate Keenan, the Haymarket Gang attacked a friend of Keenan's named Thomas Hickey, in Barney Kummel's saloon on Eleventh Avenue. Hickey was prepared for the assault, drew a revolver and wounded three of his assailants.

Ike the Blood, a Monk Eastman lieutenant, fared less fortunately when he ventured into a saloon at Seventh Avenue and Twenty-seventh Street. The Gophers were informed of his intrusion immediately. Ike the Blood barely had time to raise his first shot of whiskey to his lips before a couple of Gophers dashed in and shot him. He died a half-hour later on the floor of the West Thirtieth Street station.

The indignation of the Gophers may thus be imagined when another of Eastman's hetmen, Chick Tricker, launched a sizable invasion into the Tenderloin, which the Gophers regarded as being under their protection. This meant war, and war it soon was.

Tricker was described by Lewis as "a purple patrician of the gangs." When Eastman was sent to prison, and Kid Twist, Eastman's chief lieutenant, was killed, the Eastman gang was divided into separate commands under Tricker, Jack Sirocco and Big Jack Zelig. Aside from his responsibilities as a gang leader, Tricker kept what Lewis described as a "house of call" at 128 Park Row, a noisome dive not far from the doors of New York's leading newspapers. Wrote Lewis, "There he sold strong drink, wine and beer, and the thirsty sat about at sloppy tables and enjoyed themselves. When night came there was music, and those who would —and could—arose and danced."

In 1909, Tricker decided to branch out, move uptown and into the Tenderloin, which was becoming sedate compared to its nights of glory before the Reverend Dr. Parkhurst and his companions made their celebrated foray. He bought the Stag Café, at 32 West Twenty-eighth Street, from Dan the Dude, and renamed it the Café Maryland. That was insolent enough for the Gopher chieftains, but Tricker also brought up from the Bowery a score or more of his most formidable underlings. These lads were soon cutting into the Gophers' assault-and-robbery business and other prerogatives. It could also have been said—outlandish as it may seem—that Tricker's Café Maryland was giving the district a bad name. Before 1909 was out, three of Tricker's henchmen were shot to death in the barroom when gunplay broke out over a woman.

What provoked the Gophers beyond all endurance, however, was the bold and unprecedented action of one of Tricker's amorous lads. He reached deep into Gopher territory and came up with a toothsome plum named Ida the Goose, who was immediately installed as the reigning trollop of the Café Maryland. "Ida the Goose," Asbury stated, "was a noted beauty of the underworld and had been the beloved of a long succession of Gopher captains, so that her defection caused much comment. The Gophers indignantly demanded that she return forthwith to Hell's Kitchen, and when she refused to desert her new lover they sent an emissary to deal with Chick Tricker, and threatened to regain the lady by force of arms. Tricker refused to interfere, and the West Side ambassador retired from the conference seething with anger. . . ."

One probable reason for Tricker's intransigeance in refusing to send Ida back to her old neighborhood was that two of the Gophers' leaders, Marty Brennan and Newburgh Gallagher, were languishing in the Tombs at that time. In May of 1910, Gallagher had been shot twice in the groin by a reckless citizen named William Lennon. True to the sometimes underestimated law of the underworld, Gallagher told the police to go to hell when they demanded the name of his assailant.

By August of that year, Gallagher had recovered from his

wounds. He and Brennan caught up with Lennon in a saloon at Eleventh Avenue and Forty-fifth Street and shot him to death. The police had little difficulty in solving that murder. So the Gophers' two stanchest fighters and ablest strategists were awaiting trial on murder charges in the Tombs while their followers were trying to decide how to counter Tricker's challenge to their sovereignty. On November 10, 1910, Gallagher and Brennan were sentenced to Sing Sing for terms of nine and one-half to nineteen and one-half years.

It must have been with considerable satisfaction, however, that Gallagher and Brennan had read the morning papers of October 7 in their cells. The front page of the *World* featured an account of the happenings of early that morning at the Café Maryland. About 1 A.M., Morris Richel, a bartender, was quoted as telling police, "twelve to fourteen young men dashed through the swinging doors" and opened fire with their revolvers on approximately fifty patrons seated at the tables and standing at the bar. Four men were killed instantly in the fusillade. No one could offer the police any reason for the gunmen's descent on the café.

By the next day details of the slaughter on West Twenty-eighth Street became somewhat less confused. Only five young men, the *World* reported, had shot their way through the Café Maryland. The city was alarmed at the bold manifestation of gang activity. Chief Inspector Max Schmittberger, the old boodler of pre-Parkhurst days who had survived all the various shakeups in the police department, issued a soothing communiqué to the *World:* "The outbreak at the Café Maryland was an exceptional one and had no bearing on the honest desire and effort of the police to drive such unlawful organizations out of the city." The city was more mystified than soothed by this statement.

More details of the quadruple killing in Tricker's headquarters became available on succeeding days. The purpose of the raid, of course, was to restore the prestige of the Gophers and retrieve Ida the Goose. The Gopher execution squad had boldly walked in, ordered beer at the bar, and coolly taken note of the table around which half a dozen Tricker henchmen and Ida the Goose were seated. Tricker himself had the good fortune to be absent that night. The Gophers calmly finished their beer and waited until their leader said, "Well, let's get to it," and like good efficient workmen each drew two revolvers, advanced toward the Tricker men's table and blazed away at their enemies. Ida, ordinarily a rattle-brained creature, had the good sense to hit the deck a split second before the Gophers cut loose. She was quite certain her old friends hadn't dropped around just to have a quiet beer and admire the new décor.

After that first shattering fusillade, Ida cautiously rose from her hiding place under the table. Another survivor tried to hide behind her wide skirts as she faced the gunmen. He was, in fact, her current protector! She had to make a quick decision: turn her lover over to the Gophers or both of them would be shot. Ida, being a girl with an advanced sense of self-preservation, twitched her skirts aside, shoved her lover toward his enemies and said, "Say, you, come out and take!"

One of the Gophers stepped forward and put a bullet through the brain of the terrified man sprawled on the floor. The job was done. No innocent bystanders had been so much as scratched by a ricochet. A good deal of Tricker's woodwork and glassware had been damaged, not to mention the injury done to public confidence in the establishment, but otherwise the Gophers' reprisal had been a model of restraint and efficiency. Tricker soon closed the Café Maryland and went back to the East Side, a sadder and poorer man.

As the Gophers left the café on completion of their mission, Ida the Goose trailed behind them at a respectful distance, "glowing with pride that such a great battle had been fought for her favors."

The raid on the Café Maryland was a striking example of the Gophers' fighting powers and intensity of purpose. Perhaps, in fact, it was a little too impressive, gratifying though it must have been for the Hell's Kitchen gangsters to hear themselves praised throughout New York's gangland for their prowess. The trouble was, it also impressed the public, which began to demand the breaking up of the street gangs which had been terrorizing large sections of the city for generations. A shift in the political winds made a cleanup of the street gangs almost a necessity. The political influence which had in great measure protected the Gophers in their own bailiwick was now withdrawn, and the police were permitted to break up the gang in any way they could. With Gallagher and Brennan on their way to Sing Sing, the task was that much easier.

Simultaneously, the New York Central organized a special task force of railroad police to take action against the gangsters who had been looting the freight cars and warehouses in its yards at Thirtieth Street and Eleventh Avenue almost since the day the first depot was opened there. Many of the railroad police's recruits for this assignment were former policemen who had taken their beatings at the hands of the Gophers and who relished this chance to get even. The New York Central, not unexpectedly, has no records available on this campaign against the Gophers and other gangsters who bit the dust during the reprisals. Platoons of railroad police clubbed, sapped and kicked their way through Hell's Kitchen for several months. Every time a Gopher's head popped up on the street he was run down and knocked senseless. Those gangsters who were jailed for some offense which the police were only too glad to supply, were hospitalized for concussions, abrasions and fractures. From then on, the boundaries of the New York Central yards were practically sacrosanct.

11

Growing Up in Hell's Kitchen

SHORTLY before the First World War, teams of social workers subsidized by the Russell Sage Foundation descended on Hell's Kitchen with the assignment of determining what social and economic conditions made street gangs, crime and violence endemic for generations in the tenement and water-front districts of the Middle West Side. Statistics did not then obsess the sociologist, and the reports of these workers were full of human interest. Many of them went about their job with a reportorial zest for legwork and ringing doorbells, some of them lived in Hell's Kitchen for up to two years to get close to their subject.

One phase of the inquiry concerned the boy of the streets and how he grew up to be a trooper in the Gophers or one of their slightly less murderous successor gangs.

Some indication of the harshness of his lot could be obtained from occasional newspaper essays on child life in Hell's Kitchen. The New York *Herald*, having interviewed a schoolteacher with many years of experience in a Hell's Kitchen school, reported this exchange between herself and one of her tough little pupils:

"Young Murphy," demanded the teacher, "did you give your mother that note I sent to her by you yesterday?"

"Yes'm," the boy said.

"What did she say?"

"She didn't say nothin'. She gimme a slam in the jaw."

"Murphy, don't talk like that in this school. If your mother chastized you, say so. But don't say that she slammed you in the jaw. Now, once again, what did your mother say?"

"She didn't say nothin'. She gimme a slap in the puss."

And there was the more tragic story (New York *Evening World*, April 10, 1911) of twelve-year-old Johnny Moran whose father had died of dropsy, who had watched the body robbed by a playmate, who had himself taken "the old man's watch," and then gone out to play in the street as though nothing had happened. A *World* reporter talked to the boy in Children's Court and wrote this description of him: "His chest is sunken and his shoulders slope; his furtive little gray eyes are deep set under a bulging brow, topped by a shock of hair of no particular color; his small fingers are cigaret-stained, and his clothes look as though their origin had been the ash barrel." The reporter quoted Johnny as relating:

"Me old man was sick a week and three days. I didn't know what wuz the matter wid him, and he didn't neither. He just laid around and groaned and his legs swelled awful. His name? He wuz named John, too, and he was a night watchman, when he woiked down to the dock at Thoity-seventh Street. Yes, sir, he drinked some mostly before he went to work in the evenin'. But it didn't seem to bother him. No, sir; he never treated me bad; hardly ever licked me.

"The old man never had nothin' to eat, 'cept what I bringed him the first day he wuz sick. Yes, sir, I went to school every day. I wuz afraid the troont-officer'd get me. The old man didn't mind —he just stayed by himself. No, sir, nobody come to see him, and he never told me to git nobody. After school I'd play in the streets with the other fellows and I'd git some milk and buns. I didn't want much—wuzn't hungry—and the old man never seemed to want anything.

"Thursday night he wuz took woise. I slept on a bundle of old things in a corner and in the night I heard the old man git up and go in the kitchen and sit down there. He groaned somethin' awful . . . and I couldn't sleep and I told him to shut up. Then, after a while, he stopped groaning and when I got up to go to school I see he wuz nearly all in.

"He told me to tie a rope around him and try and pull him into the bed and I did, but it wuzn't no use. Then I went out and got a roll and a glass o' milk and when I come back he wuz half way onto the bed, and he didn't answer when I spoke to him. I called him four or five times, but he never answered, and so I went to school. I didn't want the troont-officer to git me.

"Yes, sir, I knowed he wuz dead, but I had to go to school. Then after school was out, I told some of the fellers and two of 'em went up in the room with me, and one of 'em—he wuz a big boy—took five dollars out of the old man's pocket and I took his watch. The big boy wouldn't give me none of the five dollars and he and the other kid run away.

"The next day I got hungry and I told the janitor and he told the cops and they come and got me and took the old man's watch to keep for me. Yes, sir, I'm sorry the old man's dead. He wuz good to me. No, sir, me muther is dead. She died when I wuz a year old. . . . What'll they do with me, Mister?"

The Sage Foundation's study of the conditions under which boys such as the orphaned Johnny Moran grew up to ask the question, "What'll they do with me," was published in its *West Side Studies*, and provided a graphic picture of Hell's Kitchen with its roaring elevated railway, its North River docks, its Death Avenue (Eleventh Avenue) with the New York Central's freight trains running on the surface of the thoroughfare. "In street after street are the same crowded and unsanitary tenements; the same untended groups of children playing; the same rough men gathered round the stores and saloons on the avenue; the same sluggish women grouped on the steps of the tenements in the cross streets.

The visitor will find no rambling shacks, no conventional criminals' alleys; only square, dull, monotonous ugliness, much dirt, and a great deal of apathy.

"The very lack of salient features is the supreme characteristic of this neighborhood. The most noticeable fact about it is that there is nothing to notice. It is earmarked by negativeness. There is usually a lifelessness about the streets and buildings, even at their best, which is reflected in the attitude of the people who live in them. The whole scene is dull, drab, uninteresting, devoid of the color and picturesqueness which give to so many poor districts a character and fascination of their own. Tenth Avenue and the streets west of it are lacking in the crowds and bustle and brilliant lights of the East Side. Eleventh Avenue by night is almost dark, and throughout the district are long stretches of poorly lit cross streets in which only the dingy store windows shine feebly. Over the East River great bridges throw necklaces of light across the water; here the North River is dark and unspanned. . . . The casual little horse car which jingles up Tenth Avenue four times an hour is typical of the West Sider's home, just as the Draft Riots of 1863 were typical of his temper. . . .

"The district is like a spider's web. Of those who come to it very few, either by their own efforts or through outside agency, ever leave it. Now and then a boy is taken to the country or a family moves to the Bronx, but this happens comparatively seldom. Usually those who come to live here find at first (like Yorick's starling) that they cannot get out, and presently that they do not want to. It is not that conditions throughout the district are economically extreme, although greater misery and worse poverty cannot be found in other parts of New York. But there is something in the dullness of these West Side Streets and the traditional apathy of their tenants that crushes the wish for anything better and kills the hope of change. It is as though decades of lawlessness and neglect have formed an atmospheric monster, beyond the power and understanding of its creators, overwhelming German and Irish alike."

Boyhood, in these surroundings, was not likely to be idyllic.

A child's playgrounds were the streets, the tenement roofs, the rubbish-strewn vacant lots, and in the summertime the noisesome waters of the North River, tinged pink by the drainage of pig, sheep and cattle wastes from the near-by slaughterhouses and infested with blood-sucking limpets. To the Sage Foundation's fact-finders, the mixture of tenements and industrial establishments in Hell's Kitchen meant that "the demands of the family and the needs of industry and commerce are eternally in conflict. The same streets must be used for all purposes; and one of the chief sufferers is the boy. . . .

"The philosophy of the West Side youngster is practical and not speculative. Otherwise he could not fail to notice very early in his career that the world in general, from the mother who bundles him out of an overcrowded tenement in the morning, to the grown-ups in the street playground where most of his time is spent, seem to think him very much in the way. All day long this fact is borne in on him. If a wagon nearly runs over him the driver lashes him with the whip as he passes to teach him to 'Watch out.' If he plays around a store door the proprietor gives him a cuff or a kick to get rid of him. If he runs into someone he is pushed into the gutter to teach him better. And if he is complained of as a nuisance the policeman whacks him with hand or club to notify him that he must play somewhere else. Moreover, everything that he does seems to be against the law. If he plays ball he is endangering property by 'playing with a hard ball in a public place.' If he plays marbles or pitches pennies he is 'obstructing the sidewalk'; and craps, quite apart from the fact that he is gambling, constitutes the same offense. Street fighting individually or collectively is 'assault,' and a boy guilty of none of these things may perforce be 'loitering.' In other words he finds that property or its representatives are the great obstacles between him and his pleasures in the street."

Despite the adult unfriendliness pervading them, the streets from earliest childhood were the most constant and impressive part of a boy's existence. His education began there long before he learned the alphabet. All his pleasures were to be found there, just as a farm boy would find his in the fields, creeks and woods around his home. The everlasting variety of life in the streets attracted him morning, noon and night—now a funeral procession, a few minutes later a fire company galloping in answer to an alarm; a cop subduing an unruly drunk with his nightstick, followed by a shift in scene to a crap game on the sidewalk; a chase after a runaway horse, followed by a gang raid on a fruit stall and a thrilling flight from the Neapolitan fruit vendor; a gang fight over the tenement roofs, followed by a stolen ride on one of the freight trains on Death Avenue.

The Hell's Kitchen boy roved all over the district from Eighth Avenue to the river in search of amusement, but the docks were his favorite haunt. "All the year around at some time of day or night," it was observed, "you can find him on the docks. In the summer they provide a ball ground, in the winter coal for his family, and always a hiding place from the truant officer or the police. Here along the riverfront he bathes in the hot weather, encouraged by the city's floating bath which anchors close by, and regardless of the fact that the water is filthy with refuse and sewage. In the stifling evenings, too, when the band plays on the recreation pier and there are lights and crowds . . . he is again drawn to the water."

Up on the tenement roofs, most of which were adjoining for a solid block and divided only by parapets, the boy created another world of his own, freer and safer than the streets, healthier than the waters around the docks. Every boy knew the roofs as familiarly as he knew his own home. They were his refuge and his escape. And they provided two other forms of amusement, kite flying and the keeping of homing pigeons. In those days the tenement roofs of New York were as cluttered with pigeon coops as today they are with television aerials. Many of the boys kept their pigeons in their homes and took them up to the roofs daily for exercise, after training them to return to their own coops. The pigeons were also trained to fly around the neighborhood and bring back strangers to add to their owner's flock. A pigeon fancier's standing was measured by the number of birds he was able to acquire, usually by raiding other flocks.

The center of a boy's life, however, was the gang to which he belonged, almost of necessity, from an early age. His gang provided him with the rough affection he could not find at home. It also engaged a loyalty he could bestow on nothing else in the life which surrounded him. The gang became another home and family to him. His loyalty to the gang and the block of tenements around which it was organized drew even the boys of gentler inclination into the vicious street fighting which was an integral part of a gang's activities.

To a physician who had long been a resident of Hell's Kitchen, the gangs of the pre-First World War era and their methods of fighting seemed to be getting more dangerous every year. The doctor's apprehensions on this score were confirmed some years later when the boys he watched fighting outside his home with bricks and clubs took up more effective weapons as the liege men of bootlegging gang leaders. The physician observed that "now it seems they will stop at nothing. They carry knives, clubs, and even, I have heard, revolvers. Sometimes arrests are made, but they never amount to anything, for the boys are always released without punishment. If an outsider tries to interfere, both gangs ordinarily turn on him. They terrorize the neighborhood with their fights, breaking windows and injuring passersby with stones. Only recently one of these fights broke out almost in front of my house, and a score or more, most of them armed with beer bottles, were engaged in it. I got a boy by the shoulder and asked him what he was doing with the bottle. 'Oh,' he said, 'I am just taking it to the store to get it filled.' Then he laughed in my face and the rest of the gang burst out laughing. I could do nothing with them, and had to retire to my office."

A "spirit of cowardice" dominated these gang fights, it was noted by the social workers, who observed that "the strength of the boy is the strength of the gang, and under its protection unspeakable horrors take place for which it is impossible to place responsibility." Likewise they were inclined to panic if one or two of their fellows showed signs of weakening. "An unexpected move by the enemy at bay will rout an attacking party of four times their strength. Half a dozen boys caught at a disadvantage will charge unscathed through a gang of nearly two score, who fly in all directions at this unexpected display of bravery. . . ."

There was little in most of the boys' homes to bring out any latent decency of character or to refute the hard lessons learned in the streets which were their jungle, their habitat and their training grounds for the lives to which they were almost invariably committed by circumstance. The fathers worked long hours and found surcease at the corner saloon; the mothers often had to work also and were harried by a succession of younger children; older brothers and sisters were often indifferent or preoccupied by their own affairs.

A boy's diet in the days before the pure-food laws was likely to be a lot less than nourishing. With parents and older brothers and sisters preoccupied with other matters, the Hell's Kitchen boy usually picked up at least one meal a day outside the home. Crushed fruit, stale cake and rolls were sold to children at half price. These would be supplemented by candy which was said to be a mixture of "glue, glucose, aniline dyes and coarse flour" which would "upset the digestion of children far better nourished than they." One storekeeper specialized in selling cider to children at one cent a glass. He blithely explained that the cider was so spoiled that "no one but a kid would drink it."

(At least one former resident of Hell's Kitchen, who was growing up there at the time, is inclined to dispute the gloomy reports of social workers on dietetic matters, and recalls with considerable nostalgia, "We didn't do so bad in the eating line. Milk in those days was two quarts for a nickel. The meat on the family table was loaded with nourishment, even if it was cheap. Without knowing it at the time, we were eating better than the nabobs on Fifth Avenue who stuffed themselves with pheasant, steak and all kinds of rich sauces. The reason was, beef hearts, lamb kidneys, calves' liver, the lights and other organs were something the butchers were ready to throw on the floor. They were hardly regarded as fit for human consumption. We bought 'em for a few cents a pound. No wonder we were tough in those days.")

Urgent family necessity often made small boys expert at what was technically petty larceny. Their elders encouraged them to scrounge around the neighborhood for coal and wood in the wintertime. Most families simply didn't have enough money to buy fuel. "The line of least resistance is worn smooth in this neighborhood," a social worker commented, "and it is easy and natural to fall in with the parental fiction that the fuel which reaches the tenement has miraculously dropped from heaven." The coal and wood, of course, had to be stolen from the railroad yards and docks where lighters and barges brought them from the Jersey shore.

"From stealing for his family the boy naturally proceeded to stealing for himself. Somehow a boy had to lay hands on the money to buy cigarettes and pay his way into the 'moving' pictures." Nickelodeons were beginning to compete with the pool-rooms and dance halls for the adolescent's small supply of pocket money.

Social workers, perhaps a little too severely, concluded that the only law recognized by the Hell's Kitchen boy was that of "the Texan or Corsican vendetta."

Life in Hell's Kitchen was harsh enough for the male sex, but it often approached martyrdom for the female. From the threshold of adolescence on to marriage and premature responsibilities the girls of Hell's Kitchen were trapped in a situation that rarely promised any hope of happiness. The burden of "keeping the family together" often fell upon them at a very early age, and only increased with the years. It was a wonder that there were not more shawl-covered women rushing the growler for themselves or having their nips at the Family Entrance of the saloon where their menfolk found a measure of surcease from their troubles.

Social workers intent on studying the "neglected girl" found that a more devious approach was required than for those who investigated the "lawless boy." The lady sociologists opened a

club for adolescent girls on Tenth Avenue so they could be observed more or less at ease and offguard. The sociologists "found
it impossible to be on an intimate footing with them in their
homes. The atmosphere of family life was far too often one of
mutual recrimination and reproach, and the visitor was likely to
find herself in the embarrassing position of a court of appeals.
Picture an evening spent in the company of the two Katie
Murphys mother and daughter, thus: Mrs. Murphy, sitting with
folded arms in the rocking chair, rehearses the story of Katie's
sins. Katie leans against the back of the sofa with dropped eyelids
and a face as expressionless as putty. Meanwhile, the mother
runs on, zealously driving nails in her own coffin as far as the
girl's affection and confidence are concerned. Harassed by the
problem of feeding, clothing and housing six children on eight
dollars a week, Mrs. Murphy has little strength or imagination left
for the subtler problem of how to handle an adolescent daughter."

The girls were spared little; the harsher facts of life in Hell's
Kitchen applied to them as well as the opposite sex. While the
girls preferred to travel in gossipy little cliques or form clubs
which unconsciously parodied their more elegant models in an
upper stratum of society, the street gangs made their influence felt
on the girls as well as the boys. The Gophers had been disbanded
a few years earlier, in 1910, but the exploits of their leaders, most
of whom were behind the walls of Sing Sing and Dannemora,
were still the talk of Hell's Kitchen. "At one of the first club meetings, a tall, attractive girl arose and proposed as a name for the
club, the Gopherettes. As a motto, she suggested, 'Hit one, hit
all.'"

Hell's Kitchen had become so notorious by that time that vaudeville comedians used it as a source of humor. One of the gags
cruelly and briefly captured the essence of girlhood in the district:

Teacher: "Why weren't you in school yesterday, Margaret?"

Margaret: "Please, ma'am, I couldn't be here. I had to be in
court."

Teacher: "Court? Why, what do you mean, Margaret?"

Margaret: "Please, ma'am, I couldn't help it. Me father killed me mother night before last."

The attitude of the community toward the adolescent girl was that "the chances are she will 'never give you worry and trouble like a boy.' But if she does, she will give vastly more. The sting of her shame is felt to be keener than any boy can inflict. And with very few girls in our neighborhood is 'trouble' of this sort beyond the range of the possible. Therefore the sense of family responsibility is far more alert in her behalf than on her brother's account."

Or as one Hell's Kitchen matron put it, "You've got to keep your eye on a girl. It's different with a boy. He can take care of himself. But you never can tell, if you don't keep watch, when a girl's going to come back and bring disgrace on you."

The girls were sent to work at just as early an age as the boys, and seemed to resent it more. Among the girls who joined the sociologists' club on Tenth Avenue and became unwittingly subjects of scientific inquiry, the majority constantly complained of headaches, weariness and ill health. "One great reason was the immoderate pace at which the lives of such girls are hurried on. Long hours of work are thrust upon them. Long hours of play are seized with petulant insistence. To wrap packages from 7 A.M. to 5:30 P.M. within the walls of a factory, then several times a week to dance until 2 or 3 A.M. in the stifling closeness, the noise and excitement of a public hall, is not an unusual program. . . . With the girl who keeps up her train of pleasures, only a rebellious season now and then when she sleeps long mornings, saves her from exhaustion." None of the twenty girls was without some physical defect, and one of them was found to be suffering from trachoma.

The girls learned early in life that neither their education nor their leisure would be allowed to stand in the way of family necessities. When a new baby came into the household, the oldest schoolgirl in the family was usually detailed to care for the infant, since the mother and her older daughters had to continue at their jobs. One member of the girls' club told how her eleven-year-old sister, the second daughter of the family, took charge of the family during the mother's illness. "You ought to have seen how she run our house. Gee, but she was that strict, believe me. I couldn't have a cent of my own money. She cried if my father didn't give her his pay and she made him do it, too. She'd give him his quarter for shaving money, not a cent more. And she bought everything and run things herself while my mother was away sick for nine months."

There was another eleven-year-old girl named Sissy Donovan, who took over in much the same fashion when both of her parents fell ill. "You'd ought to have seen her," her mother told a social worker. "She let down her skirts and done up her hair. She was just a little bit of a thing. She come out one morning and said, 'Ma, I'm going to work as well as Mame.' We laughed at her but she set out. So that day she came back and sure enough she'd got a job in a chewing-gum factory wrapping packages. There was a gramophone and at lunchtime all the girls danced. Oh, she had a grand time, believe you me. There was a lot of little girls whose mothers was poor. When the inspector'd come, they'd hide Sissy under the table. We almost died laughing when she brought home her first week's pay—eighty-five cents! Now, what do you think of that? She come in here and give it to me as proud's if it'd been dollars instead."

Many of the Hell's Kitchen's girls went to work when they were still young enough to be called by their childhood names—Tootsie, Baby, Sissy. Only work of the least skilled and lowest paid classifications was available to them, folding sheets in the many bookbinding concerns in Hell's Kitchen, packing or wrapping in the equally plentiful candy, cookie, biscuit and cigarette factories, marking clothes and sheets in the steam laundries, running errands for milliners and dressmakers. The jobs to which these girls were assigned were the "sort of lightweight machine work from which the last drop of individuality has been squeezed out. Their chief characteristic is a degree of monotony in which no discipline for the young worker is possible because their effect is stupefaction. The work soon palls on the girl's restless spirit." One girl, oppressed by the monotony of her job after five months at her machine, cut the power belt just to get out of a day's work. Such rebellions, however, were infrequent, and most of the girls accepted their lot with a matter-of-fact attitude. "Heaven Will Protect the Working-Girl" became a popular song when it was published in 1909, but the working girl depended more on herself than divine intervention in solving her problems. Jobs were plentiful enough for girls willing to work in a store at $3.50 to $5 a week or in a factory at $4 to $7 a week, with a ten- to twelve-hour working day, six days a week.

When she chose to rebel against the rule that a girl must contribute all but a few cents of her pay to the family's common fund, she was most likely to splurge on some scrap of finery wildly unsuitable to her circumstances. One girl whose five-dollar weekly wage was the sole support of her family spent a whole week's pay on a hat with a willow plume. "We starved for that hat," her mother said bitterly, unable to comprehend the desperate cravings behind her daughter's one moment of irresponsibility. "Just plain starved for it, we did."

Among the Italians who were coming into Hell's Kitchen in ever greater numbers following the turn of the century, there was much less family discord. The Italian father was the undisputed boss of the household. His daughters came straight home after work, were forbidden to loiter in the streets or go to dance halls, and were courted under strict chaperonage only by young men who had the father's approval.

Whatever their racial or national origins, the Hell's Kitchen girls placed their ultimate hopes on marriage as the means of liberating themselves. They gave little thought to the possibility that they would be trapped in the same unremitting struggle for survival as their parents. Most of the girls married between the ages of sixteen and nineteen, somehow certain that their adolescent hunger for "good times" would be appeased the moment they were freed from the restraints of their parents' homes. New and more urgent problems soon arose. The dapper, high-spirited and flippant lads they took as husbands, already accustomed to the solace and comradeship of the corner saloon, were usually the first of their problems.

Almost immediately after marriage, the girls found that the truism of their neighborhood—"a woman just can't afford not to work"—was bitterly realistic. When children were born, this necessity became even more pressing, for the children would have suffered if they refused to take jobs. "By overworking themselves," it was noted, "they made their earnings clear gain for their families."

Preoccupied with his own hard life, the Hell's Kitchen husband offered little in the way of companionship to his wife. Some German and French workingmen in the district made it a practice to take their wives and children on excursions to the country Sundays and holidays, a survival of old country customs. Otherwise husbands and wives seldom went out in each other's company. Social workers recognized this segregation of the sexes and did not even attempt to include the fathers in meetings arranged in connection with their children's schools (a sort of forerunner of the Parents-Teachers Associations). "The father," it was said, "is left to go to the corner saloon."

Women learned very early in marriage that life was rigged against them. Older women and those careless of their reputations might slip into the Family Entrance of a saloon, but fewer of the younger ones with family responsibilities frequented the bars. Few men denied themselves this daily respite from toil and trouble. "Go down on the far West Side on a cold winter night," a social worker suggested, "station yourself on a sheltered corner, and watch the laboring man as he comes from work and turns into the corner saloon. See him push open the glass door and, still carrying his spade, pass from Eleventh Avenue to Elysium. Seen at such close range, the overwhelming lure of the saloon for its victims is easy to realize. It is also easy to see why the problem of the workingman's leisure time, brief as it may be, is of such terrible importance. . . . But the wife of the workingman who goes out daily to earn has not even this brief hour of freedom."

Whether the husband was German or Irish, different as they

may be in temperament, strong drink was likely to be the chief disturbing factor in family life, with "the more serious German dwelling side by his side with the easy-going Irish. . . . Teamster Henschel, with his dark rebellion, and Timson, the cab driver and drunken philosopher, meet as neighbors on the common stairs. Nowhere is the difference between the German and the Irishman more strikingly revealed than where the effects of long continued poverty and drink are to be observed. The German poor man tends to cruelty, and the Irishman to brutality. In German homes were tragedies unrelieved by humor, and in Irish homes, brutalities enhanced by an easy-going acceptance. The German wife under the influence of want and overwork tends to melancholy, while the Irish wife slides down into indifference and slovenliness, and sometimes takes to drink."

The Irish and the Germans, in the second generation then largely populating Hell's Kitchen, had intermarried to a great extent. Thus there were frequently such christening oddities as, say, Herman O'Brien or Michael Vincent Schultz.

Dissimilar as they were, the Irish and the Germans tended to accept each other with a surprising measure of tolerance. "In particular families representing a German and Irish union there was no tendency, even in an atmosphere full of reproach and recrimination, to blame the faults of either party upon his or her nationality. A German mother-in-law, for instance, was complaining that her son had married a poor housekeeper, an Irish girl from a neighboring tenement. When she was asked whether she thought this might be due to her Irish habits, the old woman took up the cudgels at once in behalf of the Irish, declaring that they were just as good housekeepers as her own countrywomen. Another German mother whose daughter had married an Irish longshoreman who was turning out badly, was never once heard, in all her bitter denunciation of the young husband, to attribute his faults to his race."

The home of the Hell's Kitchen wife was usually a three- or four-room flat, including a sitting room, a combination kitchen and dining room, and one or two bedrooms. Space was necessarily at a premium, and such space-saving furniture as folding cots, chiffoniers and drop-leaf tables were popular. A sewing-machine bought on the installment plan was also to be found in most of the cold-water flats of Hell's Kitchen, but "this was evidence of the sewing-machine agent's industry rather than the amount of sewing done in the family." Sewing was a craft little practiced among the women, who bought most of the family's clothing ready-made from the stores on Ninth and Tenth avenues.

The working mother was able to do much of her shopping from pushcarts and roving vendors whose odd chatter heralded the arrival of fish, fruits, vegetables and other commodities on the block. On Saturday nights, under the Ninth Avenue El, Paddy's Market held sway between Thirty-ninth and Forty-second streets. It was one of the few landmarks of Hell's Kitchen that could be termed picturesque. Those three blocks under the El were clamorous with wheedling, pleading, bickering and cursing voices as the local Irish and Germans matched wits and bargaining ability with the Jews and Italians of the Lower East Side. Much of the food displayed on the pushcarts had been rejected in other parts of the city and would rot if not sold that night. The peddler's theory was that this uncomfortable fact should have no bearing on his prices, while the buyer's gambit was to pretend that the food was so close to putrefaction that the peddler ought to pay to have it carted away. Nicked dishware, factory rejects, flawed merchandise and "notions" of the sort later taken over entirely by the five-and-ten-cent stores were also on sale.

To an outsider, the Hell's Kitchen mother's attitude toward children may have seemed ambivalent. Each new baby meant illness, expense, "taking the food out of the mouths of the other children." According to the Sage Foundation's findings, abortions were common and "unsuccessful attempts were even commoner," with the result that unethical doctors, midwives and vendors of patent medicines carried on a large and illicit business in the district. An infant that died in childbirth, his mother would say, was "better off." Yet once a child was born and survived the perils of infancy he was well loved. His mother was willing to work twelve hours a day, six days a week to keep the home together. "She meets her responsibilities," it was observed, "with a matchless heroism."

The children of working mothers too young to attend school were a constant problem. Some of them were cared for by relatives while the mother was away at her job. Day nurseries were not yet common. Only two were established in Hell's Kitchen by the year 1914 and could accommodate only 120 children between them. The mothers distrusted them as they distrusted anything pertaining to an "institution." They preferred to leave their children with relatives, friends or neighbors.

The working mother, when seeking employment as an adult, found that she could count on little more than she had earned as a child. On a rough average, she earned about $6 a week, compared to a man's average wage of $12 a week. Many of the women, of course, were forced to work because of the death or injury or other incapacitation of their husbands. Drink turned other men into loafers living off the earnings of their wives and children, but their number was not so large as may be imagined. A survey made shortly before the First World War showed the leading causes of the death or incapacitation of husbands in Hell's Kitchen to be as follows: tuberculosis, 35 per cent; pneumonia, 13 per cent; work accidents, 11 per cent; heart diseases, 4.8 per cent; insanity, 3.4 per cent, and alcoholism only 2 per cent. Many men were crippled temporarily, depriving their families of support in the days before workmen's compensation became effective, in performance of the hazardous jobs most of them filled as longshoremen, teamsters, construction workers, iron-foundry hands.

Many of the women worked in twine factories which had been operating in Hell's Kitchen for generations, some of them taking their first jobs in such establishments at the age of nine or ten. A twine factory operated by an English couple named Garth had an unusual reputation for decent treatment of their employes. Mrs. Garth "mothered the girls a great deal" and provided "a healthy influence over the younger spirits." The girls and women employed there wept the day the Garths' factory closed down, and not only for the loss of their jobs.

None of the jobs available to women could be considered easy, pleasant or remunerative, even by pre-First World War standards. Cleaning women spent eight to ten hours a night in the midtown buildings, scrubbing floors on their calloused knees. The twenty women employed to clean the Metropolitan Opera had to sweep the place down with whisk brooms seven days a week—acres and acres of red plush in the orchestra, balcony and galleries.

Laundry work was no less arduous and even less well paid. One of the hardest jobs in a steam laundry was "shaking out" the damp heavy sheets and other items of wash, for which the women were paid $4.50 a week. A State Factory Commission report on the steam laundries said the work "retains all the worst features of domestic drudgery and adds the further evils of long hours, speeding, and dangerously unhealthful conditions." The report cited as one example of "scientific management" the laundry whose experts figured out the problem, "If ten women shake 6,925 towels in five hours, how many towels can one woman shake in one hour"—and thus set up a quota which a woman had to maintain or lose her job.

Candy-dipping may have seemed a pleasant occupation to adolescent girls but they soon learned better. The State Factory Commission's 1912 report also described the conditions under which candy-dippers worked: "The chocolate rooms are generally cooled by refrigerating pipes, and their temperatures are sometimes as low as sixty degrees. . . . The lower temperature may seem comfortable for a time, but it is found to be chilling when the worker sits from ten to twelve hours without exercise. . . ."

Women in the great Manhattan hotels worked "inhumanly long hours," investigation showed, with many putting in sixty-five to seventy-two hours a week as chambermaids and cleaning women. Going into domestic service was a slightly more pleasant occupation, providing the lady of the house was not too demanding, but it paid only $10 to $15 a month, plus the privilege of carrying home castoff clothing and scraps from the kitchen. A woman working in a factory or hotel could earn about twice that much.

It was for the sake of their families that the women of Hell's Kitchen placed themselves on the slave-labor market and endured its privations and humiliations. "The last penny of their earnings is absorbed by their homes. Visit one of them on Saturday night and see how she spends her wages. The money which the woman has earned through the week on her hands and knees is spent in the Tenth Avenue stores and comes back into the home in the form of meat for Sunday's dinner, warm clothing for the children. . . ."

12

From Tenth Avenue to the Argonne

WITH the outbreak of the First World War, and consequent higher wages and increasing unionization, there was a noticeable improvement in conditions on the Middle West Side. Even in Hell's Kitchen, the striped silk shirt, which distinguished the newly prosperous worker in those days, began to make its appearance.

The unions managed to force wages up from the prewar average of about $12 to $20 and higher in the more skilled occupations. The first Teamsters Union local was organized in the tenement flat of Thomas F. Burke in West Thirty-ninth Street. His son, William Burke, a New York *Times* employe, remembers how his father and fellow unionists crowded into the Burke home to hold their meetings, because they didn't have the few dollars necessary to hire a hall. Willie Burke, whose proudest possession is the brass badge given his father as a charter member of that local, also remembers that his father worked seven days a week for seven dollars a week driving coal wagons. His father worked from 6 A.M. to 6 P.M. daily, and on Sunday was required to go to the stables to curry, feed and water the team he drove.

Rents, of course, rose with the wage scale. Railroad flats on

Tenth Avenue went up to $20 a month, according to social worker Clara Byrnes (*Block Sketches of New York*), as soon as the workingman began receiving a fairer price for his labors. The slum landlords, and the huge estates behind those landlords, were raking in tremendous profits. Otho G. Cartwright (in *The Middle West Side*, a part of the Sage Foundation's *West Side Studies*) estimated that the land was worth $25,000,000. "But," he noted, "the Astor Estate does not sell any more land. It gives leaseholds for twenty-one years, with the privilege of two renewals—at the end of which time the land must be surrendered to the owners.

"Tenement builders on such leases must therefore make their houses pay not only the original investment in full, so that the houses may be pulled down at the end of sixty-three years without loss, but must derive an income therefrom in addition to the return of the capital. Moreover, at each renewal of the lease it is the custom to increase the ground rent, so that the tendency of rentals for tenement flats built upon this land is almost inevitably upward."

It hardly takes an economist to analyze this squeeze-play between landowner and landlord and tenant and determine which has profited the most from a century of accommodating the poor in tenements.

By the time of the First World War, too, the streets were considerably safer. The bigger gangs were broken up. The "shenango"—Hell's Kitchen terminology for a lad who worked on the docks two or three days at a time when there was a slack period in burglary and allied trades—was still around but he no longer carried himself with such a confident swagger as before the Gophers were broken up. The police, social agencies and churches were succeeding in making the streets safer. One of the more redoubtable scourges of lawless youth, wayward girls and erring husbands was Father Bergen of St. Raphael's Church in the heart of Hell's Kitchen, older residents of the district recall.

Regularly, a few minutes after nine o'clock in the evening, Father Bergen would take a horsewhip and conceal it under his clerical black overcoat. Then he would stride up and down the streets of his parish. Young men and women found loitering in hallways were flayed on the spot. Toughs hanging around street corners were sent scuttling for home with the buggy whip whistling around their ears. Anyone offering resistance soon learned that he had made a grievous error. The priest was extremely talented with his fists. He never stopped to inquire whether the subject of his ministrations was Catholic or Protestant, it is recalled, and dealt out condign punishment with a fine impartiality.

This duty done, Father Bergen would then repair to the saloons in the neighborhood, grasp any parishioner who should have been home with his family by then, and pitch him out the door.

He was a tough priest in a tough neighborhood—even men of the cloth were assaulted and robbed on the streets of Hell's Kitchen, returning late at night from administering the sacrament to some dying sinner—and immensely respected, not only for his fistic talent, among the people of his parish.

Many of the boys who would have been recruited by the Gophers, had they been allowed to continue in existence, joined such neighborhood clubs as the Bear Association, the Twin Oaks, the Royal Oaks, the Yankee Doodle Boys, the Raleigh Athletic Club, the Liberty Athletic Club and the Go Ahead Boys.

More employment for the thousands of longshoremen living in Hell's Kitchen and Chelsea came about with the extension of the Chelsea piers from Twelfth to Twenty-second streets at a cost of $15,000,000 to the city. The great passenger liners of Cunard, White Star and other North Atlantic lines docked at the foot of West Side streets, discharging their voyagers into the limousines dispatched from Fifth Avenue hotels and Long Island estates.

The district's great experience with high drama, undoubtedly, was the night of April 18, 1912, when the *Carpathia* docked at Pier 54 at the foot of Fourteenth Street with the survivors of the *Titanic.*

The night of the *Carpathia's* arrival, more than thirty thousand persons thronged the streets around Pier 54, only two thousand of them holding passes issued at the Customs House for relatives of the survivors and persons having official or journalistic business at the scene. Police lines had to be established in Ninth Avenue to keep the morbidly curious from pushing their way onto the already crowded pier.

It was dark by the time the tugs nosed the *Carpathia* past the seawall of the Battery and up the North River. Suddenly she loomed into view on the dark misty surface of the river, silhouetted against the blaze of electric signs on the Jersey shore.

The thronging thousands remained silent while the *Carpathia* was docked and the gangway lowered. Then came the first of the *Titanic*'s survivors, a woman clad in a sailor's oilskins and with her face white and strained with anguish as she stumbled down the gangway. A "low wailing," animal-like, went up from the crowd. The woman collapsed in the arms of a man who had been waiting for her at the foot of the gangway. Other survivors followed her off the *Carpathia*, some of them carried into the thirty-five ambulances waiting on the pier, some finding space in the fleet of eight limousines sent over by the Waldorf-Astoria. The young widow of Colonel John Jacob Astor, who went down with the *Titanic*, was escorted to an automobile in which the silk shades were quickly drawn. Hysteria of joy and hysteria of sorrow mingled on the brilliantly lighted pier as families were reunited and as others learned there would be no reunion. Many residents of Hell's Kitchen, children at the time, vividly remember that night.

During the Edwardian years something of an artistic and literary colony established itself on West Twenty-third Street. Its citadel was the Chelsea Hotel, which was fashionable enough to shelter such personages as President Chester Arthur, the Prince of Wales (before he became Edward VII), and the Duchess of Athol, yet reasonable enough to attract the upper strata of Bohemia.

At the Chelsea a suite of nine large, high-ceilinged rooms with massive wood-burning fireplaces in each room could be leased for $1,200 a year, seven rooms for $900 and three rooms with foyer and bath for $400. The hotel's guests included artists Charles

Melville Dewey, Gordon Stephenson and Joseph Cummings; actress Annie Russell, and such writers as Henry Sydnor Harrison (*V.V.'s Eyes* and other best-sellers of the time), O. Henry and Edgar Lee Masters, not to mention the contemporary high priest of American letters, William Dean Howells. Perhaps it was this lingering literary atmosphere that attracted Thomas Wolfe to the Chelsea more than a score of years later. Wolfe produced his earliest and best work there, and his towering figure was a familiar sight in Chelsea and Hell's Kitchen.

For a well-born young lady dabbling in the arts it was considered most daring to move into the effervescent little world of West Twenty-third Street. In the *Age of Innocence*, Edith Wharton described the pious affront with which the gentry of Fifth Avenue learned that one of her characters, Ellen Olenska, had taken a house in that street, inhabited only by artists, musicians and "people who wrote."

O. Henry gathered much of the material for his short stories along the North River water front and the streets behind it. Another celebrated writer of the time who found inspiration, or at least ideas for the characters of his realistic novels, was David Graham Phillips, best known today for *The Great God Success,* an early assault on the commercial gods of American life, and for *Susan Lenox: Her Fall and Rise*, which many years later provided a motion picture vehicle for Greta Garbo.

Phillips' earliest acquaintance with Hell's Kitchen came as a reporter for the *Sun* and the *World,* when he was assigned for a time to cover the old Eighteenth Precinct station in West Forty-seventh Street, sharing a basement headquarters across the street from the station with such future notables as Richard Harding Davis, Charles Somerville and Louis Weitzenkorn. Phillips' novels attacked the corruption in politics and business which he had witnessed at first hand as a reporter, and by the time of his sudden and violent death at the age of forty-four, in 1911, Phillips was one of the most popular of American novelists.

One night in January of that year, Phillips sat around a table at Shanley's, one of the Broadway lobster palaces, with Bat Masterson, Alfred Henry Lewis and Dick Butler, the dock walloper turned politician. Phillips and Butler agreed before parting that night to meet the next day and make a tour of Hell's Kitchen so Phillips could gather material for a story on longshoremen. On his way to meet Butler, January 23, Phillips was confronted in the street by a lunatic musician named Fitzhugh Goldsborough, who fancied that Phillips' writings defamed American womanhood and particularly his sister. Goldsborough shot Phillips six times and the writer died the next day. . . .

When Europe went to war in 1914, the people of Hell's Kitchen, except for the small segments of those with French or English blood, were largely unsympathetic to the Allied cause. The majority of them were of Irish or German descent. The attitude of many Germans, particularly the newer arrivals, which loyally changed when the United States entered the war on the Allied side, was naturally biased in favor of the Central Powers. As for the Irish, they were so bitterly anti-British, so continually conscious of British oppressions on their native island, that Kaiser Wilhelm and the "Hun hordes" were not immediately viewed with any degree of anathema. No innocent German baker was ever chased down the streets of Hell's Kitchen by overwrought patriots, no bewildered dachshund was ever stoned there for reasons of state. The Irish were further embittered in 1916 when the British brutally suppressed the Easter Rebellion and executed all the leaders they could lay hands on.

Dick Butler, who was president of the New York District Council of the International Longshoremen's Association during the war, later revealed how German agents, working through Irish-American sympathizers, tried to engineer a strike of the twenty thousand longshoremen employed in the Port of New York and thus prevent the loading of munitions and foodstuffs bound for the Allies in Europe.

Butler was tipped off to the plot by William T. Flynn, chief of the United States Secret Service, then a much harried man whose job it was to run down hundreds of rumors, betrayals and false alarms of pro-German activity every week. "Anybody who spoke with a Teutonic accent," Butler recalled, "was liable to be arrested for blowing up bridges or dropping bombs on Wall Street."

Flynn's information was that German agents, through intermediaries, were preparing to offer leaders of the longshoremen's union a million dollars to call a four-week strike. It was a crucial period of the fighting along the Western Front, and a slackening of the supplies being sent to France and Great Britain might have been enough to turn the scales in favor of the Central Powers. This was just after the suppression of the Easter Rebellion, and both the Germans and the Irish-Americans, Butler said, "would have been delighted if we shut munitions and other supplies off from the Allies and England took a good beating from the Germans."

True to Flynn's information, Butler shortly thereafter was approached by the representative of a group of wealthy Irish-American merchants in Boston. Not only were the union leaders to receive a cool million, but the longshoremen themselves would receive $10 a week while on strike.

Butler and other officers of the union turned it down, and one of the officers, not Butler, leaked the story to the New York *World*. Shippers using the Port of New York were considerably relieved to learn that the dock workers would remain loyal. Butler, however, was irked that the story reached the newspapers, knowing that for the duration his union would be unable to call a strike for higher wages or better working conditions without being suspected of having been bribed by German agents.

The *World* saluted the loyalty of the longshore union with an editorial reading in part: "Most of the members of this organization are poor and all are hardworking. If they could have been hired to strike and to riot, the foreign commerce of the United States might have been paralyzed, atrocious crimes might have been committed and charged against unionism, and public sentiment in this country relative to the war might have been very emphatically influenced. . . ."

The sinking of the *Lusitania*, the terrific explosion at munitions-

laden Black Tom Island supposedly engineered by German sabo-
teurs, the German intrigues in Mexico and other heavy-handed
maneuvers against American neutrality finally swayed public
opinion, even in the strongly anti-British Hell's Kitchen, toward
the Allied cause. The boys of the district did more than their
share of the fighting in Europe. The social worker Clara Byrnes
(Block Sketches of New York City) told of counting 123 service
stars as she walked along one block of Tenth Avenue during 1917.

The 165th Infantry, a regiment attached to the famous Rainbow
Division, was Hell's Kitchen's Own. It was better known, of
course, as the Fighting 69th or the Fighting Irish. By the time the
First World War ended, it was by all odds the most publicized,
and rightly so, regiment in the American Expeditionary Forces.
The 69th New York was officially designated as the 165th Infantry
but even the unsentimental and hard-cased General John J.
Pershing, as A.E.F. commander, recognized that it was entitled to
be known under the name it had made famous through sheer
courage and self-sacrifice. Few men of the First World War became better known to the country as a whole than Father Duffy,
the regimental chaplain; Major William "Wild Bill" Donovan,
subsequently regimental commander and still later head of the
Office of Strategic Services during the Second World War, and
Sergeant Joyce Kilmer, the New Jersey poet.

The 69th had served with unusual distinction in the Civil War,
the Spanish-American War, and for nine months along the Mexican border in 1916. Its single most celebrated battle action was
the hopeless charge against Marye's Heights at the battle of
Fredericksburg; after the assault, the slope was littered with the
green sprigs that the Fighting Irish wore in their caps. The regiment also performed with notable gallantry at Antietam, Chancel-
lorsville and Gettysburg. One of the 69th's senior officers during
the First World War said that "it was the easiest to handle in war,
the hardest in time of peace," and the inscription on the regimental banner, "Gentle when stroked, fierce when provoked," was
not merely military braggadocio. The youth of Hell's Kitchen,
many of whose fathers and grandfathers had served with the regi-

ment, largely composed its ranks, along with Irishmen from other parts of New York. Still, some of the names on the regimental roster were distinctly non-Celtic. A sampling of the Fighting Irish would have to include names such as Schmidt, Stumpf and Schmedlein; Larsen and Malmquist; Gardella, Menicocci and Tricario; Rodriguez and Garcia; Van Pelt and Vanderdonck. In addition, there were almost eighty men of the Hebrew faith in its ranks.

Immediately after the United States entered the war the 69th was inducted into the regular army, the "federalization" taking place only four months after it returned from service on the Mexican border. The regiment was brought up to fighting strength and trained to the point of combat readiness. In November of 1917, it disembarked from its transports in France, and soon thereafter was moved to billets north of Lunéville, close to the main lines of the Western Front. The Germans' summer offensive of 1918, the final throw of the dice for von Hindenburg and von Ludendorff, made it imperative for the Allied command to commit whatever American troops were available in the Champagne sector.

While the 69th was undergoing its final training just behind the lines, certain personalities in the regiment began making themselves felt through sheer force of character. Major Donovan, a former Buffalo lawyer, was one of the more vigorous and efficient field officers. Sergeant Kilmer was particularly respected by his men for having turned down the chance to enter an officers' training school. And Father Duffy's cheerful presence was welcomed from one end of the regimental camps to the other.

The Reverend Francis P. Duffy was undoubtedly a man of exceptional breadth, tolerance and understanding, quite as much the shepherd of the flock to Protestants and Jews as to members of his own faith, yet with no suspicion of the proselytizer. He was a handsome, square-jawed, level-eyed man of middle years; without the Roman collar and the clerical black broadcloth of his premilitary days he would have appeared to be a successful football coach or a gentleman farmer; in uniform he was plain soldierly.

He was born in Coburg, Ontario, forty-six years before the 69th went overseas; and before the war had served in the parish of Our Savior Church in the Bronx. Later he became as much a part of Hell's Kitchen as the Belgian stone which cobbled Tenth Avenue.

The war correspondents who attached themselves to the Rainbow Division as one of the few United States units in France likely to see action in the near future made him famous in the newspapers back home as The Iron Man, The Fighting Priest, Front Line Father Duffy and The Miracle Man. Those men of the 69th who knew him back in the Mexican border days told the correspondents anecdotes about Father Duffy that only enhanced his growing legend. Captain John J. Mangan, then regimental supply officer, recalled how the chaplain was always miserable on horseback. "We had lots of fun with him on the border when he was just beginning to ride," Captain Mangan said. "Somebody, I forget who, took pity on the Padre and presented him with an old rattletrap Ford. Father Duffy was delighted. 'I'm deeply grateful for this,' he said, 'for, though I hate to say it, Henry Ford made a better horse than God.'" Captain Mangan also recalled that on the 69th's return from the border the regiment was assigned to escort the Vice President at the second inaugural of President Wilson in Washington. "It was a terrible windy day, and the Padre, as usual, had a rough time of it on horseback. At the end of the parade somebody made a remark about Wilson, what a terrific strain it was for a man to be President in those difficult times. Father Duffy said, 'I wish I were President, then I could get off this horse.'"

His great love of New York and the theater endeared Father Duffy to a stout owlish young sergeant who was at the front for *Stars and Stripes,* another man destined to become a legend, Alexander Woollcott by name. Woollcott wrote that mostly Father Duffy preferred to ignore the war and the ruined country around them in his conversations. "He liked nothing better than to sit in a shell-hole with Clancey and Callahan and Kerrigan and talk about New York. I have stood beside him ankle-deep in the

Argonne mud and, above the noise of the rain pattering on our helmets, heard him speculate about the gleam of Fifth Avenue in October sunshine and say how he would like to see once more that grand actress who called herself Laurette Taylor, but who, mind you, was born a Cooney."

The 69th first went into the line along a rather inactive sector of the Lorraine front. Corporal Martin J. Hogan of Company K recalled (in *The Shamrock Battalion of the Rainbow*) how Father Duffy "told us in the simple soldier language which he used so well and with which he helped us steady ourselves often later in the writhing line of battle that we were 'up against our great task now and must not miss a trick.'" From then until the 69th was relieved, Father Duffy was in the trenches night and day. Later, when he was promoted to chaplain of the whole 42nd Division, he kept returning to the 69th as though he were homesick.

As divisional chaplain, Captain Mangan related, "he saw to it that all the denominations got chaplains from their own denominations. One day, outside of Baccarat, he called a meeting of all the sky pilots at headquarters. He asked me to give them a good lunch—he delighted in calling me the regimental housekeeper—and I made the arrangements. The house where the meeting was held was opposite the Padre's billet. In the middle of the affair, he left for a moment to get some papers and I met him as he crossed the street. 'How is it going?' I asked him. 'Fine, Jack, fine,' he said. 'I've got all of them on red wine and three of them on the hard stuff.'"

During the spring days of 1918 when the 69th was learning its trade under occasional bursts of machine-gun fire from the German trenches and occasional shelling from the enemy artillery, in the Baccarat sector, the most dramatic moment came one brightly moonlit night. The 69th was being relieved, and its column left the line as another column marched up from the rear. To their great excitement, the men of the 69th discovered that the men in the other column were part of the 77th Division, New York's Own, as it was called. There was much bragging and name-calling as the columns passed each other. The 69th was proud of the fact it was an all-volunteer outfit, and disparaging of the fact the 77th Division was composed of draftees. Old friends tried to identify each other in the march-past. Up and down the columns arose such cries as:

"Where's Company K of the 69th?"

"Where's Company I?"

"Anybody here from Greenwich Village?"

"Anybody here from the old Gashouse?"

"I'm from the Village . . . which John Kelley did you want?"

Somebody from the 77th boasted loudly that "the Germans will find out what American soldiers are like when we get a crack at them."

Father Duffy overheard Sergeant Mike Donaldson (who became one of the Fighting 69th's three Congressional Medal of Honor winners, the other two being Major Donovan and Sergeant Richard O'Neil) bellow indignantly in reply, "What are you giving us—we were over here killing Dutchmen before they pulled your names out of the hat."

"Well, thank God," roared back a defender of the 77th, "we didn't have to get drunk to join the army."

"There was some excitement as old neighbors would identify each other," wrote Woollcott (*While Rome Burns*), "and one unforgettable moment when Father Duffy saw two brothers meet. In their emotion they could only take pokes at each other and swear enormously. Then, lest all these ructions draw the attention of the enemy artillery to this relief, order was somehow restored and the march went on, mingling prohibited, speech of any kind forbidden." The passing regiments softly hummed "The Sidewalks of New York" as their columns swung past each other in the moonlight, the song saying what the men could not say. Then they hummed George M. Cohan's hymn of the homesick New Yorker, "Give My Regards to Broadway." "The last words I heard," Father Duffy wrote in his autobiography (*Father Duffy's Story*), "as the tail of the dusty column swung around a bend in the road, were 'Herald Square, anywhere, New York Town, take me there.' "

One of Father Duffy's closest friends in the regiment was Joyce Kilmer, whose transfer to the 69th from the 7th Infantry he was able to effect. Father Duffy later wrote that Kilmer "had a romantic love of death in battle," the same sort of lyrical feeling about war that dominated his English counterpart, Rupert Brooke. Father Duffy wrote of Kilmer, "He is very much a soldier . . . prouder of his triple chevron than he would be of a colonel's eagles in any other outfit. If they do not let us commission officers within the regiment, he will come out of the war as Sergeant Kilmer, a fine title, I think, for any man, for it smacks of the battlefield with no confounded taint of society about it. . . . He has worked himself into various midnight patrols and Captain Anderson has told me to advise him that he lacks caution in taking care of himself, but as Kilmer has told me the same thing about Anderson, I feel helpless about them both. . . ." Father Duffy's forebodings were justified soon enough when young Kilmer was killed in action.

By mid-July the Rainbow Division was transferred to a potentially more active sector around Châlons-sur-Marne, where it was attached to the French Fourth Army. The Germans were preparing for a last mighty onslaught, one more drive on Paris, before the weight of the growing American Expeditionary Force could make itself felt and the war irretrievably lost to the Central Powers. The crack division of the German Imperial Guard were concentrated on the Champagne front for this all-out offensive by the weary and decimated armies of Kaiser Wilhelm. The night of July 14, wrote Corporal Martin Hogan, the firing from the German lines suddenly ceased and "things were abnormally, unpleasantly quiet. . . . It seemed almost as though the war had stopped. It wasn't natural; it wasn't comfortable to sleep in the trenches, when the guns had ceased to speak."

When the German artillery "spoke" again, it was with a terrific drumfire barrage—"shock on shock," wrote Corporal Hogan, "the shells exploded until for very noise one could go mad."

Under this shattering barrage, with trenches and other field-works crumpling, Father Duffy still made his parochial rounds, "pausing to speak a few words with each man in the line," Hogan recorded. "His face radiated a cheerful calm which made the hell around us seem unreal. He might just as well have been walking down the silent aisle of some majestic cathedral for all his face told of heeding danger or wrought-up nerves."

On came wave after wave of the shock troops of the Prussian Guard, battering in vain against the positions held by the 69th and the other regiments of the Rainbow Division. "Clubbed rifles were splintered against skull and shoulder bone, bayonets were plunged home, withdrawn, and plunged home again."

The German plan of operations called for their spearhead divisions to reach the Marne by the evening of July 15, and elsewhere on that front they were making headway against the French Fourth Army.

But the fighting 69th not only stopped the Kaiser's elite troops in their tracks but proceeded to drive them back three miles.

Now the 69th had become shock troops, a fire brigade summoned wherever the German offensive threatened to get out of hand. Late in July they were sent to defend the line of the river Ourcq—which was promptly renamed the O'Rourke by the men of the 69th. Here, with the rest of the Rainbow Division, they shattered the assaults of four German divisions, the 4th Prussian Guards commanded by Prince Eitel Friedrich, son of the Kaiser; the 201st German, the 10th Landwehr and the 6th Bavarian. Many times in later life Father Duffy told of the wounded soldier of the 69th who, like his comrades, wondered at the presumption of the French in calling such a trickle of water as the O'Rourke a river. He waved aside a canteen offered him, saying, "Give it to the O'Rourke. It needs it more than I do."

Wherever the 69th went into action, Father Duffy was to be seen, offering whatever comfort he could to Catholic, Protestant and Jew alike, hearing confessions in village squares as the Rainbow moved toward the front, presiding over burial services, giving the last rites of the Church, then going up into the lines with the battalions once again. He had time, too, for a many-sided compassion few men could dredge up within themselves in that desperate summer. Following the battle along the Ourcq, there were many German bodies blackening under the sun. No one wanted to be bothered with giving the enemy a decent burial; that was a job, at any rate, for rear-echelon troops. But Father Duffy cajoled and pleaded and bullied the men into digging a trench for the German dead. Then he himself began dragging their bodies into the trench, until the men were shamed into helping him with the task. Little wonder that he was awarded the Distinguished Service Cross, the Distinguished Service Medal, the Croix de Guerre and the ribbon of the French Legion of Honor. Or that Colonel Douglas MacArthur, as chief of staff of the Rainbow Division, half seriously proposed an impossibility— the elevation of Chaplain Duffy to command of the 69th. MacArthur himself noted that "it was one of the few times in the history of the American Army when the suggestion was made that a minister of the Gospel be converted into the commander of a fighting unit." General Frank R. McCoy agreed that Father Duffy was the "heart and soul of the regiment—and the funnybone too." The regimental command passed to Colonel Donovan.

It was his "funnybone" that endeared him to the men in the ranks. Once he went AWOL to get them some of the things they needed from the quartermaster's stores, one of the essentials being packs of playing cards. Another time he came upon a group of soldiers who were cursing with an expert fluency after a rough night in the lines. They stopped suddenly when they caught sight of Father Duffy. "Go ahead, boys," he said. "You've had lots of trouble. The Lord won't mind a little of that."

The 69th saw action at Château-Thierry and helped launch the counteroffensive which "finally broke the Germans' pride and their hearts." Then the battle of the St. Mihiel salient. Then the hellish forest of the Argonne, where hundreds of the 69th were killed and wounded. One of the wounded was Colonel Donovan, whom Father Duffy, with the utmost exasperation, had always been telling that a regimental commander's place during a battle was in the command post and out of danger.

Father Duffy saw Colonel Donovan being carried in a blanket to a dressing station and hurried over in great distress.

"Ah, there, Father," said Colonel Donovan, "you thought you'd have the pleasure of burying me!"

Father Duffy shook his fist at the colonel. "And I will yet," he shouted.

Until a few hours before the Armistice of November 11, the 69th was in the thick of action, losing a third of its numbers in killed and wounded. It cracked the vaunted Kriemhilde Line at Grandpré, cut the Sedan-Metz railroad line and on November 7 carried Hill 346 before Sedan with the bayonet. Company D of the 69th was selected to join in the occupation of historic Sedan with the 40th French Division, but there was a mixup in orders and the gesture was not completed.

With the end of the war, the 69th moved into the Rhineland and joined the occupation forces in seeing to it that Germany disarmed herself, restored order among the elements trying to seize power in the new republic, and kept the peace.

One of the signal honors bestowed upon the regiment as it relaxed from the arduous summer and autumn of 1918 was a personal inspection by General John J. Pershing. For this occasion, at least, the stern old cavalryman attempted to unbend a little, play the father of the regiment. He inspected the 69th on St. Patrick's Day, 1919. As he approached the ranks, Blackjack Pershing turned to a staff officer and loudly inquired, "What regiment is this?"

"The 165th Infantry, sir," replied the officer, giving the 69th's official designation.

"What regiment is this?" the general demanded again.

"Oh . . . the 69th New York, sir."

"The 69th New York," said General Pershing. "I understand now."

The dialogue may or may not have been written by a public relations officer, but it went over big with the 69th.

According to Father Duffy, the general's attempt at public benevolence backfired on him a little later in the review. The commander of the A.E.F. paused before one Irish dough- boy with three wound stripes on his arm, and inquired, "Well, my lad, and where did you get those?"

"From the supply sergeant, sir," replied the warrior with a straight face.

On the late-April day the 69th landed in New York the city prepared to pay its most impressive honors. The regiment—minus its 859 dead and most of its two thousand wounded—marched up Fifth Avenue through five miles of cheering crowds. The roaring welcome of millions of their fellow citizens was so deafening, it is recalled, that not even the larruping rhythm of "The Garry- owen," the 69th's favorite marching song (and General George A. Custer's, too, along with his ill-fated 7th Cavalry), could be heard above the tumult. On the regimental banner were sixty-one silver bands denoting separate engagements and sixteen streamers sym- bolizing major battles in which the regiment participated from the Civil War to the end of the First World War. The last bat- talion in the line of march was made up of seven hundred men invalided home before the regiment itself was repatriated. To the people of Hell's Kitchen watching their sons, brothers and husbands marching up New York's proudest thoroughfare it was an unforgettable day.

The 69th was disbanded and its officers and men returned to their civilian occupations. Not a few of the men, particularly those whose peacetime job had been sheer drudgery, did so re- luctantly; some of them were attracted by the high pay and ex- citement offered by the rapidly expanding bootleg liquor gangs. Whatever their peacetime course, the men of the 69th knew they had won a secure place in the nation's military history. The 69th was one of a handful of American units, first in France, which demonstrated the tremendous morale and fighting power of the new United States regiments and supported General Pershing in his determination that the A.E.F. would fight as a whole and under American command rather than being committed piecemeal to various French and British armies, a matter of great historic consequence.

Father Duffy, too, returned to the less exciting tasks of a peace-time career, but obscurity never swallowed him up as it did most of his comrades. From the end of the war until his death more than a dozen years later, he was one of the authentic heroes of New York, one of its leading celebrities, in a time when most such fame was based on something as frivolous as flagpole sitting or operating a night club with piratical flamboyancy. Father Duffy returned to the duties of a parish priest, but his rectory was like none other in the world.

In 1920, he was appointed pastor of Holy Cross Church, which is on West Forty-second Street between Ninth and Tenth avenues. Thus he was to serve out his life in Hell's Kitchen, where so many of the men of the Fighting 69th had been recruited. He took over a parish deep in debt, most of its people too poor to contribute very much to its upkeep. To pay off its debts Father Duffy under-took a fund-raising campaign and collected $250,000—much of it coming from Protestants and Jews.

To Alexander Woollcott and many others, he was the first citizen of New York. In *While Rome Burns,* Woollcott wrote of him, "This city is too large for most of us. But not for Father Duffy. Not too large, I mean, for him to invest with the homeliness of a neighborhood. When he walked down the street—any street—he was like a *curé* striding through his own village. Everyone knew him. I have walked beside him and thought I had never before seen so many *pleased* faces. The beaming cop would stop all traffic to make a path from curb to curb for Father Duffy. Both the proud-stomached banker who stopped to speak with him on the corner and the checkroom boy who took his hat at the res-taurant would grin transcendently at the sight of him. He would call them both by their first names, and you could see how proud they were on that account. Father Duffy was of such dimensions that he made New York into a small town."

It was Father Duffy's sense of humor and his humanity which

endeared him to so many kinds of people. There were undoubtedly other chaplains of the First World War who had conducted themselves as bravely and generously, but Father Duffy was the sort of man who found himself the center of anecdotes wherever he went and whatever he did, and anecdotes are the warp and woof of legend. One of his fellow officers of the 69th was fond of recalling how Father Duffy raised two thousand francs for an aged French village priest. Father Duffy presented the French priest with the money on one condition—that he go to Paris and "blow every centime of it on a roaring good time." The old priest protested that he couldn't spend all that money on himself, he'd have to think of a wiser use for the windfall. Father Duffy finally made him promise to take it to Paris, but remarked later, "He won't do it. I'll bet you that when he dies, ten or fifteen years from now, he'll have every sou of that two thousand francs left. You know, in some ways, it's a great handicap to be a Frenchman." The only time Father Duffy was observed to weep overseas, the same officer recalled, was after the battle of the Ourcq and he went over the battlefield searching for the regiment's dead. He knelt and burst into tears when he found the body of a soldier whom he had baptized as a baby.

He kept a list of all veterans of the 69th, no matter what their faith, and sent each of them a letter at least once a year. When he returned from Rome with five thousand rosaries blessed by the Pope, he sent them out to the first 4,999 names on his mailing list, regardless of their religion or lack of it.

His visitors at the parish house of Holy Cross—a block and a half down the street from the theatrical blaze of Forty-second near Broadway, in the years when that intersection was still the capital of show business—were an odd assortment that attested to his love of the theater, literature, the arts, and most sports. Playwright Marc Connelly brought him the first draft of *Green Pastures* to read in his study. Edna Ferber, the novelist, was a faithful correspondent and frequent visitor. His friends also included Otto Kahn, Fiorello LaGuardia, Governor Al Smith, Bernard Baruch, General Pershing.

And there were less notable callers, many of them seeking assistance, financial or spiritual. After one boozy but winning vagrant was sent on his way satisfied, Father Duffy turned to another priest and said helplessly, "Joe, why do they make sinners so nice?"

One of his more worldly distractions was attending prize fights. He attended the second Dempsey-Tunney fight as a strong partisan of Gene Tunney. While Tunney was taking the famous long count with Jack Dempsey towering over him, a companion begged Father Duffy, "Pray, Father, pray." The priest explained later, "I started to pray, but suddenly I stopped. I thought it wasn't fair for an Irishman to have help in a fight." Father Duffy apparently had overlooked the fact that Dempsey, too, was of Irish descent.

Father Duffy died June 26, 1932, at the age of sixty-one. New York gave him one of its most impressive funerals. In the funeral procession which moved from Holy Cross to St. Patrick's Cathedral three days later, hundreds of war veterans, policemen and firemen marched behind the cortege. Six artillery horses drew the purple-draped caisson bearing his casket, followed by rank on rank of generals and of senior officers from the old 69th. The procession moved through Times Square, stilled at midday. Twenty-five thousand persons crowded into and around the cathedral for the services.

Five years later a statue of Father Duffy was unveiled in Times Square with ceremonies testifying to his undiminished place in the memory of an otherwise fickle metropolis.

The nine-foot greening bronze still stands looking south from the head of Times Square, toward his old parish of Holy Cross.

If Hell's Kitchen has a saint, an unofficial saint, he is Father Francis Patrick Duffy.

13

Duke of the West Side

ITH the end of the war came Prohibition, and with Prohibition came a number of significant changes in Hell's Kitchen, particularly among the scofflaws who had been fighting the cops and fending off honest employment for generations. Speakeasies proliferated throughout the district, the bootleg gangs took over many of the warehouses, and many a Hell's Kitchen lad, instead of engaging in profitless forays against the police, joined up with Owney Madden or Dutch Schultz to make his fortune as a rumrunner. Almost any midnight convoys of trucks loaded with booze trundled along Tenth Avenue, bound for a warehouse and eventual distribution to the speakeasies catering to New York's undiminished thirst. Up front, in a touring car, on guard against hijackers, would ride a Hell's Kitchen bucko with a submachine gun in his lap. Occasionally the convoy would halt at a street corner, and a cop would be paid off for averting his official gaze.

A woman resident of Hell's Kitchen told a *Telegram* reporter there were "more speakeasies than kids in Hell's Kitchen, and there are easy two hundred kids to a block. . . . The corner saloon days was better." The reporter investigated her charges and found that "Hell's Kitchen fathers patronize the speakeasies and Hell's Kitchen children spend their pennies on candy at the counters in front that serve as blinds."

But most of the people in Hell's Kitchen were able to look upon Prohibition without any excess of resentment. The leaders of the bootleg gangs were generous employers, and a young fellow engaged in transferring liquor from rumrunners which slipped down from Canada or up from the Bahamas was likely to be prosperous enough to support several generations of his family.

Prohibition agents making a rare sortie into Hell's Kitchen were likely to be roughly handled, as they learned early in the game. The revenuers received the same sort of greeting in the district as they did in the moonshine country of Tennessee or North Carolina. In 1922, three federal agents attempted to raid a speakeasy at 766 Eighth Avenue and were forced to retreat under a shower of bottles and glasses. The same evening they forced their way into a suspected groggery at 683 Ninth Avenue, and this time were sent flying when the proprietor hurled a five-gallon earthen demijohn at their heads.

Soon after the war ended, the police were served notice that the toughs of Hell's Kitchen were no longer willing to fight with bricks and fists. Until then the shooting of a police officer was a remarkably rare event. In 1921, however, Patrolman Dan Neville was shot and killed in a vacant lot on West Thirty-seventh Street between Tenth and Eleventh avenues—a few blocks from the site of the original Hell's Kitchen. Three years before Neville's partner, John Nolan, had been killed by a brick hurled from a roof. Neville, following his partner's death, had been fanatically devoted to breaking up the gangs. Detective Sergeant "Boots" Trojan told a reporter (New York *Telegram,* September 4, 1921) that the police expected a lot of trouble from lads who had learned to use a gun in the A.E.F. "It was the war that taught the gangsters how to use guns," Trojan said. "They all went overseas and came back with medals, because they sure knew how to fight. They used to fight with bricks and their fists, but now they're going in for guns."

Armed or not, the lawless element learned to respect one of the Hell's Kitchen cops. Patrick H. Diamond, known as The Iron Claw, disdained to draw his service revolver in making an arrest, no matter what the circumstances. He was reputed to wear out a couple of nightsticks a week. When this weapon broke in his hands, he would haul out a cargo hook—hence his sobriquet—and "continue the argument," as a New York *Sun* reporter noted. Patrolman Diamond captured the redoubtable Red McCaffrey barehanded during the investigation into the Dan Neville murder, for which one Bill Hoey was eventually tried. Still, when Diamond retired from the force and returned to his native County Derry, there were no hard feelings in the district. More than five hundred men gathered at the Old Homestead restaurant at Twenty-third Street and Eighth Avenue for his farewell dinner. Among them, the *Sun* reported (May 10, 1927), were policemen, gangsters and politicians, "probably as unique a group as has been gathered together in this city for many years."

By that time the old "Hell's Kitchen precinct," the West Thirty-seventh Street station, had been closed down and its functions absorbed by the West Thirtieth and West Forty-seventh Street stations. Known as the "slaughterhouse" to the people of the neighborhood, whose sleep had been disturbed by the howls coming from its interrogation chambers, the character of the old station house was changed abruptly. It was taken over by policewomen as a center for their welfare work. White curtains screened the windows, and flower boxes appeared on the ledges beneath the bars. In the former office of the precinct captain, Mrs. Mary E. Hamilton, director of the center, established herself and a canary in a wicker cage. The back room, where patrolmen had lounged off-duty and occasionally walloped a prisoner to keep their hand in, was fitted out with a Persian rug and library tables displaying the latest magazines.

Another symptom of the passing of an era was the violent death in August, 1923, of Goo Goo Knox, once the stanchest of the Gopher Gang's street fighters. A bullet cut him down on West

Fifty-second Street near Ninth Avenue. Goo Goo, the police said, was a casualty in one of the current bootlegging wars.

A study of the newspaper files for the 1920's indicates that there was still an occasional flareup of the old cop-hating spirit that had made the whole district west of Eighth Avenue a battle-ground. On one occasion, a policeman walking his beat on West Forty-fourth Street ran into more trouble than he anticipated when he stopped a group of boys from playing a "toddle-top" game. This was a gambling enterprise based on the antics of a put-and-take top. Twenty-eight housewives in the block on Forty-fourth Street between Tenth and Eleventh avenues imme-diately banded together to express their displeasure with Patrol-man Frank Reilly. Down from the rooftops came a barrage of flowerpots, crockery, pieces of furniture and pails of water, de-scending with the marksmanship for which the neighborhood was famous. The West Forty-seventh Street station had to call out the reserves to rescue Patrolman Reilly and put an end to the hostilities.

Such occurrences by this time were so rare as to bring a nos-talgic lump in the throats of old-timers in the district.

Among the quality folk of the Hell's Kitchen gangs, the name of Owen Victor Madden became pre-eminent. A graduate of street fighting, he somehow acquired a certain amount of polish between Tenth Avenue, Sing Sing, and the gaudier Broadway night clubs where he later held sway as The Duke of the West Side. He had earned the title. His manner may not have been exactly ducal, but among the hoodlums with whom he associated on matters of business he stood out as a model of suavity, quiet tailoring and almost courtly behavior. He was the prototype of the hoodlum turned celebrity. Otherwise-respectable people fawned on him and were grateful for a kind word in the 'twenties when a man's best friend was his bootlegger. Owney, through various mishaps and mistakes, learned that violence, even in the underworld, should be applied with discretion. Which may be one reason for the fact he has lived to a ripe and quite untroubled old age.

In his much-troubled youth, however, Owney inherited the leadership of a surviving remnant of the old Gopher Gang. He was born in England but was of Irish descent, brought to this country by his parents at the age of eleven. He quickly became expert in the use of the revolver, the blackjack, the leadpipe and the brass-knuckles. By the age of seventeen he was known around Tenth Avenue as Owney the Killer, and by the time he was twenty-three, according to Herbert Asbury, he was credited, probably inaccurately, with five murders. Old playmates of his say he wasn't nearly so homicidal as the authorities made him out to be.

He must have had certain forceful characteristics, whether expressed violently or not, early in his career; when the old Gophers were broken up by the regular police and the New York Central's special police, he seized his first opportunity. Somehow he had escaped the general roundup of toughs in Hell's Kitchen. He had a cherubic smile and the general appearance of an altar boy, so he might well have been overlooked. For the next several years he ruled one faction of the surviving Gophers while Buck O'Brien ruled another. Madden's territory extended from West Forty-second Street southward to around Fourteenth Street, the boundary of the Hudson Dusters and the Marginals; O'Brien ruled from Forty-second to Fifty-ninth streets west of Broadway. Unlike the old Gophers, Madden's gang refused any peace treaty with the Hudson Dusters and often battled in the streets with them.

After one of his early arrests, he boasted that he had never done a day's work in his life and, at the request of a police reporter, wrote out an account of how he spent his time as a princeling of the underworld. Quoted by Asbury in his compendium of New York gang histories, it was a brief and fascinating document on the early life and times of a rising hoodlum. It read:

"Thursday—went to a dance in the afternoon. Went to a dance at night and then to a cabaret. Took some girls home. Went to a restaurant and stayed there until seven o'clock Friday morning. . . . Friday—spent the day with Freda Horner. Looked at some fancy pigeons [like many Hell's Kitchen boys, he flew pigeons from his rooftop]. Met some friends in a saloon early in the evening and stayed with them until five o'clock in the morning. . . . Saturday—slept all day. Went to a dance in the Bronx late in the afternoon, and to a dance on Park Avenue at night. . . . Sunday—slept until three o'clock. Went to a dance in the afternoon and to another in the same place at night. After that I went to a cabaret and stayed there almost all night."

Whether the rap was homicide or hijacking, the authorities rarely managed to keep their hands on Owney Madden for very long. When he was still in his teens, he quarreled with a clerk named William Henshaw over a girl. Someone shot Henshaw in a trolley car at Sixteenth Street and Ninth Avenue; there were plenty of witnesses—at the moment—and they all agreed that Henshaw's assailant was Madden. Furthermore, police said, Henshaw told them the name of the gunman just before he died in the New York Hospital. This time, in the opinion of the detectives working on the case, they had Owney the Killer sewed up in an airtight case; all they had to do now was catch him. Ten days later Madden was spotted on Tenth Avenue and the police gave chase. Madden led them over the tenement roofs, a world of its own which he knew like the inside of his pockets. The police surrounded the area and finally ran him to ground.

By the time Owney Madden, blandly smiling, was brought into court, the witnesses against him had vanished, the state's case had evaporated, and the charges were dismissed.

Ever a sociable fellow, Madden established a place called the Winona Club where good fellows could get together. Unfortunately some of his fellow clubmen lacked Owney's refinement. There was drinking, gambling and wenching on the premises, and all these pursuits led to some ferocious brawling and furniture-smashing. The neighbors kept protesting, only to be confronted by Madden's angelic smile. Finally the cops came in force.

Madden and his fellow clubmen barricaded themselves inside, and a voice identified as Madden's was heard over the tumult, shouting, "We'll shoot the gizzard out of any cop that tries to break in." This unfriendly sentiment was quickly followed by a shot that just grazed one officer's ear.

A moment later, Madden outmarshaled for once, a detachment of police broke down the rear door and clubbed into submission everyone on the premises. His lawyer pointed out in court that Owney was still a minor, a misunderstood waif of the slum streets, and the judge merely placed him under a $500 peace bond.

Madden and his group of freebooters subsequently enlarged their scope of operations from simple thuggery and burglary to extending "protection" to businessmen in their territory.

Owney's success in these endeavors naturally aroused the jealousy of rival gang leaders, and he was warned that an attempt to "knock him off" was inevitable. Owney, who had the fierce courage of a dock rat, dismissed all such warnings. Nobody, he believed, would have the guts to go up against him. In this matter, he sadly underrated the opposition.

On the evening of November 6, 1912, Madden, whose slender and dapper figure cut an admirable swath through the dance halls of the West Side, went unaccompanied to the old Eldorado, renamed the Arbor Dance Hall, on West Fifty-second Street near Seventh Avenue—well out of his organization's territory.

Owney held court in the balcony of the dance hall, occasionally bestowing a few words on lesser hoodlums who came up to his table obsequiously, drinking his whiskey at an unhurried pace, and inspecting the girls down on the dance floor.

A pretty girl came up and began talking to him, distracting him from certain sinister activities on the balcony. Ten or twelve strangers had drifted up there and deployed themselves at near-by tables. Suddenly they began closing in on Madden's table. Madden looked up, and realized immediately that he was surrounded by enemies.

Owney jumped to his feet and reached for his revolver, yelling, "Come on, you guys. Who'd you ever bump off?"

He didn't have a chance when the shooting started.

By the time the police and an ambulance had arrived, Owney

lay sprawled alongside his table with a half-dozen bullets in him. The ambulance doctor shook his head at all those strategically placed perforations, and suggested it might be a good idea to stop by the morgue on their way back to the hospital, because it looked as though Madden couldn't live more than a few minutes. Owney confounded the interne by refusing to give up the ghost and continuing to cling to life once he reached the hospital.

Detectives who came to his bedside received the standard answer: "It's nobody's business but mine who put these slugs in me. The boys'll take care of them."

Inside a week three men suspected of having taken part in the attempted assassination were lying dead in the gutters of the West Side.

Madden spent a long time convalescing from his wounds—long enough for several of his underlings, principally Patsy Doyle, to get ideas about succeeding him as gang boss of Hell's Kitchen. Doyle, who spread the word that Madden would be crippled for life by his wounds, already bore a grudge against Owney. Freda Horner, the girl mentioned in Madden's indiscreet memorandum on how he spent his days and nights, had originally been Patsy Doyle's girl. Doyle's ego was bent all out of shape when she announced that she preferred Madden.

Owney, of course, had heard all about Patsy Doyle's ambitions to take over the gang leadership, and decided on immediate remedial action. A few days after Madden left the hospital Doyle's unconscious form was found in the street. He had been blackjacked and almost killed.

Doyle retaliated soon thereafter by blackjacking, knifing and shooting Tony Romanello, one of Madden's most trustworthy lieutenants.

The Doyle-Madden feud sputtered away for months, and the whole West Side waited for the blowoff. Most of the betting was on Madden. But he refused to be hurried; like most gangsters he had a vast fund of patience when it came to paying off an old score.

Madden finally decided to play on that self-destructive vanity of Doyle's. Word was sent to Patsy through intermediaries that Freda Horner had wearied of Madden and would like to return to her former place in Patsy's affections. Patsy swallowed the story in one eager gulp. He was told to meet Freda in a saloon at West Forty-first Street and Eighth Avenue, the night of November 28, 1914.

Patsy strolled into the barroom at the appointed hour and found a girl friend of Freda's, Margaret Everdeane, seated at a table in the rear. Margaret told Patsy that "Freda'll be along any minute now."

Just then the barkeep called over to Doyle, "Patsy, there's someone here that wants to have words with you."

"Who?" asked Patsy, starting to turn toward the bar.

"Me," said a voice behind him.

Patsy turned around and was confronted by two men, one of whom jammed a revolver into his midriff and fired three times. Patsy stumbled through the swinging doors and died in the gutter of Eighth Avenue.

This time the police and the district attorney's office managed to weave together a case against Madden as the instigator of Doyle's murder, and also took the precaution of sequestering their principal witnesses. It was the girls who turned against Madden. Freda Horner and Margaret Everdeane, agreeing to testify for the state, told how Patsy had been lured to his death in the barroom. Johnny McArdle and Art Biedler were taken into custody as the actual slayers, Madden as the man who had ordered the execution.

Owney, with his political connections, was made quite comfortable in the Tombs while awaiting trial. He was given a double cell all to himself and a room service that would have been the envy of any Fifth Avenue hotel. Guards and trusties vied for the honor of serving him. About that time Dick Butler happened to be in trouble himself, and was taken to the Tombs to await the jury's verdict on charges that he and several other Hell's Kitchen characters had sprung Harry K. Thaw, the millionaire playboy who killed Stanford White, from the Matteawan asylum for the criminally insane. Butler told (in *Dock Walloper*) how Madden, an old friend, invited him to share his cell the night before the jury acquitted him on conspiracy charges. Madden, whom he characterized as "always good to the poor" and the man "who saved many a West Side pauper from potter's field," poured him a drink of whiskey for a nightcap, and in the morning ordered orange juice, boiled eggs, toast and coffee for his guest's breakfast. Among other amenities, Owney had a bed with a mattress in his cell. "Owney sure was boss of the place," Butler wrote admiringly.

In court, however, Madden was treated less gently. He was given a sentence of ten to twenty years in Sing Sing, with McArdle going up for thirteen years and Biedler for eighteen. At the same time the law went after the members of his gang. By the end of the year, New York Police Department records show, sixteen members of the Madden gang were in jail on an assortment of charges.

Owney Madden spent the next eight years at Sing Sing, being released on parole in January, 1923. It may have seemed that the world had passed him by, that other big shots of the underworld had cornered the bootleg liquor and rumrunning markets, but Owney was a nimble fellow and soon made his way back to eminence in the rackets. Hijacking was regarded as a loathsome occupation by respectable, well-established crooks, but it was a quick way to make a score and convince the ruling mobsters that Owney Madden would have to be taken into account. Several months after being paroled from Sing Sing, Madden was arrested on a charge of hijacking $25,000 worth of liquor in White Plains. The charges were dismissed for lack of evidence.

About that time George Jean "Big Frenchy" de Mange, one of the reigning figures of the Broadway mob and owner of the Club Argonaut, decided Madden had better be cut in or he'd tear the town apart. Besides Big Frenchy liked Madden, admired him for the gentlemanly polish and soft-spoken manners he had acquired somewhere between Tenth Avenue and his release from Sing Sing, and apparently realized that Madden would give a little class to the night clubs where cruder types might frighten off the well-heeled customers. One of Madden's greatest assets was that he never got tough unless he had to. It turned out to be one of the more successful, as well as one of the more loyal, partnerships of the New York underworld. (Actually there was little of the subterranean about the underworld of the 'twenties, when the most lucrative of the rackets, bootlegging, was so generally approved by the public.) Most of Madden's old friends from Hell's Kitchen were given employment, the New York *Herald* noting that "quite a few of them are seeing to it that whiskey from the Bahama Islands reaches the parched American throat."

In no time at all, Owney Madden was once again Duke of the West Side, the peer of Arthur Flegenheimer, popularly known as Dutch Schultz, and one of a handful of celebrities which every visiting fireman wished to have pointed out.

Another notorious product of the streets of Hell's Kitchen was a golden-haired stripling with a soft, rounded, babyish face—the prototype of the baby-faced killer as Owney Madden was the very model of a gentleman-gangster—named Vincent Coll. He soon became celebrated as Mad Dog Coll, and was accounted the most vicious killer in American criminal history. By the age of twenty-three, he had become so dangerous that the underworld, both for its own protection and as a public relations gesture, coldly and precisely sent him to his death.

Coll and his brother Peter, a year older, were born in County Kildare, orphaned at an early age, and brought to New York by their older sister, Florence. They lived in a tenement near Twenty-fifth Street and Eleventh Avenue. Even as a boy in short pants Coll was the terror of the neighborhood, with a temper that scattered much bigger and older boys when he took after them with bricks and fists. At the age of thirteen he was arrested as a "disorderly child" and sent to the Mission of the Immaculate Virgin. A year later he was caught trying to break into a store and sent to the more strictly disciplined Catholic Protectory. At seventeen he was arrested for carrying a revolver, and was sent to the still stricter House of Refuge. Even that institution was not equipped to handle the likes of Vincent Coll, and he was passed along to the Elmira reformatory. That prison was so overcrowded that Coll was paroled, sent back for violating his parole, and paroled again.

Coll had not yet begun to shave regularly when he braced Dutch Schultz for a job guarding the latter's convoys of beer trucks. Not only that, but he persuaded Schultz to put his brother Peter, a less violent and less ambitious boy, on the same payroll. Coll was still under voting age when police charged him with having killed a speakeasy owner who refused to buy Schultz's product. Coll, probably through Schultz's considerable influence, was freed of the charge.

Vincent Coll was undoubtedly a cold-blooded and efficient triggerman, but Schultz soon learned he couldn't be kept under control. He was too ambitious, too resentful of taking orders, too dangerous to have around. Coll proved it when he and Carmine Barelli, also a Schultz gunman and an old schoolmate of Coll's in Hell's Kitchen, pulled off a job on their own. They robbed the Sheffield Farms dairy in the Bronx of its $18,000 payroll. Schultz didn't like to have independent contractors on his payroll, and upbraided Coll for pulling the robbery on his own.

Instead of crawling, as he was expected to do, Coll flabbergasted Schultz with a demand that he be admitted to a partnership. "No more hundred and fifty bucks a week salary, Dutch," the presumptuous youth said. "I want a piece of all your beer sales and a cut on all the new joints we take over. I want a piece of the business, Dutch."

"I don't take in nobody as partners with me," Schultz said. "You're an ambitious punk, but you take a salary or nothing. Take it or leave it."

"Okay, I'm leaving it," Coll said.

In the next few weeks, Coll let Schultz know that he meant business. He proposed to set himself up as a rival gang leader in Schultz's territory, which included most of New York that wasn't under the control of Owney Madden and Big Frenchy de Mange, and canvassed other hirelings of Schultz to throw in with him. Without exception they shuddered and told him to forget the whole suicidal idea. Among those he approached was his old boyhood friend, Carmine Barelli, who also turned down Coll's proposal and furthermore went to Schultz with the details of Coll's plan to cut into Schultz's territory.

Learning of this betrayal, Coll, in the best tradition of his calling, proceeded to work out plans for Barelli's immediate removal from the scene. The bait in his trap was to be May Smith, a taxidance hall girl and Barelli's girl friend. Coll persuaded her that he wanted to make up with Barelli but that the latter was being foolishly stubborn. He said he wanted May to arrange an "accidental" meeting without Barelli's knowledge. May was touched at the thought of reconciling two old pals, and arranged to be walking with Barelli a few nights later near her home in the Bronx.

Coll kept the appointment at two o'clock in the morning of February 13, 1930, with two friends, Patsy del Greco and Frankie Giordano, waiting in an automobile with him near May Smith's home. The couple came up the street, and Coll slipped out of the car.

When confronted by his old friend, Barelli took one look at the revolver and began to beg for his life. Coll cut off his pleas with two bullets in the abdomen.

Then he turned to May Smith.

The girl, correctly interpreting the look on Coll's face, started to run down the street. Coll brought her down with two shots, then walked over and fired another bullet into her head. Always a careful workman, he also put a bullet into the back of Barelli's head for good measure, and strolled back to his car.

The police picked him up for questioning, but there were no witnesses and Coll stood up to all the back-room battering the police could hand out. The arm-weary cops turned him loose. With the prestige gained from this successful defiance of both the law and Dutch Schultz, Coll was able to gather an organization around him.

Coll and his hoodlums soon managed to make life miserable for both Schultz and Madden. He hijacked Schultz's beer trucks, wrecked his speakeasies, managed to carve out a small piece of territory for himself wedged in between Schultz and Madden, and began to muscle in on the Harlem policy racket, one of Schultz's most lucrative enterprises. In the matter of eliminating Coll, Madden wisely deferred to Schultz; he knew it was going to be a long tough war, and wanted no part of it unless his own major interests were threatened.

It was quite a slaughter on the streets of upper Manhattan. Coll and his mob killed ten of Schultz's henchmen. The Dutchman retaliated by killing Vince's brother and five other members of the Coll gang.

All this, by underworld standards, was legitimate warfare. Coll's next moves, although he didn't exactly plan it that way, outlawed him even among outlaws. First, needing money to continue his campaign against Schultz, he decided to make Owney Madden his involuntary financier. Vincent Coll had learned long ago that it's bold generalship that pays off.

His scheme was to kidnap Big Frenchy de Mange and hold him until Madden paid the ransom for his dearest friend and closest associate.

On the evening of June 15, 1931, Coll and his most trusted gunman, Frank Giordano, waited outside de Mange's Club Argonaut in West Fiftieth Street until the bulky victim hove into view. Coll, with a gun in his side pocket, walked up to him with a large friendly smile.

"Hiya, Vince," Big Frenchy greeted him. "How's tricks?"

The smile vanished from Coll's face. Big Frenchy saw that Coll had a gun pointed at his vast midriff through the coat pocket.

"Start walking," Coll said. De Mange had no alternative but to comply, and a moment later was being sped to a furnished flat in the Bronx which Coll had arranged for the hideout.

Later that night, in his office in a West Forty-seventh Street building, Owney Madden received a phone call from Coll. He already knew that Big Frenchy had been kidnaped.

"The tab for Frenchy," Coll announced, "is fifty grand."

"Too steep," said Madden.

"Get it up by midnight, or something is liable to happen to Big Frenchy."

Coll showed up alone and unarmed in Madden's office at midnight. All that Madden had been able to raise on such short notice was $35,000. Coll shruggingly accepted it. As he left, Madden uttered a classic of understatement: "That was very unwise, Vincent." Later that night Big Frenchy was returned to the Club Argonaut unharmed.

The kidnaping threw Dutch Schultz into a panic, and he holed up for days in Polly Adler's de luxe whorehouse with a squad of his most reliable triggermen standing guard night and day. Gunmen imported from various out-of-town underworlds by Schultz and Madden combed the city for Coll, but he, too, had gone for cover.

It was about this time that Coll fell in love with a girl from the old neighborhood, a tall, dark-eyed and comely girl named Lottie Kreisberger. She was born in Germany but brought up on Tenth Avenue. She had engaged in her first love affair at the age of ten, was arrested on a robbery charge at fourteen, and married a thug named Joe Kreisberger at sixteen. After Kreisberger disappeared and was presumed dead, she set up light housekeeping with Sammy Medale, a Schultz gunman. Then she met Coll, and they fell violently in love with each other. Medale discreetly stepped aside. Fickle as she had been in the past, Lottie stuck to Coll for the rest of the time allotted to him.

In the continuing war against the Schultz mob, Coll selected as his next target a slippery character named Joey Rao, who was head of Schultz's policy games and other gambling enterprises in Harlem. Rao, knowing he was marked for the slaughter, was said to have kept a pocket full of pennies for distribution to the children on the block around his headquarters, the Helmar Social Club in East 107th Street, so that he was always surrounded by swarming children on the street and Coll's gunmen wouldn't dare open fire on him.

On the afternoon of July 28, 1931, Rao was lounging in front of his headquarters, surrounded, as usual, by the neighborhood children. He was accompanied by two bodyguards. A touring car came around the corner and its occupants opened fire on Rao and his protectors, heedless of the children playing around them. When the fusillade was over, a five-year-old boy lay dead on the sidewalk and four other children were wounded. Rao and his bodyguards escaped without a scratch.

Everyone in town knew that Coll and his lieutenants had done the shooting. In the tall black headlines, Coll was christened the Baby Killer and the Mad Dog. Madden and Schultz each offered $25,000 rewards to any hoodlum who would knock off the psychotic killer who was giving the underworld such a bad press.

The law finally caught up with Coll in October when police arrested him with Lottie in a West Twenty-third Street hotel. Coll and Frank Giordano were tried on charges of having murdered the five-year-old boy. The Mad Dog was still prosperous enough to engage the city's top criminal lawyer, Samuel J. Leibowitz, as his counsel at the trial. As it developed, Leibowitz was worth every cent of his fee. The state produced one Samuel Brecht as its star witness, Brecht testifying that he was an eyewitness to the shooting and identifying both Coll and Giordano as being among the gunmen. Leibowitz, however, noted Brecht's furtive manner and his habit of talking out of the side of his mouth, a trait developed by most jailbirds. He investigated Brecht's background, then calmly blew the case right out from under the district attorney's office. Brecht, the counselor revealed in court, was an ex-convict known as a "professional witness" who had performed a similar rôle recently in St. Louis. Coll and Giordano went free.

But Coll's days were numbered, the city was swarming with high-priced talent assigned by Schultz to "get Coll." Walter Winchell reported in his column, with perhaps only the slightest exaggeration, "Five planes brought dozens of machine guns from Chicago Friday. . . . Local banditti have made one hotel a virtual arsenal and several hot spots are ditto because Master Coll is giving them the headache."

Not at all abashed by his unpopularity in the underworld, Mad Dog Coll laid bigger and better plans for the future. He called Owney Madden, who had been such an easy touch the previous summer, and announced that unless Madden came up with $100,000 he would be kidnaped and held for that sum in ransom. Owney could make it easy on himself and pay "the tab" in advance, avoiding the discomforts and uncertainties of a kidnaping. Madden thereupon called a conference of the underworld's top brass in a midtown hotel. At this council of war it was agreed to work on the weakest member of Coll's gang and obtain information on his movements, and simultaneously to divide the city into zones with squads of gunmen waiting at various locations to cut Coll down the moment he was pinpointed. Then Owney went to Florida for a vacation, not exactly scared out of town, perhaps, but finding a change of climate essential for reasons of health.

On the night of February 8, 1932, Coll and a bodyguard stopped off at a drugstore in West Twenty-third Street near Eighth Avenue, not far from the tenement where he and his slain brother had been raised by their sister.

Coll was in the phone booth, his henchman lounging at the soda fountain where two other patrons were having coffee, when an automobile with four men pulled up at the curb outside. Three of the men deployed themselves around the drugstore entrance, while the fourth man, carrying a Thompson submachine gun in his right hand, entered the store.

The gunman nodded to Coll's bodyguard, who swiftly climbed off his stool, headed out the door and disappeared into the night. Presumably he was the one who had put Coll on the spot.

Then the tommy-gunner announced to the patrons and employees of the store in soothing tones, "Everybody keep cool now. Don't lose your heads and nobody will get hurt."

Coll was still jabbering away over the phone in the booth.

The gunman moved deliberately to the phone booth, clicked off the safety, raised the barrel and fired a short burst through the glass. He paused, corrected his aim, fired another short burst—

then another. He looked into the booth, where Coll had been chopped almost in half, and strolled out of the drugstore.

At twenty-three, Coll's career had ended as violently as it had begun on the streets of Hell's Kitchen. His entire estate, it was found, was $100 in cash pinned inside Lottie Kreisberger's brassière.

Owney Madden and Dutch Schultz survived the Mad Dog's reign of terror, but luck was running out for them, too. Schultz was subsequently shot and killed. Madden, still on parole for the murder of Patsy Doyle in 1915, was arrested as a parole violator later in 1932 and spent another year in prison. Shortly after his release, the newspapers carried stories saying that a million dollars had been offered the state parole board to lift his parole, which did not expire until 1935. By that time Madden had had enough of the rackets. He retired to Hot Springs, Arkansas, where he married the postmaster's daughter in 1935. Since then he has lived an ostensibly respectable life, although occasionally a newspaper insists on referring to him as an "elder statesman of the underworld." The only time he returned to New York was for his mother's funeral about ten years ago.

Madden is now seventy-six years old, an age splendidly defiant of whatever actuarial estimates have been compiled on the life expectancy of a gangster.

14

It's Not the Same There Any More

URING the furious public-building activity of the 'thirties, the face of Hell's Kitchen, along with many other "depressed areas," underwent plastic surgery. The wrecker's ball and jackhammer cut wide swathes through the district and scores of "old-law" tenements were smashed to rubble. It was a time when the socially conscious were concerned over the fact that "one third of the nation" was ill-housed, a time of ferment that passed soon enough with the distraction of other causes. Before the frenzy passed, however, various governmental agencies combined to change the look of Hell's Kitchen; their principal project was the destruction of sixty-two ancient tenement buildings to accommodate the approaches to the Lincoln Tunnel under the Hudson.

A survey conducted by the New York *Herald-Tribune* (September 2, 1934) indicated that most of the doomed structures were about to topple through sheer decrepitude. "Stores and a few industries have come in and the limits of the slums have narrowed considerably. But the Tenement Department finds that condi-

231

tions in those tenements remaining are some of the worst in the city. Many of these buildings have been standing for eighty years, and it is said that for thirty years some of them have been unimproved and in general disrepair." A series of disastrous tenement fires the winter before had helped along the slum-clearance campaign of that summer.

One approach to the Lincoln Tunnel was Dyer Avenue between Ninth and Tenth avenues from Thirty-fourth to Forty-second streets, and another path through the old tenements was cut along Thirty-ninth Street, right over the original site of Hell's Kitchen, where Bully Morrisey and Battle Annie Welsh used to conduct their forays.

Another aspect of the face-lifting to which Hell's Kitchen was subjected was the New York Central's West Side improvement program. From its Thirtieth Street yards to Sixtieth Street the railroad's trackage on the West Side was dropped below the street level and grade crossings were eliminated. The freights then rumbled below the surface between Tenth and Eleventh avenues, and Death Avenue was no more. The parish priests of the district had been tireless in circulating petitions to have the surface tracks on Eleventh Avenue removed. This, of course, meant the passing of one of the few picturesque characters in the section—the Death Avenue cowboy who rode on his horse ahead of every locomotive. Reporters found an old flagman in his shanty at Thirty-eighth Street and Eleventh Avenue; his name was John Murphy, Hell's Kitchen-born and the father of twelve children brought up in the same neighborhood. Already a note of nostalgia was creeping into newspaper stories about Hell's Kitchen and Murphy was quoted as saying, "It seems like yesterday when Dolly used to come chugging out of the 30th Street terminal. She was a steam locomotive. Her single car carried the line's only passengers. But to the neighborhood, she was just Dolly. People used to set their watches by her whistle. She started her run to Spuyten Duyvil daily at 12:30 P.M. She was always crammed with swells who had country estates in Harlem."

Another casualty of the civic betterment campaign was Paddy's

Market, the pushcart bazaar under the Ninth Avenue El on Saturday nights. It had been the market place of Hell's Kitchen for half a century, but the demands of the Lincoln Tunnel project and the official impatience with all that was shabby but picturesque, doomed it. The Department of Public Markets and the Port of New York Authority ordered the pushcart merchants to stay away from Ninth Avenue. A hardy and argumentative breed, as their customers could testify, the hucksters took their case to the courts, lost, and were evicted. One group retreated to West Thirty-ninth Street, another to West Forty-first Street, but business was poor among both groups. People simply learned to go to stores and dispense with the indubitable joys of haggling.

Also eliminated from the scene late in the decade was the Ninth Avenue Elevated. Residents had been cursing it for decades but some began to miss it once the wreckers removed it. A Ninth Avenue elder complained the "older people can't sleep" without the familiar racket of the El trains outside their windows. But a ten-year-old girl told a *World-Telegram* reporter, "I like it, not having the El outside. The sunshine comes in the window—sometimes—in one of our rooms."

In the generally progressive atmosphere of the 'thirties, the landlords, too, were getting particular about how their tenants conducted themselves. The Guaranty Trust Company evicted fifty families from what the *World-Telegram* described as a "crime-ridden" tenement at 754-756 Eighth Avenue. Several murders had been committed on the premises, and police had received many complaints of gambling conducted there before the trust company cleaned the place out.

In a few years, Hell's Kitchen had simmered down to the point where a fight between two women of the district, who whacked away at each other with ax handles in a dispute over a rooftop clothesline, was referred to as "a nostalgic affair" in one newspaper's headline over the story.

Commercially and industrially, the Middle West Side was becoming important and respectable, although only a few years before it was noted mainly as a breeding place of crime and disorder. Its strategic location on the North River water front, and the network of New York Central, Pennsylvania and Erie railroad lines webbing Hell's Kitchen, were mostly responsible for this. Twenty steamship lines in the trans-Atlantic service were now using the West Side piers, discharging a total of 750,000 passengers annually. The freight cargo was important, too, with one steamship company alone unloading 800,000 tons a year. Three new 1,100-foot piers were built to accommodate the huge luxury liners recently commissioned by the British and French steamship companies. In addition to this more glamorous traffic, there were the 90,000,000 passenger trips across the Hudson annually by ferry.

Industry, finding the section well served by rail and sea transport, arrived in strength. The National Biscuit Company (Nabisco) had bakeries and plants scattered all over Chelsea. The Sheffield Farms milk plant at Fifty-seventh Street and Eleventh Avenue was the world's largest. The Knickerbocker Mills processed more than a million pounds of spices annually at its factory in West Twenty-sixth Street.

With the onset of respectability, both the business people and the residents of the district began to object to the common—and apparently ineradicable—designation of Hell's Kitchen. They protested, with reason, that the name should really have been applied only to that block in West Thirty-ninth Street where it originated. The West Side Chamber of Commerce made this point in 1937, and pointed out that the designation was "objectionable to the honest people who own property or make a livelihood on the West Side." A priest at St. Raphael's Church entered his strenuous objections to the Hell's Kitchen label, and the New York *Times* tried to console him in an editorial, which pointed out, "What saves the situation is that nobody knows where 'Hell's Kitchen' is—any more than the average New Yorker can tell where Greenwich Village or Yorkville ends, where Chelsea or Harlem begins." Unappeased by this conciliatory note, property owners of the area began circulating petitions to rename Ninth, Tenth and Eleventh avenues, their new names to be South Columbus,

South Amsterdam and South West End avenues, respectively. The campaign was unsuccessful.

Still it should have been of some satisfaction that Hell's Kitchen was getting a better press; newspaper stories about the district were now produced by feature writers instead of police reporters. A *Times* reporter told of visiting the miniature farm established on the roof of the West Side Center of the Children's Aid Society in West Thirty-eighth Street. The children, he observed, worked hard at maintaining their kitchen and flower gardens, despite the constant raids of sparrows and pigeons. To scare off the marauders, the children built an eight-foot scarecrow which they named Frankenstein. "The children let their movie-influenced imaginations run riot," the reporter wrote, and one glimpse of the scarecrow "would probably frighten away any winged thing smaller than the prehistoric roc."

Considerable attention was attracted to the "Tenth Avenue Charm School" established for the young ladies of the section at the Theodore Roosevelt Recreation Center. What Battle Annie and Euchre Kate would have thought of such a place, where a girl wasn't even taught how to defend herself in a fair fight, may be imagined. The columnist Edwin C. Hill, who had covered the old Tenderloin precinct, inspected the place and remarked, "Like the little girl in Shaw's *Pygmalion*, the girls are schooled in the 'general technique of becoming a lady,' with training in diction, in decorum, in the niceties of speech modulation and in becoming dress and the care of the person. And who knows but that this one or that one may yet curtsey to the queen? It can happen here."

Columnist Hill, however, couldn't help remembering the less genteel days of Hell's Kitchen. "One feels sure that almost anything can happen here when he thinks of charm in Hell's Kitchen. It used to be as charming as a cage full of man-eating tigers, plus a couple of train wrecks and an Armenian massacre. Studies in posture covered the crouch and the swing from the heel. Poise was attained with a chunk of railroad iron in the street corner tête-à-tête. Diction was the unsullied gang idiom in which the

youngsters needed no tutoring. And any drink milder than blue
vitriol was for sissies. And now it looks as if the district would
become New York's Chautauqua. But there's one little furtive
survival of the old days. Here and there, in a little old fly-specked
drugstore, you'll find leeches for sale. Leeches for black eyes were
fast sellers, thirty or forty years ago, especially on Sunday nights
or Monday mornings, after the weekend bare-knuckle and brass-
knuckle tournaments. Hell's Kitchen doesn't need them any more,
but there is an occasional call from outlying districts, still bel-
licose and not yet charming."

Milton Bracker of the New York *Times*, on a similar tour of
duty, found that Hell's Kitchen had changed considerably beneath the surface. It was no longer overcrowded, and fifty thousand persons lived where one hundred and fifty thousand had
formerly fought for breathing space. Writing in the *Times* of
November 12, 1939, Bracker noted that, "In many respects the
sector is physically unchanged. But it is no longer psychologically
outside the law and no one knows that better than the force at
West 47th Street, where veterans no longer have to double up
on beats within three blocks of the station house. . . . The 'bar-
and-grill' has replaced the saloon. The names in the dim hallways
are still mostly Irish, but many are Italian and Polish, too. The
waterfront dominates the economic setup, with probably forty
per cent of the population on relief. With many of the oldest
tenements in worse shape than ever, a native away twenty-five
years might come back today, slant his eyes to the monotonous
roof line, the fire escapes, the flapping wash, the doorstep socials
and the noisy youngsters, and decide, 'It's just about the same
old place.' But it isn't. For the basic change has been from one
side of the law to the other. West Siders, instead of baiting the
Police Department, have begun literally to join it. The gangs
have dwindled; the thuggery of the misnamed 'dry' era is only
a memory. Education has been a prime factor; another, in an
area with only one settlement house to eleven on the East Side,
has been the work of the Stryker's Lane Community Center. . . ."
The community center, located in West Fifty-fourth Street, was

actually the headquarters of a number of neighborhood clubs whose activities were carefully but not obtrusively guided and supervised. "The Lane developed into a sort of state capital where elected representatives cope with joint problems. A house council—like three-fourths of the paid staff, strictly from the neighborhood—is the governing body. Whenever a group keeps up an outside room too—similar to the cellar clubs of the Lower East Side—a Lane certificate is displayed. The cop on the beat knows that that document on the wall means a load off his mind."

From time to time since the 'thirties art colonies have tried to establish themselves in Hell's Kitchen's upper reaches, but they seldom last long. In 1935 a group of thirty painters and sculptors took over a $25-a-month loft at Fifty-fifth Street and Twelfth Avenue, next to the city incinerator and one flight above the Bermuda Restaurant ("Ladies Invited"). "In the memory of the oldest resident of the waterfront, it was the first invasion of the arts into a district devoted to warehouses, abattoirs and slums," wrote a New York *Herald-Tribune* reporter.

The artists spent two months cleaning up the place, pawned watches and rings to install windowpanes, plumbing and heating. "We're not the usual Washington Square crowd," their leader was quoted as saying. "We're here for art's sake and for art's sake only."

The colonists put up a sign which faced the Furness-Bermuda Line's pier and which they hoped would attract wealthy tourists bound for or returning from the West Indies. It read: "Art down here! Exhibition of Murals, Decorations and Paintings. Before you go forth with bags and all, visit us!" It was a forlorn sort of cry; the voyagers preferred the certified bohemianism of Greenwich Village or the elegance of Fifty-seventh Street galleries, and the colony soon dwindled and finally disappeared.

Subsequently there was another artistic invasion of the district, with the establishment of the Hell's Kitchen Art Galleries at 460 Tenth Avenue by Frank Shevlin, who was born in the neighborhood and owned a prosperous trucking company. It opened with a showing of the works of Johann Pogrzeba, a Polish refugee.

John Sloan, the leading figure of the West Twenty-third Street colony, praised his painting, and the newspapers complimented the gallery itself as being "as elegant as anything on Fifty-seventh Street," but the venture failed to survive. Reporters interviewed a wide-eyed garage foreman named Jimmy O'Donnell, who commented: "Wonder what Newburgh Gallagher, Marty Brennan and Bull Montana would say if they walked in now. Boy, this was a tough district then. Fights, gangs, shootings. But those guys grew up. Their kids are now cops, lawyers and doctors."

The descendants of the old breed of Hell's Kitchen, many of them, have indeed prospered.

The succeeding generations spread out over Manhattan in an amazing variety of pursuits. One of the Donohues married into the Woolworth millions, and another became a bishop. The Mc-Clanahans proudly watched James McClanahan become one of the city's leading bankers. Malcolm Stevenson, the polo player, was descended from an old Hell's Kitchen family. From the same neighborhood came James J. Braddock, onetime heavyweight champion of the world, and Justice Owen McGivern of the State Supreme Court; Frank Farrell, onetime owner of the New York Yankees, and Ben Duffy, now vice chairman of the executive board of Batten, Barton Durstine & Osborn, Inc. Duffy worked his way up from copy boy to the presidency of the advertising agency before his semi-retirement due to illness in 1957. Another ex-heavyweight champion, Gene Tunney, worked as a checker on the Chelsea docks before joining the Marines during the First World War. Jeffrey Farnol, the English novelist, lived in Hell's Kitchen while struggling to become a writer.

Show business has had its quota of recruits from Hell's Kitchen, too. Alice Faye, the daughter of Irish and German parents who raised her on Tenth Avenue, bolted out of P.S. 84 with truant officers hot on her trail. They neglected to search backstage at the Capitol Theater, where she talked her way into the Chester Hale dancing troupe. A few years later she was a movie star. Ruby Keeler tapped her way into Texas Guinan's floor shows, Broadway musicals, an early marriage to Al Jolson, and finally stardom in Hollywood. During the 'twenties and early 'thirties, the chorus lines of Broadway night clubs and musical comedies were liberally sprinkled with pert little Irish girls from Hell's Kitchen. Many celebrated actors, among them James Cagney and Pat O'Brien, who shared a hall bedroom, found quarters in Hell's Kitchen both inexpensive and handy to the producers' and agents' offices. George Raft, born of German-Italian parents, was born in the district and in a recent magazine series confessed to having been a street fighter in his youth and later a friend of Owney Madden, Big Frenchy and Dutch Schultz.

During the Second World War, the old Fighting 69th, now firmly designated the 165th Infantry, was reactivated and brought back memories of the regiment's gallantry in France a generation before. Among its recruits were Christopher Kilmer, the son of Joyce Kilmer, and a grandson of O'Donovan Rossa, the hero of the fight against Tammany in the 'seventies.

It was a hard-luck regiment during the Second World War. The boys may well have been as courageous as the men of the Fighting 69th but they had fewer opportunities to demonstrate the fact. In the first place the 165th Infantry was allowed to molder away in the Hawaiian Islands for thirty-odd months after the war began, which sapped regimental morale. Then it was attached to the 27th Infantry Division and became involved in one of the war's most unpleasant inter-service controversies when its commanding general was removed by his Marine Corps superior for failing to show the aggressiveness in action demanded by Marine doctrine. Before that, however, at least one native of Hell's Kitchen, himself a Marine, wondered what had happened to the legendary toughness of the old 69th. He was temporarily stationed with his unit on the island of Iheya Jima during the opening phases of the Okinawa invasion, as was the 165th Infantry. One day the Marine was lolling on a grassy knoll when he was approached by a soldier of the 165th who inquired, "Pardon me, can you tell me where I can defecate?" The ex-Marine avows that, during his youth in Hell's Kitchen, the word had never been heard in that neighborhood.

The 165th landed on Makin Atoll in the Gilbert Islands on November 20, 1943, and its commander, Colonel Gardner Conroy, was almost immediately killed by a Japanese sniper. The regimental chaplain, Father Stephen J. Meany, of Brooklyn, lived up to the Father Duffy standard by crawling out between the lines to rescue a wounded man. He, too, was wounded when a sniper's bullet struck the medallion of the Virgin Mary he was wearing and ricocheted through his chest and arm.

The new commander of the 165th, Colonel Gerard Kelley, was born and bred in the old Gas House district on the East Side, and was a graduate of West Point. In the dispute then raging over whether a boy from the city streets or one from the ranch and farm country made a better soldier, Colonel Kelley not unexpectedly ranged himself on the side of the city-bred, and asserted that the New Yorker was a better fighter than the Texan. "They [the New Yorkers] are more adaptable," he told newspapermen. "On the city streets you run into new tough situations every day. You learn to fight your way out—or talk your way out. I've learned both. These city-bred boys of the old 69th, going out to the jungle to fight, encountering new tough situations at every step, adapt themselves quickly."

It was during the invasion of Saipan in the Marshalls that the 27th Division's commander, Major General Ralph Smith, was relieved for not pushing his regiments into action aggressively enough. Yet the 165th Infantry saw hard fighting and took heavy losses before the island was secured. It was given the assignment of rooting the Japanese out of their fortified caves and ravines northwest of Tanapag Harbor, and was not supplied with hot food and coffee until twenty-three days after going into action. The 165th captured Aslito airfield June 18, 1944, and participated in the successful assault on Mount Tapotchau, in which Colonel Kelley was wounded. Many in the regiment claimed that the shrapnel rained down on them by the Japanese artillery was scrap iron from the old Ninth Avenue El.

Hell's Kitchen men returning from military service found that many of the piers where they sought employment a few blocks from their homes were firmly under the control of what was formally known as Local 824, International Longshoremen's Association, but more familiarly known as the Pistol Local. This local was loaded with ex-convicts and hoodlums, yet controlled the "richest" piers in the Port of New York—those from Forty-second to Fifty-seventh streets where the luxury liners docked, the Cunard's *Queen* ships, the French Line, the United States Line's *America* and *United States*, the American Export Lines' *Independence* and *Constitution*—and discharged millions of dollars worth of cargo annually.

The ex-servicemen found that they not only had to work very hard under frequently dangerous conditions, but submit to the domination of gangsters and pay tribute to them in various forms. Testimony before the State Crime Commission a few years ago developed an ugly picture of how the racketeers ran the Pistol Local. The real power in the local was wielded by Mickey Bowers, whose police record showed thirteen arrests between 1920 and 1940 and a conviction for bank robbery in Jersey City; John Keefe, the vice president of the local, was also an ex-convict. The chief witness against Mickey Bowers was Dominick Genova, who was introduced to the local's strong-arm squad by his former prison mate, John "Apples" Applegate. Genova told how he pulled out of the Bowers group when he was ordered to kill a milkman who had offended Applegate in a barroom dispute over a woman. (The milkman, John Wice, was killed by machine-gun fire in West Forty-seventh Street on June 14, 1947.)

Genova also testified that Bowers was slashed by one Tommy Gleason, a rival for control of the Pistol Union, as he left a bar in West Forty-seventh Street in 1944. The ex-convict recalled that Bowers later told his henchmen, "Well, he [Gleason] is going to have to go." Less than two weeks later, Genova testified, Gleason was shot and killed as he "took a snooze" in a Tenth Avenue undertaking parlor, a rather convenient location for an assassination.

Bowers was not at all reluctant to display his power and influence, even while under investigation. The Pistol Local called a work stoppage on all its piers as a protest against issuance of subpoenas by the Crime Commission, and in 1953, just to show how it could arbitrarily crack down on the employers, it ordered the Cunard liner *Mauretania* to dock at Pier 90 instead of its usual berth at Pier 92. Cunard submitted without a protest. The Crime Commission concluded that Bowers and his gang "ruled by murder and mayhem," and the United States Attorney's office in New York labeled them a "major menace" on the water front. But they stayed in power, and are still in power, even though Bowers was sentenced to the federal prison at Leavenworth for evasion of income taxes in 1956. His little empire on the Hell's Kitchen docks—with its royal prerogatives of conducting the gambling, loan-shark and policy-game rackets and the pilferage from cargo and luggage—presumably will be awaiting its master when he is released from prison around 1960.

Today Hell's Kitchen and much of Chelsea are still "depressed areas," a tenement and industrial district, while the old Tenderloin has been taken over by the garment factories and shows no sign of having once been the sinfulest section of New York.

Many of the old landmarks are gone, many others survive. The "old-law" tenements, some of them dating back to the Civil War, still stand out like rotten teeth against the horizon. In the avenues back from the docks, there are still gas reservoirs, packing houses and stockyards. Along West Forty-first Street between Eleventh and Twelfth avenues the New York Stockyards, with tier on tier of corrugated iron-sided pens for cattle, still stands with all its pungent aroma. Another of the old buildings still standing is the Valentin Loewer Brewery, built in 1869, a vast red-brick pile on West Forty-first Street between Tenth and Eleventh avenues, abandoned many years ago. Its greening copper-sheathed cupola houses a shattered clock, and a statue of Gambrinus, the mythical inventor of beer, presides over an empty yard where the barrel-laden drays hauled by teams of Percherons used to convey an endless stream of lager for thirsty throats throughout the city. The brewery is a pigeon asylum now, with broken windows and cobwebbed vats. Prohibition simply didn't end soon enough for Valentin Loewer, his descendants and his brewmasters.

All through those streets, indeed, can be found the traces of their antic history. The red-brick Chelsea Hotel is still in operation, with its iron fretwork balconies and its suggestions of Victorian elegance. Jim Fisk's Grand Opera House, just down West Twenty-third Street at the corner of Eighth Avenue, is now the RKO Twenty-third Street Theater, offering films instead of comic opera and alternating blonde and brunette choruses. On the second, third and fourth floors, few signs remain of Jim Fisk's embattled Erie Railroad enterprises; a poolhall and bowling alley occupies the second floor, and the third and fourth floors have been closed off, a likely promenade for the shades of Fisk and Josie Mansfield and Edward S. Stokes. Yet there may still be seen the iron doors, twelve feet high and twelve inches thick, which withstood the battering of Fisk's creditors and other enemies, with the intertwined "E R" initials still emblazoned on their outer surface. The iron statuary lamps of Fisk's day, now holding electric lights, are in their places on the wide staircase leading to the floors above.

The old Hell's Kitchen precinct house in West Thirty-seventh Street is now the Civil Jail of New York, where the city's alimony dodgers are detained until they see the error of their ways. It is still a sad place, but not so noisy as when it was known as the "slaughterhouse." Opposite the jail is a tenement row, also built around 1870, with ornamental iron balconies like those in the Vieux Carré of New Orleans, one of the handsomest tenement façades in the city.

Ninth Avenue from Thirty-fourth to Forty-fourth streets remains the shopping center of the district. The people still like to do their shopping out in the open, and the avenue is one vast sidewalk mart. Most of the stores spread their merchandise over the sidewalks in fair weather, offering mounds of vegetables, battlements of fruits, baskets of mussels, clams and oysters. Other establishments specialize in olive oil, pasta and all sorts of imports from the Mediterranean countries, and there are pork stores, Italian pastry shops, mill-end and remnant stores, fish stalls, tiny variety stores with everything from diaper pins to inexpensive evening dresses on sale. The atmosphere of Paddy's Market lingers on.

The ancient walls of P.S. 127, in West Thirty-seventh Street between Tenth and Eleventh avenues, still shelter succeeding generations of schoolboys and girls, as they did before the Civil War, when dreamy-eyed pupils watched the sails beating their way up the Hudson and walked home through the meadows of Bloomingdale Farm. The river view, however, is blocked off by factories and warehouses, and the boys of P.S. 127 can no longer hurry over to Eleventh Avenue when school's out to beg rides from the Death Avenue cowboys who rode ahead of the trains. And no longer are the classrooms filled with row on row of Irish and German children: twenty-six nationalities recently were listed among its pupils. Newer and perhaps worthier heroes than, say, Owney Madden or Newburgh Gallagher, have risen among the children of Hell's Kitchen, and such legends as "I am Wyatt Erpp [sic]—Whitey" and "Elvis is a doll" are chalked on the sidewalks and building walls. Television aerials have replaced pigeon coops on the tenement roofs.

No, it isn't the same there any more. Hell's Kitchen is no longer a danger area on the police map, even while juvenile gangs in the Bronx, Brooklyn, Queens, and upper Manhattan are battling in the streets and arousing the same sort of concern the Hell's Kitchen gangs did before the First World War.

Tenement life is much the same as it has been for generations, deplorably so, but many of the older residents cling to the block which is as much home to them as any tidy New England village is to its natives. Their children have moved to the suburbs, and even to the gentleman-farmer counties of Connecticut and Pennsylvania, but the older people can not be persuaded to join the exodus. Hell's Kitchen is still hellish in some of its aspects, but it has been home to generation after generation for almost a century.

Acknowledgments and Bibliography

THE AUTHOR is indebted to such veterans of Hell's Kitchen as Willie Burke, Frank McCauley, Joe McGovern, and many others who gave themselves up to reminiscence but who, of course, share no responsibility for what use the author made of their reminiscences. Also to a number of colleagues on New York newspapers, including Charles Roland, Robert E. Berry, Joe P. Faulkner, Bill McCullam, James D. Horan, Bob Spellman, Bill Michelfelder; they likewise bear no responsibility for what is written here.

Following are the sources of published material:

BOOKS

Anonymous. *Snares of New York, or Tricks and Traps of the Metropolis*, New York, published sometime in the 1880's
Asbury, Herbert. *The Gangs of New York*, New York, 1928
Berger, Meyer. *The Eight Million*, New York, 1942
Brace, Charles L. *The Dangerous Classes of New York*, New York, 1872
Brown, Henry Collins. *Brownstone Fronts and Saratoga Trunks*, New York, 1935
Brown, Henry Collins, editor. *Valentine's Manual of Old New York*, New York, 1919
Butler, Richard J., and Driscoll, Joseph. *Dock Walloper*, New York, 1933

Byrnes, Clara. *Block Sketches of New York City,* New York, 1918

Crapsey, Edward. *The Nether Side of New York,* New York, 1872

Dictionary of American Biography, New York, 1931

Duffy, Francis P. *Father Duffy's Story,* New York, 1919

Flick, Ella M. E. *Chaplain Duffy of the 69th Regiment,* Philadelphia, 1935

Fuller, Robert H. *Jubilee Jim,* New York, 1928

Gardiner, Charles W. *The Doctor and the Devil, or Midnight Adventures of Dr. Parkhurst,* New York, 1894

Hart, Smith. *The New Yorkers,* New York, 1934

Hogan, Martin J. *The Shamrock Battalion of the Rainbow,* New York, 1919

Jacobs, Bruce. *Heroes of the Army,* New York, 1956

Lening, Gustav. *The Dark Side of New York Life,* New York, 1873

Lewis, Alfred Henry. *The Apaches of New York,* New York, 1912

Longchamp, Frederick. *Asmodeus in New York,* New York, 1868

Lynch, Denis Tilden. *The Wild Seventies,* New York, 1941

Morris, Lloyd. *Incredible New York,* New York, 1951

Moss, Frank. "Story of the Riot," New York, 1900

Mott, Hopper Striker. *The New York of Yesterday,* New York, 1908

O'Brien, Fitz James. *Life, Stories and Poems,* Boston, 1880

Parkhurst, Charles H. *My Forty Years in New York,* New York, 1923

Raymond, Allen. *Waterfront Priest,* New York, 1955

Report and Proceedings of the Senate Committee Appointed to Investigate the Police Department of the City of New York (the so-called Lexow Committee), Albany, 1895

Rider, Fremont. *Rider's New York City,* New York, 1924

Riis, Jacob A. *How the Other Half Lives,* New York, 1900

Rovere, Richard. *Howe and Hummel: Their True and Scandalous History,* New York, 1947

Stoddard, Lothrop. *Master of Manhattan: The Life of Richard Croker,* New York, 1931

Talmage, T. DeWitt. *The Masque Torn Off,* New York, 1882

Walling, George W., *Recollections of a New York Chief of Police,* New York, 1888

Warren, John H., Jr. *Thirty Years' Battle with Crime, or the Crying Shame of New York, as Seen Under the Broad Glare of an Old Detective's Lantern,* New York, 1874

Werner, M. R. *Tammany Hall,* New York, 1928

West Side Studies, 2 vols., published under the auspices of the Russell Sage Foundation, New York, 1914

Wilson, Rufus Rockwell. *New York: Old and New,* Philadelphia, 1903

Woollcott, Alexander. *While Rome Burns,* New York, 1934

Works Progress Administration. *New York City Guide,* New York, 1939

NEWSPAPERS

All of New York: *Times, Herald, Journal, American, Herald-Tribune, Journal-American, Tribune, Sun, Evening Telegram, Post, Evening Mail, Globe, World-Telegram*

MAGAZINES

Harper's Weekly, Leslie's Weekly, The New Yorker, The West Sider